PERMANENT RACISM

Key Issues in Social Justice: Voices from the Frontline

Series Editors: Kalwant Bhopal, University of Birmingham, **Martin Myers**, Universirty of Nottingham, **Karl Kitching**, University College Cork and **Kenzo Sung**, Rowan Univeristy

How do issues of social justice, inclusion and equity shape modern day society? This series delivers a forum for perspectives from historically marginalised and minoritised communities to challenge contemporary dominant discourses about social justice, inclusion and equity in the social sciences and aligned disciplines.

Also available

Transformative Teaching and Learning in Further Education: Pedagogies of Hope and Social Justice
By **Rob Smith and Vicky Duckworth**

Hidden Voices: Lived Experiences in the Irish Welfare Space
By **Joe Whelan**

Forthcoming

Low-income Female Teacher Values and Agency in India: Implications for Reflective Practice
By **Ruth Samuel**

Disrupting the Academy with Lived Experience-Led Knowledge
Edited by **Maree Higgins** and **Caroline Lenette**

Find out more

policy.bristoluniversitypress.co.uk/key-issues-in-social-justice

PERMANENT RACISM
Race, Class and the Myth of Postracial Britain

Paul Warmington

First published in Great Britain in 2024 by

Policy Press, an imprint of
Bristol University Press
University of Bristol
1–9 Old Park Hill
Bristol
BS2 8BB
UK
t: +44 (0)117 374 6645
e: bup-info@bristol.ac.uk

Details of international sales and distribution partners are available at policy.bristoluniversitypress.co.uk

© Bristol University Press 2024

British Library Cataloguing in Publication Data
A catalogue record for this book is available from the British Library

ISBN 978-1-4473-6016-2 hardcover
ISBN 978-1-4473-6017-9 paperback
ISBN 978-1-4473-6018-6 ePub
ISBN 978-1-4473-6019-3 ePdf

The right of Paul Warmington to be identified as author of this work has been asserted by him in accordance with the Copyright, Designs and Patents Act 1988.

All rights reserved: no part of this publication may be reproduced, stored in a retrieval system, or transmitted in any form or by any means, electronic, mechanical, photocopying, recording, or otherwise without the prior permission of Bristol University Press.

Every reasonable effort has been made to obtain permission to reproduce copyrighted material. If, however, anyone knows of an oversight, please contact the publisher.

The statements and opinions contained within this publication are solely those of the author and not of the University of Bristol or Bristol University Press. The University of Bristol and Bristol University Press disclaim responsibility for any injury to persons or property resulting from any material published in this publication.

Bristol University Press and Policy Press work to counter discrimination on
grounds of gender, race, disability, age and sexuality.

Cover design: Liam Roberts Design
Front cover image: Unsplash/Patrick McManaman

To the Critical Race Theorists. All nations.

Contents

Series editor's preface		viii
List of abbreviations		x
Acknowledgements		xi
Preface		xii
1	Introduction: 'no place in our society'	1
2	Race: real and unreal	22
3	Permanent racism: Derrick Bell's racial realism	45
4	Postracial Britain	69
5	Against antiracism	95
6	Whatever happened to the Black working class?	117
7	Conclusion: Black futures	144
References		151
Index		173

Series editor's preface

Kalwant Bhopal (University of Birmingham, UK)

Debates about social justice, inclusion and equity in the early twenty-first century have become increasingly more contentious and problematical. This should not come as a surprise and reflects Western social, economic and political climates driven by neo-liberal narratives; the rapid expansion of European Union membership followed by signs of its impending potential dissolution; such as the election of Donald Trump as 45th President of the United States of America in 2016; and, the growing populism of nationalist political parties in almost every western democracy. At the same time the global south has seen economic expansion on a scale undreamt of a generation ago that threatens to undermine the hegemony of the West.

This original book series delivers a forum for marginalised and minoritised perspectives in the social sciences. It challenges contemporary dominant discourses about social justice, inclusion and equity from the perspective of marginalised and minoritised communities. Drawing upon the work of researchers, theorists and practitioners from Europe, the US and the Global South, the series adopts a broad interdisciplinary approach including disciplines such as education, sociology, social policy and childhood studies. The titles in the series are published on broad topics, underpinned by research and theory.

The series draws upon definitions of social justice that identify the marginalisation and exclusion of groups and communities of people based on their difference from the majority population. The series seeks to understand how such processes should be disrupted and subverted. Social justice in this respect is both the subject matter of the book series but also its practical contribution to academic scholarship. By providing an outlet for scholarship that itself emerges from under-represented voices the books published in the series contribute to addressing rather than simply commenting on social justice issues. The series centres social justice, inclusion and equity as a key focus; gives voice to those from marginalised communities and groups; places a spotlight on the work of under-represented (minority ethnic, religious, disabled, female, LGBTQIA+) academics; and challenges hegemonic narratives that underpin western discourses about how best to reach a socially just world.

A key strength of the series includes a broad range of topics from different disciplines in the social sciences including education, sociology, social policy, gender studies, migration and international relations, politics and childhood studies. The series draws on themes which include race/ethnicity, gender, class, sexuality, age, poverty, disability and other topics which address and challenge inequalities. It includes a range of different theoretical perspectives including addressing intersectional identities.

Permanent Racism explores how racism continues to be an everyday feature of life. It uses Critical Race Studies and Black Atlantic thought as a framework for understanding lived racial experiences and politics in Britain. Drawing on the scholarship of Derrick Bell and Kimberlé Crenshaw, Warmington counters disinformation about Critical Race Theory by reminding us of what it is and what it is *not* – and specifically outlining why it represents a challenge to current discourses of postracialism and the demonisation of antiracism. Furthermore, Warmington reminds us why it is vital to acknowledge how communities of colour have been erased from the cultural definition of the working class. In each of the chapters, Warmington powerfully and eloquently analyses why the centering of race remains vital to understanding issues of social justice and equity and why the need for focused anti-racist thought and action continues to be vital in a cultural and political climate in which racial inequalities are normalised.

List of abbreviations

BLM	Black Lives Matter
CLS	Critical Legal Studies
CRED	Commission on Race and Ethnic Disparities
CRT	Critical Race Theory
EHRC	Equality and Human Rights Commission
FSM	Free School Meals
NHS	National Health Service
ONS	Office for National Statistics
RRAA 2000	*Race Relations (Amendment) Act 2000*

Acknowledgements

I am grateful to friends and colleagues who offered encouragement either directly or indirectly during the writing of this book, at what was a challenging time for many of us. Many thanks to: Michael Apple, James Avis, Centre for Global Learning at Coventry University, Centre for Identities and Social Justice at Goldsmiths College, Centre for Research in Race and Education at the University of Birmingham, Charlotte Chadderton, Lyn Clouder, Sean Demack, David Gillborn, Karen Graham, Emily Henderson, Remi Joseph-Salisbury, Vini Lander, Zeus Leonardo, Helen Mabhikwa, Ian McGimpsey, Shamim Miah, Open University BME Researchers Group Seminar, Kevin Orr, Laurence Parker, John Preston, Race Empire and Education Collective, Farzana Shain. Thanks also to Kalwant Bhopal, Martin Myers, Karl Kitching and Kenzo Sung (Key Issues in Social Justice) and colleagues at Policy Press for commissioning this book and supporting the production process: Laura Vickers-Rendall, Jay Allan, Annie Rose, Amber Lanfranchi, Millie Prekop, Caroline Astley, Zoe Forbes, Freya Trand, Sophia Unger. And thanks most of all to the Warmington and McLoughlin families, with much love to Jeanette, Aisha and Eli.

Preface

This book is about Britain, the politics of postracialism and the 'permanence of racism'. It is about the ways in which, instead of transcending race and racism, postracial claims too often provide new ways of voicing racism – and, we should also say, new ways of *doing* race, since race is not an inherent human quality; it is less something we 'are' than something we 'do' and that is 'done to' us. Today the image of Britain as a postracial or non-racial society is, to poach Orwell, a characteristic fragment of the national scene. We are urged by politicians and pundits to 'move on' from the failed multicultural approaches of the past and warned that demands for race equality may have gone too far. In the years since the landmark public inquiry into the Metropolitan Police's mishandling of the investigation of the murder of teenager Stephen Lawrence, the *Macpherson Report*'s (1999) focus on structural and institutional racism has gradually been eroded. Instead, a facile postracialism has come to inform Britain's politics, social policy and public debate. In the wake of the Black Lives Matter (BLM) protests of summer 2020, the postracial project has accelerated, becoming a kind of state-sanctioned postracialism.

The facile mode of postracialism is rooted not in a desire for social transformation, but in political convenience. It is an expression of Britain's long held wish for a kind of racial closure, wherein demands for racial justice to come to a conclusive end – not, mark you, to see the end of *racism* but to erase from the domestic conversation the politics of race that have complicated British identity since the second half of the 20th century. Today, we gloss over the fact that up until the 1980s there was still a fraction of British society that clung to the belief that communities of colour could literally be removed en masse from British society. Today those dreams of closure have been replaced by postracialism's discursive erasures, its unseeing of racism. The features of state postracialism are its colourblind ideology, an accompanying 'anti-' or 'contra-' antiracist discourse and the disqualification of communities of colour (and the complications of race) from Britain's class matrix.

Some 30 years ago the US critical race scholar Derrick Bell reflected on his own times, in which the hopes and energies of the civil rights movement had, he believed, dissipated because of undue faith in the state's promises of formal equality and the continuing deferral of lived racial justice. He wrote:

> The goal of racial equality is, while comforting to many whites, more illusory than real for blacks. For too long, we have worked for substantive reform, then settled for weakly worded and poorly enforced legislation, indeterminate judicial decisions, token government positions, even holidays. I repeat. If we are to seek new goals for our

struggles, we must first reassess the worth of racial assumptions on which, without careful thought, we have presumed too much and relied on too long. (Bell, 1992: 13–14)

Derrick Bell was one of the founders of Critical Race Theory (CRT), an inspirational though currently much maligned body of scholarship. Bell will haunt this book, alongside other writers working in CRT and in the wider flow of Black Atlantic thought, but the book is grounded in Britain's recent history. Bell warned against seductive postracialism, reminding us that racism continues to be present 'in the real lives of black and white people, not in the sentimental caverns of the mind' (Bell, 1992: 198). He added the sobering conclusion that, given its political usefulness, racism is not likely to be abolished any time soon. Struggles against racism were, Bell argued, entrenched in 'a pattern of cyclical progress and cyclical regression' (Bell, 1992: 98). He therefore urged an unsettling paradox: that those who are committed to racial justice should start from the position that in the world we have constructed over the past half millennium, racism is best regarded as a permanent feature of society (Bell, 1993). In other words, we should set aside the insistence that 'we shall overcome', set aside belief in the arc of the moral universe. There is, as yet, no postracial domain.

This book has a particular concern with the ties between race, racism and colour. Not all forms of racism are colour-coded. In Britain, discrimination against Gypsy, Roma and Traveller communities is rife, some of it state-sanctioned. Anti-Jewish racism persists in multiple forms; we most certainly do not live in a world that is 'post-' antisemitism. This book does not focus exclusively on anti-Black and anti-Brown racism but its analysis was conceived and developed in what now seems a very brief window of discourse between the BLM protests of summer 2020 and the very British backlash that quickly followed.

In 2020, BLM's global momentum was so evident that in Britain, as in other parts of the world, the great institutions opted to express solidarity. This was, we were assured, a moment of profound and irreversible change. Yet within months the UK government issued a major report in response to the BLM protests that systematically denied the concept of institutional racism and belittled what the report called the 'well intentioned' youthful idealism of activists. The reversal was quickly sealed. BLM and associated movements were soon, more often than not, portrayed as dangerous examples of antiracism gone-too-far. The youthful idealists were now ingrates and cultural vandals, perhaps even agents of so-called cultural Marxism: legitimate targets for punishment in Britain's farcical-cum-tragic war on 'woke'. In 2022 journalist Nesrine Malik wrote that 'There is no better example of how quickly history is rewritten to suit the establishment than the aftermath of the Black Lives Matter protests' (Malik, 2022b). The politics around

BLM frightened many and we have now regressed into insisting either that antiracist social movements are unnecessary and undesirable in today's Britain or else that the antiracist coalitions built in Britain since the 1950s should be broken and replaced by politer, more domesticated forms, often the kind previously rejected by Black and Brown communities.

At the material level, the months and years following summer 2020 saw the return of mass Black youth unemployment; disproportionate minority ethnic deaths during the COVID-19 pandemic; the dire unfolding of the Windrush scandal; additions to the roll call of Black deaths during contact with the police; and the ramping up of racist rhetoric at the highest levels of government. All of this, of course, was someone else's misery. Britain had applied for postracial status and state postracialists had ready access to symbols of progress (not least the ethnic diversity of those in senior Cabinet posts). In March 2023 Baroness Louise Casey's report into behaviour and internal culture in London's Metropolitan Police Force concluded that there was institutional racism, sexism and homophobia across the force (Casey, 2023). Yet the Met's Commissioner, the Prime Minister and the Opposition all publicly distanced themselves from Casey's charge of *institutional* discrimination.

The space for critical race analysis – that is, to say more about racism than that it is just deplorable, the work of bad apples – is now vanishingly small. Maybe it is just vanishing. However, conversations set in motion about race and colour in Britain cannot be entirely foreclosed. Disputes over monuments and statues (such as that of 17th-century slave trader Edward Colston in Bristol, not too far from where I grew up) were often trivialised but they were a reminder that Britain has never been an innocent bystander in the history of colour, race and racism. 'Black' and 'White' were terms of existence invented and refined in Britain's colonies and plantations. They were, and still are, part of Britain's imperial defence plea.

None of this is to say that 21st-century Britain is simply 'a racist country' and nothing more – but to imply that Britain is postracial or a beacon to the rest of the world is an error. Neither is it the case that 'nothing has changed' since the days of the 'colour bar' and calls to 'repatriate' Britain's Black and Brown citizens. Some things have improved; some remain stubbornly resistant to change; some may even be worsening. Racism is a slippery field, in which the goalposts shift and the rules change, producing new modes for making people of colour aware that their place in Britain is contingent and precarious. Colour-coded racism remains part of Britain's social mechanism; struggles for racial justice remain, as Bell suggested, entrenched in cycles of progress and regression. In this third decade of the 21st century there has been much talk about the need for decolonisation. This book argues that our first step should be the decolonisation of antiracism itself. That decolonisation rests on understanding something of the permanence of racism.

Methods and language

In terms of general method, *Permanent Racism* utilises the resources of British cultural studies, obviating neat distinctions between the cultural and the economic, and including discussion of politics, policy discourses, education, social theory and media narratives. Using an intertextual approach, the book's method follows Bonilla-Silva (2015: 80) in examining 'seemingly disjointed examples' of social, historical and discursive phenomena to illustrate how Britain's racial grammar works. The term 'racial grammar' refers to the "deep structure", the "logic" and "rules" of proper composition of racial statements and, more importantly, of what can be seen, understood, and even felt about racial matters' (Bonilla-Silva, 2012: 174).

The idea of racial grammar is important because state postracialism aims to structure our understanding of racial matters (rearticulating them as 'non-racial') and how we feel about them (in its determining of the rules of the game and its legitimate players).

Terminology is contentious when writing about racial politics. Britain has often had difficulty even in finding ways to refer to communities of colour, particularly in policy matters, and particularly in an umbrella sense. 'Black' was favoured by many activists as a unifying term between the late 1960s and 1980s to denote the assemblage of African, Caribbean, East Asian, South Asian and Middle Eastern peoples brought about by post-Second World War immigration from the British New Commonwealth (that is, the Black and Brown Commonwealth). Subsequently, its homogenising tendencies were critiqued, not least by South Asians who felt that 'Black' primarily denoted those of African descent (but see the author's partial defence of the political usage of the term 'Black' in Warmington, 2014). Until very recently UK policy makers preferred 'Black, Asian and minority ethnic' as an inclusive term. It was an unloved phrase (particularly its acronym 'BAME') but fairly practical. In 2021 the report by the Commission on Race and Ethnic Disparities (CRED) suggested that the term BAME should be dropped by government, partly because of its tendency to conflate diverse identities and communities, but partly because of the Commission's ideological aversion to discussing institutional racism (see Chapter 4).

In the main, therefore, this book uses the inclusive terms 'people of colour' or 'Black and Brown communities' (and variations thereof). Inclusive terms are significant because this is not primarily a book that theorises particular racial or ethnic identities, but one that theorises dynamics between (mostly) colour-coded racism and state postracialism, with their patterns of progress and reversal. Where there are references to specific communities, ethnic and sometimes faith designations are used. However, it should be noted that absolute consistency is impossible because sometimes terms are taken from other writers, and historical discussion may rely on language used in policy in earlier periods. Problematic historical terms, such as 'non-White' and 'coloured' are placed in inverted commas.

In the British context, national terminology is also sometimes difficult. In the main, the book refers to Britain, meaning England, Scotland and Wales, because Northern Ireland's history of immigration and multiculturalism has been substantially different from mainland Britain's. It also carries with it the historical resonance of the 'British Empire', which is important given Britain's post-imperial reckoning with race and racism. However, sometimes discussion of government and policy requires reference to the United Kingdom as a whole (for example, the prime minister is prime minister of the UK, not Britain alone). In other instances, particular historical events or policies (that may be politically devolved) require reference to individual nations. Readers might also maintain that some of the politics discussed in this book (for instance, in relation to Brexit) apply to England more than other parts of Britain. This is arguable but it is a debate largely bracketed in this book, particularly given what we know, for instance, about minority ethnic educational achievement and rates of incarceration in Wales (Welsh Government/Llywodraeth Cymru, 2022) and the fact that in Scotland Black and minority ethnic families are almost twice as likely to live in poverty as White Scots (Meer et al, 2020).

Structure

The book is organised as follows. Chapter 1 offers an overview of key arguments, focusing on contradictions between colour-coded racism and the postracial turn in Britain. Chapter 1 introduces Derrick Bell's concepts of racial realism and the permanence of racism; it defines the key elements of the facile mode of postracialism that has come to shape policy and public debate in Britain. Chapter 2 surveys contemporary approaches in critical race studies. It explores analyses that overlap with and sometimes dispute CRT, including critical social theory; race critical theory; analyses of racial capitalism; and Afropessimism.

In Chapter 3 the focus returns to Derrick Bell and CRT. It traces the emergence of CRT out of US critical legal scholarship, explaining how Bell came to his racial realist position. The chapter ends by discussing CRT's influence in Britain. Chapter 4 shifts attention to Britain's postracial turn, focusing on state postracialism as a political retreat from the *Macpherson Report*'s emphasis on institutional racism, and as a backlash against BLM. Chapter 4 argues that Britain's current mode is a form of 'really existing postracialism': a state-sanctioned postracialism wherein symbolic achievements have overtaken actual achievements in importance.

Chapter 5 examines the symbiotic relationship between state postracialism and contemporary political and media antagonism to antiracism: 'anti-'

or 'contra-' antiracism, as it were. It reflects on how, particularly since 2020's BLM protests, critics of antiracism and multiculturalism gone-too-far have sought new discursive spaces, urging moral panics around BLM, CRT and the trial and acquittal of the Colston Four. Chapter 6 considers an accompanying means by which Britain has sought a conclusive end to problems of race and racism: by discursively erasing people of colour from Britain's social class matrix, positioning Black and Brown people in opposition to Britain's authentic White working class, as a 'legitimate grievance'. Chapter 7 concludes by reflecting on the politics of race and racism in relation to Britain's post-*Macpherson*, post-BLM reversals. It returns to the dialectic between pessimism and possibility that informs Bell's insistence on the permanence of racism.

1
Introduction: 'no place in our society'

Racism has no place in our society. At least, that is what we are told. In any given month the 'no place' mantra will be recited by politicians, journalists, campaigners and celebrities. We repeat it to show how much we deplore racist chanting on the football terraces or social media trolling over the casting of some sci-fi blockbuster. The problem is, however, that for centuries racism has had a very real and active place in our societies. Historically, racism has been a cataclysmic tool: as powerful an invention as any weapon of mass destruction or model of artificial intelligence. It has structured nations and empires across the globe, facilitated the mass movement of populations and the genocide of peoples. Released from the Pandora's box of Atlantic slavery and European colonialism, colour-coded racism, in the historically specific form of White supremacy, shaped the modern world from its outset and it has remained current as a tool for structuring power under capitalism.

Today racism fuels nationalist dreams of building borders to keep out 'others'; paranoid 'great replacement' theories; authoritarian social policies and 'anti-woke' political discourses. At the daily level it informs our experiences of education, employment, health, criminal justice, migration and political representation. Racism remains a valuable political recruiting tool, helping to frame questions of national identity, justifying state violence, rationalising environmental extraction and determining which communities are seen as deserving of resources and compassion, and which are seen as dispensable. The 'no place' mantra cannot alter this historical truth. Speaking in postracial terminology does not birth a postracial society.

Colour-coded racism persists, but in 21st-century Britain, and in other White majority multiracial nations, postracial ideology is preferred over racial justice. We are encouraged to view racial injustices and inequalities through a 'colourblind' lens, as not being about race and racism at all and, in fact, as being caused by 'anything but racism'. This facile postracialism is rooted not in a desire for social transformation, but in political convenience. Insofar as it has now been appropriated in government and policy, the facile mode has become the ideological basis of a form of *state postracialism*, promoted in policy discourse and sympathetic media, through state and state adjacent bodies.

The features of Britain's state postracialism are its facile, colourblind ideology; a parallel 'contra-' antiracist discourse; and the disqualification of communities of colour from Britain's social class matrix. Our state postracialism is an expression of the desire for demands for racial justice to be hauled to a conclusive end: to erase from domestic conversation the politics of race that have complicated British identity and are now adjudged to have gone too far. Those hard headed enough to suggest that colour-coded racism still creates fundamental fault lines in British society will be met with consoling counter examples: the appointment of 'non-White' cabinet ministers; diversity in our national sports teams; grime artists at Glastonbury. In other instances, however, sanctions are preferred to celebration. Schools, universities, charities and local authorities may be threatened with the machinery of government if they are thought to align with Black Lives Matter (BLM), Critical Race Theory (CRT) or to fall short of applying 'age-appropriate balance' in teaching about race and racism.

This introductory chapter focuses on the contradictions between the persistence of colour-coded racism in Britain and the postracial turn: that is, Britain's state-sanctioned postracialism. It argues that in order to counter postracial myths, those committed to racial justice should take a realist position rooted in the lessons to be drawn from critical race studies.

Derrick Bell and the roots of Critical Race Theory

The title of this book is *Permanent Racism*. This stark phrase comes from the writing of Derrick Bell, one of the founders of CRT. Bell argued that the goals of a postracial society, while comforting to many White people, are more illusory than real to people of colour. The defining quality of Bell's social analysis was its departure from liberal models of equality and diversity, a rejection rooted partly in Frantz Fanon's understanding of racism as a permanent feature of modern social formations (Bell, 1992: x). Put simply, Bell's originating questions were about why, after decades of civil rights struggle and equalities legislation, severe racial inequalities and everyday injustice persisted.

CRT, the body of thought that Bell initiated, cohered across the 1980s in the writing of a multiracial network of US critical legal scholars, including Kimberlé Crenshaw, Alan Freeman, Richard Delgado, Mari Matsuda and Cheryl Harris, subsequently evolving into other fields, particularly education. CRT can be defined as an analytical framework for understanding the presence of racism within social and political formations. It is not primarily a theory of identity but a framework for understanding structural and institutional racism. Its focus is both on the *origins* of structural racism and its *reproduction* through institutional culture and practice. CRT's institutional starting points are legislation, policy, education and their parallel discourses: the symbolic structures in which our ideas about what constitutes, for example, 'just law' or 'good education' are embedded. CRT is far less interested either in individual prejudice or the kinds of race hate promoted by extremist groups. The fact that CRT was (and continues to be) developed by Black, Latinx,

Asian, Jewish, White and indigenous thinkers has always been a problem for malicious critics who have sought to portray CRT as somehow 'anti-White' or 'anti-western'. CRT certainly does not argue that all White people are racist or that White people are uniformly privileged in economic terms.

CRT applies concepts such as 'interest convergence', 'contradiction closure', 'colourblindness' and the 'ordinariness' of racism to counter the ideological claims to neutrality and meritocracy that are today the lingua franca of fields such as law, social policy, news media and education. As Kimberlé Crenshaw argued, our great social institutions are not mere facilitators of rule-based systems; they are complicit in 'constructing the rules of the game, in selecting the eligible players, and in choosing the field on which the game must be played' (Crenshaw et al, 1995: xxv). These are 'taken for granted' processes; CRT's aim is to make them visible. Without naming racist policies and practices, there is no way of countering them.

This is permanent

In mapping out CRT's originary framework, Bell did not suggest that nothing had ever changed and that there had been no improvements in race relations, but his concern was with patterns of progress and regression in civil rights (see Chapter 3). Policy reversals meant that too often apparent landmarks in racial justice would, within a short space of time, be hollowed out: left as zombie measures that had little effect on everyday lives. His conclusion was not that antiracist action is pointless but that positional victories – improvements in educational outcomes, increased representation in legislative bodies, positive media images – do not imply that race as a line of social conflict ceases to exist. This, by the way, was not a prescriptive analysis; it was descriptive. Bell and his colleagues did not argue that racism *should* be a permanent feature of society, only that it seemed locked into the societies we have constructed, too politically useful to be relinquished by our institutions. For Bell, this understanding was 'racial realism' (Bell, 1991, 1992, 1993, 1995b). He regarded claims that a postracial era was imminent as demonstrably absurd, but he also offered a kind of non-Marxist dialectic, predicated on the contradiction between the permanence of racism and the potential for change (Bell, 1993).

Bell's racial realism, by definition, was at odds with postraciality. Moreover, it departed from the utopianism or millenarianism that imagined racial justice in terms of an incremental climb to a shining city on a hill. It was a disruption of racial grammar, of the accepted ways of imagining civil rights struggle. Neither did Bell's analysis of the permanence of racism connote an apocalyptic scene of racial conflict or the rise of some neo-fascist new world order. Its concern was with the everyday grind of racism: the social reproduction of racial inequalities and the weak implementation and periodic reversal of race equality policies. For Bell, racism was, above all, *ordinary*; it was business as usual.

It should be noted that even some of CRT's advocates have struggled with Bell's insistence on the permanence of racism. CRT based critiques of institutional racism are sometimes topped off with hopeful suggestions that if we initiate a new organisational procedure, an innovative committee or stakeholder research project, we might remedy our situation. However, without grasping Bell's racial realism and his ideas about the permanence of racism, other CRT concepts, such as interest convergence, have little purchase. Bell's racial realism (and his philosophical pessimism) must be taken seriously if there is to be any possibility at all of addressing, let alone abolishing, current conditions of racial injustice.

British exceptionalism: 'I don't see race'

Ideas about permanent racism sit ill with 21st-century Britain's postracial self-image, but this is hardly new. C.L.R. James, the great Trinidadian historian, referred often to Britain's 'squeamishness' about addressing race and racism. Decades later, in her book *Why I'm No Longer Talking to White People About Race*, Reni Eddo-Lodge described Britain as a country 'still profoundly uncomfortable with race and difference' (Eddo-Lodge, 2017: xv), arguing that there is widespread refusal 'to accept the legitimacy of structural racism and its symptoms' (Eddo-Lodge, 2017: ix). Too often, conversations about colour, race and racism are forestalled by the claim 'I don't see race', hence our tendency to become mired in the murky talking points often used as stand-ins for race and racism in the national conversation: arguments over 'wokeness', statues, asylum claimants, fundamental British values or the fate of the 'left behind' working class. Where race matters enter public debate more directly, we see shrill anxiety over terms such as 'White privilege' or the teaching of the history of empire in schools. In truth, public debate on race and racism in Britain has long been stymied by a belief in British exceptionalism: the notion that Britain has been uniquely burdened with the challenges of multiculturalism and that 'our' racism in Britain is somehow better than 'their' racism elsewhere (particularly the US, but also other parts of Europe – hence the UK being self-described in a recent government commissioned report as a model for other White-majority nations).

Britain's postracial exceptionalism springs from a deep well. In the 1980s and 1990s British scholar Hazel Carby wrote about policies in immigration, policing and education that 'seemed to promise that race problems would have a conclusive end (returning whence they came) and protect white interests in the process' (Carby, 1999: 192). Successive UK prime ministers have urged the nation to 'move on' from models of multiculturalism, concepts of institutional racism and postcolonial embarrassment. Writer Arun

Kundnani (2007) argued that: 'The beginning of the 21st century marked a high point of progress against racism in Britain. Since then multicultural Britain has been under attack by government policies and vitriolic press campaigns with an intensity unmatched by anything since at least the 1970s' (Kundnani, 2007: 180). As state multiculturalism (its flaws notwithstanding) has withered, that regression has accelerated. With the resurgence in 2020 of BLM – in response to the murder of George Floyd – there was a brief window in which BLM seemed state adjacent. It was a window of discourse that has now passed and we are currently in a period of regression predicated upon the conviction that demands for racial justice have gone far enough.

Contradiction closure is a term used in CRT to refer to a particular kind of symbolic achievement. It is where policy or legislation initiated in response to a crisis in race relations is hailed as a finite solution to problems of race and racism. In actuality, these policies may, to use Bell's words, be 'weakly worded and poorly enforced' (Bell, 1992: 13). No matter. In the immediate term they are hailed as profound turning points, 'never again' moments. Britain's contemporary postracial turn can be understood as contradiction closure at a 'meta' level; it suggests that with the passing of time, demographic shifts and evidence from social attitudes surveys, we have irreversibly consigned racism as we knew it to the great 'elsewhere' (Warmington, 2009). In political discourse it is implied that matters of race and racism belong to other times and other places. In the ostensibly postracial world we may encounter phenomena that look very much like racism but we can reassure ourselves that what we are witnessing is, in fact, 'anything but racism'.

Postracialism: rearticulating racism

The political purpose of the colourblind 'anything but racism' mode is that it creates discursive space both to disavow and to rearticulate racism (see Crenshaw et al, 2019). In other words, it allows us to distance discourse and policy from the kinds of crude racism that most of us in theory deplore, while allowing space for racial injustice to persist under other guises, but with a non-racial disclaimer. In his book *Are We All Postracial Yet?* South African critical race theorist David Theo Goldberg argues that in denying the persistence of structural and institutional racism, postracialism has constructed a *neo-raciality* (Goldberg, 2015). That is, just as postcolonialism did not signal the end of colonialism, but rather the onset of neocolonialism, so postracialism gives space to new (or remodelled) expressions of racism. Goldberg writes:

> What the claim about postraciality as the end of race suggests, rather, is simply that a certain way of thinking about race, and implicitly of

racist expression, has been giving way to novel understandings, orders and arrangements of racial designation and racist expression. Race (as we have known it) may be over. But racism lives on unmarked, even unrecognized, potentially forever. (Goldberg, 2015: 6)

Here, Goldberg speaks both to facile 'I don't see race' postracialism and to the *permanence* of racism. Importantly, the facile concept of postracialism that underpins state postracialism does not usually claim that racism does not exist; it is not that bold. Our postracialism admits that there is still racism in society (though it is declining) and it admits that there are still social inequalities between communities. What it does is to argue for a particular relationship (or non-relationship) between racism and racial inequalities.

The assumptions of facile postracialism

Facile postracialism's key assumptions are these. First, there clearly is still some racism in society but it is declining generation on generation; it is largely a hangover from a darker past. Second, this racism is essentially external to our social structures and institutions; it is a form of prejudice harboured by malevolent or ignorant individuals – the proverbial bad apples. Third, once racism is defined in this way as an individual belief or act, the argument that racism is a structural or institutional feature is made unintelligible; concepts such as institutional racism must be bracketed or, more often, dismissed outright. These claims lead us towards a fourth, very pivotal point. If racism has declined in salience but there are still demonstrable inequalities between different communities, then in a sense there is 'more' racial inequality than there is overt racism. In one respect, antiracists would agree with the postracialists here; racial inequities are not caused primarily by individual prejudice.

However, since facile postracialism dismisses the idea of institutional racism, then existing racial inequities must be viewed through a colourblind framework: as being caused by factors other than racism, as being caused by anything but racism. These might be framed, via forms of statistical modelling for instance, as supposedly 'race free' factors or variables, such as social class, geography, markets, household income or levels of parental education. However, this kind of colourblind analysis shows a profound misunderstanding of the way that racism works and of the extent to which society is sinewed by racism. It relies on what Crenshaw et al (2019) have defined as a determined *unseeing* of racism. It refuses to grasp that parental education, for instance, is already shaped by racial inequities (Gillborn et al, 2018). Moreover, it rarely takes much time for this scratching around for 'non-racial' factors to elide into cultural deficit theses.

This is how racism is rearticulated. The disadvantages experienced by communities of colour are not said to be evidence of racial inferiority per se, but they are assumed to be shaped by deficient attitudes, values, family structures and insufficient aspiration within those communities. The colourblind framework provides the racial grammar in which such statements can be made. Colourblind accounts pivot us towards Bonilla-Silva's definition of postracialism as 'racism without racists' (Bonilla-Silva, 2010: 1), a mode wherein politicians, policy makers and media commentators are able to perform sympathy and to condemn crude racism, while underplaying the effects of institutional racism.

A powerful recent example of colourblind policy was the report by the Commission on Race and Ethnic Disparities (CRED) (2021), initiated by Boris Johnson's Conservative government in response to 2020's BLM protests (see Chapter 4 of this book). A decade earlier, the *CRED Report* (2021)'s reasoning was encapsulated by one of its advocates, a firm critic of 'old' models of multiculturalism, the journalist and author David Goodhart: 'Is British society still to blame for some of the real problems facing some young black, urban men, or are they the authors of their own misfortune or at least victims of an ideology that says they can only fail in British society, thus ensuring that they do?' (BBC, 2011: 11).

After all, if Black communities lack aspiration and hold on to defeatist attitudes, then their failures are perhaps not unjust at all but merely fated. By this logic the whole idea of racial *injustice* becomes dubious. Bell's racial realism, like that of Bonilla-Silva (2010) and Crenshaw et al (2019), lay in his recognition of this symbiosis between disavowal and rearticulation.

21st-century postracialism: a three-headed dog

Britain's 21st-century postracial turn, its state postracialism, is a mode of disavowal and rearticulation, of seeing and unseeing racism. It rests on three powerful interlocking elements. First, as discussed in the previous subsection, we have a facile iteration of postracialism, akin to what Eduardo Bonilla-Silva in the US has described as colourblind ideology (Bonilla-Silva, 2010; Bonilla-Silva and Dietrich, 2011). This facile postracialism asserts that while racism has not entirely disappeared, its social salience has declined and that race is no longer a useful lens through which to understand social inequality. It is facile because it remains premature, given the proven and entrenched racial inequalities existent in Britain. Evidence of these persistent inequalities can be seen in recent reports such as the *Lammy Review* (2017); the *Race Disparity Audit* (2018); the *Evidence for Equality National Survey* (see Finney et al, 2023); the *Independent Review into the Standards of Behaviour and Internal Culture of the Metropolitan Police Service* (Casey, 2023).

Insofar as the facile mode becomes the basis of government policy and discourse, what we are left with is a kind of state-sanctioned postracialism or, if you like, 'really existing postracialism', whose relationship to more complex, transformational theories of postracialism (see Chapters 2 and 4) is not dissimilar to the relationship between the complex ideas of Marx and the Soviet-era societies of 'really existing socialism'. The point to note about the phrase 'really existing postracialism' is that (as per 'really existing socialism') it means more or less the opposite of what one might at first think. In other words, 'really existing postracialism' (and I use the phrase with some gallows humour) does not signify a postracial society at all, but rather a combination of political expediency and flattering self-image.

There is a large body of writing on what has been termed 'really existing' or 'actually existing' socialism (see Saed, 2016). For the sake of brevity, it refers to the societies that in the 20th century claimed to organise themselves according to Marxist political and economic principles, such as the USSR and East Germany. The problem was that while Marx and Engels had offered penetrating critiques of capitalism's contradictions, they had not outlined a blueprint for an alternative post-capitalist society, and quite clearly they could not have foreseen the conditions in which 20th century Communist Party states would emerge.

Left critics of these states (particularly those writing after the USSR's savage repression of the Hungarian Revolution of 1956) recoiled from their authoritarianism and their atrocities. These critics inverted the self-designation used by states such as East Germany that claimed to have successfully produced 'really existing socialism', and instead used the term 'really existing' to signify the chasm between Marx's critique of capitalist domination and exploitation, and the repressive and exploitative states that 'really existed' in the name of Marxism. For some critics, the failures of the Communist Party states were either simply evidence of the gap between unattainable ideals and reality or else of deliberate and cynical 'deformation' of Marx's principles (Mosley, 1978: 29). Others argued that the failures of 'really existing socialism' were the consequence of the historical circumstances in which the Communist Party states were constructed: principally their accelerated creation of industrialised economies that were as wholly bureaucratised, exploitative and violent as the societies that Marx had critiqued. However, citizens of these 'really existing' socialist states were not credulous; they understood the gap between what the state professed to be and the actual daily grind of its wheels. It was, after all, the gap in which they lived.

In his book *Capitalist Realism*, Mark Fisher (2009) suggested that late capitalism had produced its own 'really existing' form. Shiny neoliberal states depicted themselves as meritocratic, economically competent and socially compassionate, with an excess of symbolic achievements to verify these claimed qualities and to support the greater claim that there was no viable alternative to capitalism. Under 'really existing capitalism' there was widespread understanding that this supposedly dynamic yet caring capitalism was not all it was cracked up to be but also an awareness of the dominance and insidiousness of the official 'really existing' capitalist line.

In a comparable sense, our 'really existing postracialism' is premised upon symbolic achievements that bear little relation to the lived experiences of communities of colour in Britain, which in many cases are still shaped by hostile immigration policies, authoritarian and unaccountable policing, and sharp disparities in employment, education and health. These ordinary miseries are, however, paralleled by an official state postracialism that reassures us that race is no longer salient and that throws up symbols of diversity and tolerance, proclaiming that 'we no longer see a Britain where the system is deliberately rigged against ethnic minorities' (CRED, 2021: 8). This state postracialism has largely superseded the 'state' or 'municipal' multiculturalism in which Britain invested during the 1970s and 1980s (see Warmington, 2014).

Second, accompanying this facile postracialism is its necessary parallel: a strident antagonism to antiracist movements. This 'anti-' or 'contra-' antiracism seeks to delegitimise antiracism, through media caricature and, more seriously, through the machinery of government. It parallels 'really existing postracialism' because if we have moved on to the postracial uplands, then those who continue to advance critical race analyses are, at best, an anachronism and, at worst, must be treated with extreme suspicion: as divisive figures, even as reverse racists. Those of us working in critical race studies are more than familiar with being told that the 'real' problem is that "people like you keep talking about racism". From both the 'post-' and 'contra-' standpoints, it is not so much racism that is the principal problem, but the antiracists who make structural and institutional racism visible. Inevitably, this reactionary take flows into wider 'anti-woke', culture war politics. Recent targets have included projects to decolonise school and university curricula, the Rhodes Must Fall campaign, BLM and CRT.

Third, Britain has found an additional way of erasing matters of race and colour-coded racism from public debate: the discursive erasure of communities of colour from Britain's social class matrix. This is apparent, in particular, in the disqualification of people of colour from authentic working-class identities. Despite Black and Brown communities being, by most measures, 'more' working class, experiencing higher levels of unemployment, lower home ownership and greater levels of poverty, Britain's current policy and media discourses depict Britain's authentic working class (the 'left behind') as White, and only White. Communities of colour are not only largely stripped of their class identities; they are also often positioned, as per Enoch Powell's old formula, as the chief cause of White working-class loss and therefore as a legitimate grievance: a vessel into which multiple resentments can be decanted. Multiculturalism has, it is suggested, produced Black gain and White deficit. This phenomenological disappearance is a profound form of elimination, for in Britain to be 'outside' class identity is a form of what Black Atlantic thinkers such as Orlando Patterson and Stuart Hall have termed 'social death' (Hall, 2017: 70) (see Chapter 6).

In considering class contradictions in post-imperial Britain, Carby argued that principal among them was 'the attempt to balance the perceived needs of the working class and the demands of capital' (Carby, 1982: 184). One means of rhetorically resolving this contradiction was the manufacture of a national interest, a 'we're-all-in-it-together' construction of national identity. Analyses such as Carby's treat 'national interest' as a political construction. It is not an objective social or economic interest but a political project to construct and maintain workable cohesion between a nation's different social fractions. It is a collective fiction, but one that has a stubborn presence both in national and international politics (Giusti, 2022). Moreover, because it is a fiction it must be constantly renewed. As such, 'national interest' has something in common with both Benedict Anderson's (1983) concept of imagined community and also with the Centre for Contemporary Cultural Studies (CCCS) Education Group's (1981) idea of political settlements: a term used to describe the ways in which different social interests negotiate points of political convergence. Settlements are unstable, multivocal and require degrees of compromise, but they are reasonably durable. In CRT, concepts such as interest convergence, contradiction closure and the permanence of racism are used to help understand the role of race in the construction (and relative stabilisation) of settlements in national interest and identity.

As Carby (1982, 1999) argued, the place of Black and Brown communities within Britain's national interest has always been ambiguous and subject to majoritarianism. In some instances, communities of colour are deemed to be 'within' (as in Britain's promotion of urban music and fashion); at other times their presence and requirements can be constructed by the state as being 'outside' or even in opposition to the national interest (as in many debates on immigration, multiculturalism, social class and national security). For Black and Brown people, Britishness is provisional and deferred. That very mobility – race as political football – ensures that communities of colour play an important stabilising role in Britain's sense of national interest and identity.

Postracialism's collective fictions

Our 'really existing postracialism' accords symbolic achievements greater importance than actual achievements. Those symbolic achievements often bear little relation to the lived experiences of communities of colour in Britain. Fisher (2009) drawing on Zizek and Lacan, emphasises the importance of 'the collective fiction, the symbolic structure, presupposed by any social field' (Fisher, 2009: 44). In postracial Britain the collective fiction of 'really existing postracialism' produces a comforting state of suspension, wherein it is asserted that in matters of colour, race and racism things have changed, even if they have not yet changed as much as we would like. The makeup of a national football team is said to herald progressive patriotism; the GCSE results of a model minority are presented as proof that barriers to achievement and social mobility have been overcome. In such instances the lives of people of colour become props by which racial progress is measured.

In October 2022 the UK gained its first 'non-White' prime minister, in Rishi Sunak. It was not an Obama moment; Sunak did not rise to leadership via general election but at a moment of economic and political disarray. He became the UK's third Conservative prime minister in less than 2 months, after the populist Boris Johnson left office amidst scandal and was replaced via the party membership's vote by Liz Truss. She resigned after only 44 days when her government's opening mini-budget led to a financial crisis. The muddled circumstances under which Sunak came to power, his reticence to speak on issues of racism and his severe lines on immigration and culture war issues (see Chapter 5) meant claims that the UK's first British Asian prime minister represented a break with the past were somewhat muted. Nevertheless, there were still references, nationally and internationally, to Sunak's postracial significance: 'A new Dawn for Britain' (*Daily Mail*, 25 October 2022); 'Here Comes the Sunak: Britain's First Asian PM' (*Metro*, 25 October 2022); 'Rishi Sunak, First Non-White and Hindu, to Take Over as UK PM' (*India Ahead*, 24 October 2022). For former Chancellor of the Exchequer Sajid Javid, it was proof that 'Britain is the most successful multiracial democracy on earth and proud of this historic achievement' (Crabtree, 2022). Labour's Leader of the Opposition, Keir Starmer, greeted the new prime minister in the House of Commons by asserting the significance of Sunak's ascent:

> 'The first British Asian Prime Minister is a significant moment in our national story. And it's a reminder that, for all the challenges we face in the country, Britain is a place where people of all races and all beliefs can fulfil their dreams. That's not true in every country and many didn't think that they'd live to see the day when it would be true here. It's part of what makes us all so proud to be British.' (Starmer, 2022)

The depiction of Britain as a place 'where people of all races and all beliefs can fulfil their dreams' was part of the postracial collective fiction. However, by February 2023 at his 100 days in office mark it was reported that Sunak was the least popular UK prime minister of the past 25 years (Walker, 2023). Given the economic woes and industrial strife that marked his coming to power, it would be wrong to attribute Sunak's unpopularity simply to racism among the electorate. However, it was a reminder of the transience of Britain's symbolic achievements in racial progress. Indeed, in some quarters the precariousness of this 'significant moment in our national story' was made all too clear. As Britain prepared to crown its new king in May 2023, commentators from the right-wing GB News channel described Rishi Sunak as 'not fully grounded in our culture' and, grotesquely, questioned whether a 'heathen' prime minister should read from the Bible at the coronation. No longer were there many claims that Sunak's premiership held much significance in the path to racial equality.

Ordinary racism

The collective fiction exists apart from everyday life, wherein communities of colour experience deferral of racial equality. Alongside the official postracial culture there are daily interactions with the state, in which, to use CRT's terms, racism is not 'post-' but 'ordinary'. Think for instance of the COVID-19 lockdown period, in which ordinary racial disparities were cruelly revealed and nervously discussed. In both main COVID-19 waves, people of colour were at higher risk than White Britons of contracting and dying from COVID-19 (Public Health England, 2020; ONS, 2020). In England, 21 per cent of healthcare staff are from 'Black and minority ethnic' backgrounds but in the period between March and April 2020 they accounted for 63 per cent of healthcare workers' COVID-19 deaths (Cook et al, 2020).

In addition, in Spring 2021 it was reported by the Office for National Statistics (ONS) that, at the end of 2020 amidst the economic downturn caused by the pandemic, 41.6 per cent of Black people aged 16–24 were unemployed, while unemployment among young White people of the same age stood at 12.4 per cent (Thomas, 2021). This unemployment figure was comparable with the mass Black youth unemployment of the early 1980s (in 1982 Black youth unemployment reached 41.8 per cent). By Spring 2022 Britain's labour market had stabilised post-lockdown, yet Black youth unemployment stood at 26 per cent, compared to 10 per cent among their White peers. Aside from brief coverage in Britain's centre-left *Guardian* newspaper, these figures went largely unremarked in political and news media debates. Britain long ago became apathetic about Black unemployment (it was one of the areas very unevenly addressed in the *CRED Report* (2021).

It is not only in the labour market that racial inequalities have become entrenched. Black and minority ethnic households are twice as likely as White British families to live in household poverty (SMC, 2020). In 2021, research by the Economics Observatory took issue with several of the claims made in the *CRED Report* (2021) about the decline in racialised disparities. Their research calculated that pay gaps experienced by Black Caribbean, Black African, Bangladeshi and Pakistani communities compared with their White counterparts had not closed in decades (Manning and Rose, 2021).

Asset gaps also persisted, with Black home-ownership rates being under half those for White families and Bangladeshi adults having on average a quarter of the wealth held by White adults (see Bell, T., 2021; see also Henehan and Rose, 2018).

In 2022 House of Commons research reported that each year between 2004 and 2021 Black and minority ethnic prisoners accounted for around a quarter of the prison population. In 2020 Black and minority ethnic people comprised around 12 per cent of the UK population but 28 per cent of the prison population in England and Wales (Sturge, 2022). In schools, rates of permanent exclusion have now remained stuck for decades with Black Caribbean pupils being permanently excluded from school at three times the rate of White British pupils (Gillborn et al, 2016; DfE, 2019). *Guardian* research from Spring 2021 showed UK schools to have recorded over 60,000 racist incidents in the previous 5 years; their report raised significant queries about the government's collection of data on such incidents (Batty and Parveen, 2021).

Given the circumstances in which the BLM movement became prominent in the early 2020s, following the murder of George Floyd during police arrest, it was particularly sobering when in February 2023 the UK charity INQUEST reported that UK government data showed Black people were seven times more likely than White people to die following the use of restraint in police custody (INQUEST, 2023). The report stated that UK governments' previous accounts of Black deaths in or following police custody had relied on partial data and had significantly underestimated fatalities. Moreover, the report's authors suggested that 'none of the [police's] accountability processes effectively and substantially consider the role racism might have played in these deaths' (INQUEST, 2023: 11). One of the report's key conclusions was that police accountability was limited by the failure to account for institutional racism: 'The idea that racism exists beyond explicit bigotry is not accounted for in the current bureaucratic and political structures. These are failing to recognise racism exists in a much deeper way in society that has roots in its power structures' (INQUEST, 2023: 12).

The readiness to recognise racial bigotry while treating 'deeper' institutional racism as unintelligible is an important dimension of facile postracialism. It allows the speaker to avoid the obvious absurdity of claiming that racism does not exist at all, while depicting racism as something existing on the margins of society, as external to our institutional cultures and practices; it does not capture what CRT describes as racism's ordinariness.

For example, in February 2023 there was a violent clash outside a hotel used by the government to house asylum seekers in Knowsley in the northwest of England. Rioters, some of whom were armed and some of whom belonged to far-right organisations, torched a police vehicle and shouted "Get them out" at the hotel's occupants. Fifteen people, including a 13-year-old boy, were arrested. It was a chilling and extraordinary event. The racism and intolerance of the crowd attacking the hotel was self-evident. However, the daily production by politicians and news media of an ambience in which violent action becomes, for some, 'logical' goes largely unremarked. Relentless headlines in national newspapers about small boat crossings and the UK government's commitment to concentrating refugees in hotels in poor districts, unable to work and unintegrated into local communities – all of that is ordinary, business as usual.

In a significant sense, CRT is not principally concerned with racism at the extremes. Britain is not heaving with shaven-headed neo-Nazis. This is not to say those types do not exist at all (they certainly do) but while antiracism and antifascism overlap, they are not identical. People of colour are aware that they might encounter knife-wielding thugs in a dark alley but they will certainly at some point encounter racist policies and practices in schooling, the labour market, policing, health provision and immigration control. This again is racial realism.

Britain: still postcolonial, still melancholy

Although our 'really existing postracialism' may be facile, it also springs from a deep well. As argued earlier in this chapter, Britain's postracialism is symbiotic both with an antagonism to antiracism and with a revisionist take on multiculturalism that discursively locates communities of colour 'outside' of class identity. In state-of-the-nation debates, Black and Brown communities are too often cast not as legitimate actors but as a *legitimate grievance*: props in a national story in which multiculturalism is viewed as a contributor to, and perhaps even the direct cause of, Britain's perceived decline and disorientation. In Britain (and perhaps in England, in particular) the ambiguous location of communities of colour is constructed, in part, via the discourses that exist around the end of empire and patterns of immigration thereafter. Racial formations based on Whiteness do not require US histories of segregation or battles over civil rights legislation. Appeals to race, both tacit and overt, pervade British culture and politics.

Two decades ago, in his landmark book *After Empire*, cultural theorist Paul Gilroy wrote about Britain as a country locked into postcolonial melancholia (Gilroy, 2004). Gilroy described Britain at the start of the 21st century as engaged in an existential quarrel with itself, as it sought the 'means to hold fear, anxiety, and sadness over the loss of empire at bay' (Gilroy, 2004: 126). The least costly forms of psychic defence often depended on revisionist depictions of Britain's imperial and colonial past: 'Though that history remains marginal and largely unacknowledged, surfacing only in the service of nostalgia and melancholy, it represents a store of unlikely connections and complex interpretive resources. The imperial and colonial past continues to shape political life in the over-developed-but-no-longer-imperial countries' (Gilroy, 2004: 2).

A central theme in Gilroy's analysis was the shift away from the models of state multiculturalism that had been, albeit imperfectly, a feature of social policy in the 1980s and 1990s (as in, for instance, the work of the Greater London Council, the Inner London Education Authority and the Macpherson Inquiry). That shift, Gilroy argued, was backed by a 'growing sense that it is now illegitimate to believe that multiculture can and should be orchestrated by government in the public interest' (Gilroy, 2004: 1).

Re-reading *After Empire* some 20 years later, it is hard to resist the feeling that in terms of postcolonial melancholia, Gilroy's Britain was still on its starter menu. At the time of that book's publication in 2004 the UK's New Labour government was, it is true, tarnished by the Iraq War, and in the EU elections the anti-immigration UK Independence Party made gains. However, elsewhere there was some cause for optimism. The UK's economy grew by more than 3 per cent in 2004, its best year since 2000 (BBC News, 2005). Northern Ireland's power-sharing agreement held and the UK government continued to increase expenditure on the National Health Service. Globally, Europe and North America were still benefitting from the economic and social stability of the 1990s, marked by relatively high growth and low inflation, and in Britain there was little in the way of industrial action. There were disturbances in northern English towns in 2001 but nothing comparable with the urban uprisings of the early and mid-1980s.

By contrast, the melancholic Britain of the 2020s is still, in terms of public services, living standards and political mood, deeply riven by effects of the 2008 financial crash and the decade of austerity policies that began under successive Conservative governments in 2010. Britain in the early 2020s is a post-crash, post-COVID-19, post-Brexit society, affected as is all of Europe by Russia's war in Ukraine. The Brexit campaign of 2016 and the UK's decision to leave the European Union saw the remobilisation of melancholic accounts of Britain's imperial past and a tightening of its 'hostile environment' immigration policies (see Tomlinson, 2019). Among the victims of the hostile environment were those caught up in the so-called Windrush Scandal (see Chapter 6).

The hostile environment persists. For example, in the dying days of Boris Johnson's premiership (2019–2022), a deal was struck to deport asylum seekers landing in the UK to Rwanda for 'processing'. This strand of immigration policy was endorsed by the succeeding prime minister Liz Truss in 2022 and her Home Secretary Suella Braverman, who explained to 2022's Conservative Party Conference: 'I would love to have a front page of the *Telegraph* with a plane taking off to Rwanda. That's my dream, it's my obsession' (Dearden, 2022). At a time of political disorientation (five different Conservative prime ministers served between 2016 and 2022), the hostile environment and its various manifestations were deployed in an important stabilising role. In June 2023 the Rwanda scheme was ruled unlawful by the court of appeal; the UK government announced plans to appeal against the decision.

Economically, Britain remains in the tightest squeeze on living standards since the Napoleonic Wars. Politicians of all stripes agree that the country faces a cost of living crisis. Between October 2021 and October 2022 the UK's GDP flatlined and annual inflation rose from less than 1 per cent to nearer 10 per cent (ONS, 2023). In September 2022, *The Financial Times* notably described the UK as essentially a poor society with some very rich people living in it (Burn-Murdoch, 2022). Whatever else we can say about Britain in the 2020s, it is no longer imperial. It is unsurprising then that matters of race and racism which, on the one hand, require Britain to acknowledge its histories of empire, slavery and colonialism, and on the other hand, require it to reimagine its uncertain present and future, provoke discomfort.

Learning from critical race studies

The initial subsections of this introductory chapter have given a sense of this book's focus on the collective fictions of Britain's 21st-century postracialism. The remainder of the chapter discusses the book's standpoint: how it approaches the task of exploring race, class and postracialism in Britain, and where it is located in terms of intellectual tradition: in critical race studies and wider Black Atlantic thought. 'Critical race studies' is the term used in this book to refer generically to critical scholarship on theories, histories and sociologies of race and racism. CRT is only one specific strand within critical race studies, one emerging from the work of Bell and Crenshaw in legal scholarship and academics such as Gloria Ladson-Billings and William Tate in education. Writers such as Jamaican critic Sylvia Wynter or US Afropessimist Frank B. Wilderson certainly work within critical race studies without sitting directly within CRT. There are other important critical race scholars, such as Zeus Leonardo, who write often about CRT, while drawing upon a diverse range of scholarship.

In the past two decades CRT has reached beyond its US origins to influence scholars in Britain and elsewhere. However, many of the founding statements of 'BritCrit' (the term derives from Hylton et al, 2011) date from the mid-2000s, in what now seems a very different moment, culturally and politically. The aim of this book is to reimagine 'BritCrit' for new times by reconsidering CRT's foundations, specifically Derrick Bell's racial realism, but also ensuring a historical grounding in the British context. This book also has an intrinsic interest in CRT, insofar as CRT has become an object of moral panic within Britain's postracial schema (see Chapters 4 and 5).

However, it does not confine its range of influences to CRT; it also explores potential dialogues between core CRT and scholars such as Sylvia Wynter, Lewis R. Gordon, Eduardo Bonilla-Silva and Charles W. Mills.

CRT and critical race studies are located within the larger flow of Black Atlantic thought, a tradition that reaches back in its written forms at least to W.E.B. Dubois, and perhaps further. Black Atlantic thinkers have examined experiences often treated as historically and sociologically peripheral. In fact, they are not peripheral but central to modern and postmodern histories of cultural production and dislocation, violent capitalism, migration and exile and, of course, racialisation. Black Atlantic thought should be no more confined in its influence than other great bodies of scholarship. Paul Gilroy has long argued that Black Atlantic thinkers have produced intellectual resources with which to develop critical understandings of Britain's social formation and the place of race within it, emphasising that 'These insights are not ours alone but will belong to anyone who is prepared to use them' (Gilroy, 2004: 61). That point should not need restating but academia in Britain is accustomed to viewing Black Atlantic and critical race scholarship as marginal. Too often in my career I have encountered colleagues who seemingly cannot see how critical race studies might have application beyond what they regard as 'minority' experiences.

Atlantic crossings

In Britain, one set of criticisms has obsessed over CRT's US origins, as if British scholars have done little or nothing by way of transfer work, by way of grounding their CRT analyses in Britain's own social and historical contexts. These responses to ongoing Black Atlantic conversations strike a jarring note, given that so many academic colleagues are lauded for incorporating the 'foreign' thought of, say, Bourdieu, Deleuze or Derrida into their work. It is hard to overestimate the academic racism in play in much of the emphasis on CRT's 'imported' status. Gramsci's work originated in local struggles within Italian communism in the 1920s, as well as in observations on the competing approaches of Frederick Taylor and Henry Ford to industrial production. Hannah Arendt drew ideas from her study of the Dreyfus Affair that divided France in the 1890s. A student of Marx would be well advised to have some understanding of divisions in Hegelianism in 1830s Germany. The work of such thinkers is regularly and rightly transferred to new contexts. Their work may well be critiqued but rarely on the crude basis that concepts developed in Germany or Italy in specific immediate contexts have no application to contemporary Britain. Different rules apply, it seems.

Academic racism notwithstanding, CRT must certainly be stretched, just as Fanon urged us to stretch Marx, so that we can understand in what instances its analyses are transferrable. One reason for scrutinising CRT's transfer is that North American CRT has uttered its key conceptual claims in both local and global registers (compare, for example, Derrick Bell's focus on US legislation with Charles W. Mills's historical analysis of the construction of racial contracts in modern social formations). There is nothing peculiar to CRT in this. All social theory originates somewhere along the line in local observations but these can direct us to the global. David Gillborn, one of the first British academics to use CRT, argued early on that: 'There is no reason, however, why the underlying assumptions and insights of CRT cannot be transferred usefully to other (post-) industrial societies such as the UK, Europe and Australasia' (Gillborn, 2008: 26).

He was correct in that CRT has generated a whole series of off-shoots, of which 'BritCrit' is only one. These off-shoots include Latinx CRT ('LatCrit': see Solórzano and Bernal, 2001); CRT scholarship on the position of East Asian groups ('AsianCrit': see Buenavista, 2016); CRT scholarship on indigenous peoples ('TribalCrit': see Brayboy, 2005); CRT analysis of anti-Jewish racism ('Hebcrit': see Rubin, 2020). There is also CRT-derived writing that explores intersections between race and sexuality ('QueerCrit': see Han, 2008) and race and dis/ability ('DisCrit': see Annamma et al, 2013). Each of these off-shoots has taken a distinctive line in trying to understand processes of minoritisation and practices of resistance. CRT has now been adopted by scholars working in Europe, South America, South Africa and Australia.

In his landmark study *The Black Atlantic: Modernity and Double Consciousness*, Paul Gilroy set out to explore the 'transverse dynamics of racial politics' (Gilroy, 1993: 4). He proposed a countercultural map of modernity as experienced in the confluence of African, American, Caribbean and European cultures over centuries of exchange; it was an attempt to understand Black cultures and histories in ways not contained by national borders. Gilroy's transnational emphasis was a determined rejoinder to the quiet crypto-nationalism that he perceived in British politics and academia, wherein historical understandings of British (or, perhaps more precisely, English) national identities too often fell prey to exceptionalism: a cultural particularism and nationalism that crowded out proper consideration of the transnational forces that shape what appear to be 'national' identities. Gilroy's concept of the Black Atlantic has been a powerful contribution to the sociological imagination. CRT has particular origins in two of the great foundations in Black Atlantic thought: the structural analysis of W.E.B. Dubois (the American-Ghanaian) and the social constructivism of Frantz Fanon (the Martinican-Algerian).

For Gilroy, the social construction of race, with its 'symbolism of colours' and associated 'language of nationality and national belonging' (Gilroy, 1993: 1– 2), was a historical force that shaped Britain's national identity but that could not be understood in exclusively national terms. For Gilroy, Black life in Bow, Butetown and Lozelles produced cultures and experiences 'in a syncretic pattern in which the styles and forms of the Caribbean, United States and Africa have been reworked and reinscribed in the novel context of modern Britain's own untidy ensemble of regional and class-orientated conflicts' (Gilroy, 1993: 3).

The politics of the Black Atlantic have been profoundly influential on the politics of race in Britain but not always welcome. Part of the reason is that, while not generally refusing political alliances, those with Black Atlantic politics have tended to produce analyses of racism qua racism and have been resistant, for instance, to treating race as an epiphenomenon of class, as merely subjective or as vaguely analogous to other equalities categories. Initial opposition in Britain to CRT from a subset of the White Left tended to rely on an analysis of race as a secondary identity (Warmington, 2020). Among conservatives there has been a determined effort to deride the Black Atlantic Left politics as anachronistic and sometimes to draw dividing lines between Black Caribbeans who drove Black Left politics in Britain and more recently settled Black Africans (Begum, 2021). Incidentally, in September 2022 when Liz Truss succeeded Boris Johnson as UK Prime Minister, there was a good deal of comment on the diversity of her cabinet and the fact that none of the great offices of the state were occupied by White men (a short-lived state of affairs, given that Truss's premiership lasted less than 50 days). A little noted point was that this diversity did not include any senior cabinet members from Caribbean backgrounds (the same applied to her successor, Rishi Sunak).

'This is not America'

I restate some of these thoughts on the Black Atlantic because, in the wake of the killing of George Floyd in the summer of 2020 and the resurgence of the BLM movement globally, Black British thinkers and activists were urged by some politicians and media commentators to stay away from what they regarded as extraneous US influences, and were warned against making inconvenient transnational comparisons. However, British thinkers were not cowed. Historian David Olusoga has written about the BLM protestors who toppled the statue of slave trader Edward Colston in Bristol in June 2020 (Olusoga, 2021). He notes both the symbolism and the political connectivity of that event. The police killing of George Floyd, an African-American man, descendant of slaves, on the streets of Minneapolis was captured by social media. The images led to a transatlantic resurgence of BLM, which in turn led to the pulling down of the statue of a slaver whose ships, three centuries earlier, had set sail for West Africa and then to the Americas as part of the triangular trade.

In addition, efforts to suggest that that the influence of Black Atlantic politics in Britain is based on a misrecognition of connections between

Britain and the US overlooks the direct family ties with the US, Africa and the Caribbean that are strong in Black British communities, and is often ignorant of the transatlantic dialogues that informed grassroots Black British politics across the 20th century (see Warmington, 2014). Black Atlantic dialogues are not merely academic or driven by social media; there is daily movement and conversation, and what may appear to be national issues are, in fact, transnational. The Black Atlantic triangle has been an uncomfortable political truth in Britain.

Chapter 6 of this book makes a case as to the enduring influence of Enoch Powell on the politics of race, class and immigration in Britain. It is not a claim lightly made and, indeed, I half apologise for again summoning this poltergeist. In his 'rivers of blood' speech, delivered in Birmingham in April 1968, the Conservative Shadow Cabinet member warned that Black and Brown immigration would bring about an apocalyptic disintegration of British life. However, an oft-forgotten paragraph of the Birmingham speech was dedicated to Powell's fearful awareness of transatlantic Black political activism. He warned that 'Nothing is more misleading than comparison between the Commonwealth immigrant in Britain and the American Negro' (Powell, 1968). According to Powell, US Black Power spoke to an entirely different history: one that apparently had no connections with Britain's imperial past. Even though Powell acknowledged that the Black population of the US 'was already in existence before the United States became a nation' (Powell, 1968), he did not acknowledge that its slaves had been inserted into a collection of mostly English colonies. In contrast, said Powell, 'The commonwealth immigrant came to Britain as a full citizen ... and he entered instantly into the possession of the rights of every citizen' (Powell, 1968). Whether this was a point of honour or regret for Powell was hard to say.

Powell's anti-Americanisms foreshadow much more recent government diatribes against US 'imports' such as BLM and CRT. In October 2020 in a debate on Black History Month in the House of Commons, an Equalities Minister declared: 'On the history of black people in Britain, again, our history of race is not America's. Most black British people who came to our shores were not brought here in chains, but came voluntarily because of their connections to the UK and in search of a better life' (Badenoch, 2020: 1011–12).

The minister did not explain the nature of those historical connections, nor what it was about those international relationships that meant Britain offered a *better life* than its former colonies. Of course, much separated this speech from the politics of Powell's times. A Parliamentary debate celebrating Black History Month would, for Powell, have signified the end times that he luridly imagined. However, as initial sympathy over Floyd's death was recast into concerns about the politics of BLM, 'this is not America' became another mantra.

Conclusion

Permanent Racism draws upon critical race studies and Black Atlantic thought as a framework for understanding lived racial politics in Britain. It is not the only framework for considering racism in Britain but it is a historically vital one that I can speak to as a child of the 'Windrush Generation' (and, believe me, no-one called us that in real time). Audre Lorde writes of the moment she learned that her 'energies for struggle were not acceptable unless I pretended to match someone else's norm' (Lorde, 2017: 41). She learned also 'that if I didn't define myself for myself, I would be crunched into other people's fantasies for me and eaten alive' (Lorde, 2017: 41). So it is that this book remains rooted in critical race scholarship. In doing so, this book synthesises some of the most challenging currents in critical race studies. Chapter 2 explores contemporary social theories of race and racism, in order to help understand what it is that we are being 'post-', 'anti-' or 'critical' about.

2

Race: real and unreal

Critical race studies treat race as a social construct, meaning that it carries a certain kind of unreality. Defining race as *socially constructed* is the default position of critical scholars; we nervously place the term 'race' in scare quotes, in order to indicate its illusory, unscientific character, but too often move swiftly on without reflecting on exactly what this means for all of us, and why race, despite its unscientific status, retains social purchase. In short, while race may be unreal – an idea or an invention – its *effects* are real and significant. Those effects are neither historically peripheral nor merely decorative; they are internal to modernity (and postmodernity) and continue to order society in profound ways. As Frantz Fanon, a key influence on Bell and his CRT peers, well understood, race is not something that exists within us; it exists *between* us, both attaching us to and alienating us from each other. So it is that this book tries to confront race as a form of sociocultural mediation, as a 'fully social relationship' (Apple, 2001: 204).

Chapter 2 begins by exploring social theories of race and racism, in order to map a framework for understanding race and racism critically, a framework through which to begin interrogating Britain's recent conversion to postracialism. This involves thinking both about the *origins* of modern ideas of race and about the *social reproduction* of race thinking and practice. In terms of origins, a central concern of critical race studies and Black Atlantic thought more broadly has been with uncovering the modern history of the idea of race and particularly its 'symbolism of colours' (Gilroy, 1993: 1). Ties between race and colour are a more recent development than we sometimes acknowledge but the emergence of colour-coded racism was an epochal turning point. Its vast imperial sweep gave rise to race science and racial essentialism. The tangle of beliefs about colour, culture and belonging continue to shape residual ideas about race and 'races' and still function as a political tool for structuring power (though we should also note the ambiguity of this socially constructed category: as something which is oppressive but also open to subversion).

The second half of Chapter 2 discusses leading edge thought in contemporary critical race studies, examining different approaches to race and criticality. These approaches include CRT but also critical social theory as applied to race; race critical theory; analyses of racial capitalism and Afropessimism. By locating CRT within wider Black Atlantic thought, this chapter shows that CRT's understanding of race and racism does not derive only from its analysis of US civil rights struggles but from a larger international body of cultural, sociological and historical scholarship.

Race and the colour line

It may be comforting to believe that racism has no place in our society but racism is, in truth, neither incompatible with nor incidental to the history of liberal democracies as they have evolved over the past five centuries. Black Atlantic thinkers as diverse as Aimé Césaire, Édouard Glissant, C.L.R. James, Sylvia Wynter, Cedric Robinson and Saidiya Hartman have examined racism as a force deeply embedded in modernity, as *internal* to it, rather than as a historical error or as something devised by the exceptionally wicked. When talking about modernity, scholars are referring not solely to the contemporary scene but to the historical period beginning around the 16th century, wherein forms of polity, democracy, human rights, science and technology recognisable today begin slowly to emerge. Think of the 'age of reason' and 'the Enlightenment' as markers.

Cultural critic and philosopher Sylvia Wynter refers to early modernity as the emergence of a western world system 'simultaneously emancipatory and subjugating' (Wynter and McKittrick, 2015: 63): a period shaped certainly by John Locke, Thomas Paine and by the French and North American Revolutions, but also by encroaching European imperialism and Atlantic slavery, institutions that required the political and psychological justifications provided by racism. Part of the Black Atlantic project has been uncovering the 'dark history of racial domination' (Shelby, 2022: xxiv) that helped forge the modern world. African, Asian, Native American and Indigenous Australian land and labour produced the resources that fuelled western nation states and their industrial revolutions. Violent domination, repeatedly enacted and re-enacted, required rationale: hence the need for the construct we know as race.

Cedric Robinson (1983) argued that modern conceptions of race and colour were indivisible from Atlanticism, since 'Blackness' was the racialised mode in which Africans were, under slavery, inserted into western modernity. Racism, colour-coded, was the ideology through which power – master/slave, free/unfree, person/property – was structured in the plantation societies of the Americas, as they emerged in the 16th and 17th centuries on the back of the largest forced movement of people in human history (see Hartman, 2021). In Britain's case, its colonisation of Barbados, Jamaica, Virginia and its other plantation territories predated 'mature' British colonialism in the Indian sub-continent and in Africa by more than a century. Over time, the Atlantic slave trade that sustained the plantation economies in British, French, Dutch, Spanish and Portuguese colonies restricted slavery to people of African descent. The grotesque innovation of these new regimes was to rationalise their social structures by the invention of a new racialised hierarchy of humanity, one that 'hardened into a color line' (Hartman, 2021: 5).

The social construct: making 'races'

By the 18th and 19th centuries, what had begun as folk beliefs about relationships between physiognomy and human worth ossified into 'race science': the project to differentiate humanity into 'biological' units of difference (Saini, 2019; Rutherford, 2020). For at least the past century, scientists, sociologists, historians and philosophers have coalesced bumpily to refute the belief in race as a scientific category. This is not to say that the battle against 'race science' has been universally won. The writer Toni Morrison reminded us of the inconvenient fact that for centuries 'every academic discipline, including theology, history, and natural science, insisted "race" was the determining factor in human development' (Morrison, 2019: 164). 'Race science' has a persistent presence in far-right politics and in the murkier social policy think tanks (see Gillborn et al, 2022). However, sustained critiques have reduced pseudo-scientific racism to something bordering on occult status (Warmington, 2009).

Race is now understood correctly as a social construct: an invention of society rather than a product of nature. It is a kind of cultural tool that does particular kinds of political work. In their *Introduction to Critical Race Theory*, Richard Delgado and Jean Stefancic explain: 'The "social construction" thesis ... holds that race and races are products of social thought and relations. Not objective, inherent or fixed, they correspond to no biological or genetic reality; rather races are categories that society invents, manipulates, or retires when convenient' (Delgado and Stefancic, 2001: 7).

Understanding it as a social construct does not mean that we have shrugged off the idea of race; far too much has been said and done in its name. Though many recoil at the suggestion, the traces of a half millennium of race thinking and practice saturate our societies and selves. Racism has been a global export and is now an everyday feature of living. What slavery, empire and colonialism bequeathed us is what the educator Mica Pollock refers to as 'fake units of diversity' (Pollock, 2004: 18). The naming and content of these fake units shift according to time and place, since their purpose is not to illuminate social phenomena but to secure power. For example, the term 'Asian' means something quite different in the UK to what it means in the US, which in itself indicates that these units are not fixed in nature. As one of my undergraduate students once said, when struggling to define race, "It's hard to say what 'race' is but you know what it is when you're using it".

The social construct thesis tells us that race is not a delineation of prior differences that exist objectively; social construction is the process of *producing* difference. For this reason, as with the UK/US 'Asian' categories, racial boundaries are not stable. Noel Ignatiev, for example, captured this idea in his book *How the Irish Became White* (Ignatiev, 2008). Ignatiev examined the processes of racialisation by which, during the 19th century, Irish Americans transitioned from being the objects of English racism in the British Isles to becoming among the most strident defenders of the colour line in the US, as they redefined themselves in social relation to African-Americans and indigenous peoples.

More recently, in the 1950s and early 1960s, the British government could not quite decide whether Cypriot communities should be categorised as 'White' or, in the official parlance of the time, 'coloured' (see Warmington, 2014). Since the 1990s in the context of the 'war against terror', Muslims have been profoundly racialised in Britain: that is, disparate ethnic, linguistic and cultural groups have, in the dominant political discourse, been accorded the attributes of a 'race' (Kundnani, 2015). Islamophobia is clearly not a theological dispute, any more than is antisemitism. When the 'racial' dimensions of Islamophobia are pointed out, it is routine for conservatives to rebut accusations of racism by responding that Muslims are not a 'race'. What the social construct thesis argues is that the other 'races' are not races either.

And yet, while race is unreal as a scientific category, it is also all too real in its social effects. Cultural theorist Stuart Hall described why the relationship between these socially constructed categories and their material effects warrants study and resistance:

> What is, of course, important for us is when the systems of classification become the objects of the disposition of power. That's to say when the marking of difference and similarity across a human population becomes a reason why this group is to be treated in that way and get those advantages, and that group should be treated in another. It's the coming together of difference, or categorization of our classification and power. (Hall and Jhally, 1997: 2)

Critical race studies seek to understand the ways in which, through the intersection of classification and power, race and racism continue to structure power and identity – and why they will not easily be uninvented.

Race, races and racism

The idea that race is an *invention* is a useful starting point for understanding the social construct thesis and the relationship between 'race', 'racism' and 'races'. When Ta-Nehisi Coates coined the canny phrase, 'race is the child of racism, not the father' (Coates, 2015: 7) he was referring to what Omi and Winant (1986) have called racial formation: the sociohistorical processes by which racial categories are invented and used to order society, producing social hierarchies that determine who has access to particular rights, status, resources and ways of being. Coates's point is that we need to invert our vernacular understanding of racism as the unequal treatment of pre-existing 'racial' groups. 'Races' are not prior to racism. What comes first are processes of conquest, subordination and exploitation. These are later rationalised ideologically by the insistence that the subordinated peoples are subordinate because they are naturally inferior. Domination of one group by another then takes on a kind of cosmic inevitability.

The invention of colour-coded racism is pivotal in the history of race. British cultural theorist Paul Gilroy has stated that the importance of the Atlantic slave trade is not that it was uniquely wicked but because of the scale of its historical effects, one of which was the creation a world in which we speak with barely a second thought about human beings as 'Black people', as 'White people' and so forth. In *Black Marxism*, his account of the development of racial capitalism, Cedric Robinson (1983) emphasised that in mediaeval Europe, Jews were distinguished from and persecuted by non-Jews, Roma from non-Roma and Slavs from non-Slavs (it is from Slav that word 'slavery' is derived). These groups were racialised, and continue to be so.

The Atlantic slave trade invented an entirely new racial category ('Blacks'), and with it a new mode of division into racial units (the modern conception of 'races'). Atlantic slavery emerged as the late middle ages passed into the early modern period, and in its forced movement of West Africans to the Americas, it wrenched those Africans from their ethnicities, languages and faiths, and conflated many peoples into a new people. The racism that accompanied plantation slavery was not ethnocentric; it was not specifically anti-Yoruba or anti-Akan. Enslaved Africans were inserted into the western world as a new social category: 'Black' people, categorised racially in a way that was largely severed from old world ethnicities and identities (Robinson, 1983). This profound historical disruption with the old world is the reason why Robinson, Morrison and other Black Atlantic thinkers, such as C.L.R. James, have referred to enslaved Africans in the Americas as the first modern people (see St. Louis, 2007).

Drawing from Fanon's structural analysis of racism, Jamaican African-Jewish scholar Lewis R. Gordon (1995: 28) reinforces this argument, pointing out that while it is fairly safe to say that a Jewish people existed prior to anti-Jewish racism and that the Irish existed prior to anti-Irish racism, 'Blackness' was something qualitatively different – not more morally wrong, but new in kind. It is, says Gordon (1995), not clear that Africans had reason to think of themselves as 'Blacks' before being designated as such within the new racial schema of Atlantic slavery and colonialism. While categories such as 'Oriental' and 'American Indian' are comparable race designations, in the case of Africans in the Americas, the wrenching away from the old world was literal and physical. This Atlantic 'Blackness' was a new category produced entirely by and for 'doing' racism (see Robinson, 1983). Colour racism served the ideology of White supremacy that paralleled slavery in the Americas. This same White supremacy in turn produced the 'race science' through which humanity was eventually categorised and understood *globally*, with even Europe's old racisms being refracted through it. Most obscenely, 19th-century racial ideology with its 'race science' assisted in shaping antisemitism into the genocidal form that it took in the 20th century.

What critical race studies, and Black Atlantic thought more broadly, have contributed has been a framework for understanding *racism qua racism*, rather than conflating race with ethnicity and nationality, or treating the politics of race and racism as an incidental feature of class history. The reason for this focus has been the Black Atlantic's concern with scrutinising its own historical conditions, what Charles W. Mills described as the 'racial contract' (Mills, 2022: 9). The Black/White polarity continues to be conceptually important in Black Atlantic thought not because Black suffering somehow trumps other racial suffering (Black thinkers did not *invent* Black/White polarity) but because historically the redefinition of people as 'Black' or 'White' and so forth indicated a new social relationship, often overriding ethnicity, faith or language. This historically specific shift requires frameworks for understanding racialised politics of difference in their modern form.

Race and identity 'from the other side'

In Britain the tendency of Black politics, informed by the history of the Black Atlantic, to focus squarely on race and racism has not always been welcome, as is apparent not only in the current demonisation of 'BritCrit' but of many race conscious Black political movements that have been active in Britain. As explored in Warmington (2014), 'Black British' politics was powerful because it defined Blackness politically and inclusively (although this definition of Blackness has been contested) and was mistrusted not only by those on the Right, who were antagonistic to antiracism, but also some on the Left who regarded race as a secondary identity that misdirected class struggle (see Warmington, 2020).

Nevertheless, over centuries subordinated people have creatively reclaimed their racialised identities in order to challenge their subordination. Kimberlé Crenshaw, one of the founders of CRT, has unpacked the social construct thesis in her work on intersectionality. She explains that social construction refers both to the act of categorisation *and* to the meanings and values that are attached to those racial categories. One thing we can read off from this is that there was no point at which Eurocentric racial categories were innocent or apolitical. However, Crenshaw also notes that:

> The process of categorizing – or in identity terms, naming – is not unilateral. Subordinated people can and do participate, sometimes even subverting the naming process in empowering ways. One need only think about the historical subversion of the category 'Black' or the current transformation of 'queer' to understand that categorization is not a one-way street. (Crenshaw, 2023: 298)

This multilateral dynamic is the reason that in critical race studies the category of race is retained. As Lucius Outlaw (1996) has cautioned, race categories are paradoxical: being scientifically unreal but also now being a component of our social realities. Outlaw concludes that the 'exploration of "race" from this other side is required before we will have an adequate critical theory' (Outlaw, 1996: 77–8).

Race as a social relationship

The definition of race as a social relationship may be less familiar than the idea of race as a social construct but it needs to be thoroughly considered. For one thing, it necessitates a shift away from the common sense understanding of race as merely a sociological category or variable, wherein it is self-evident that this group is 'White', that group is 'Black' or 'Asian' and so forth. Instead, building on the social interactionist work of Frantz Fanon and those who have succeeded him, it speaks to the need to understand race as happening 'between' people, mediating power and status.

In short, it is inadequate to treat race as a stable ontological category. In Fanon's (1967: 231) famous dictum: 'The Negro is not. Any more than the white man' – except in relation to each other, and in relation to the structures of capitalism and colonialism. Paul Gilroy describes Fanon's work as a relational analysis of the cycle in which 'Black and white are bonded together by the mechanisms of "race" that estrange them from each other and amputate their common humanity' (Gilroy, 2004: 15). However, social relationships are notoriously difficult to depict; they resist representation (unlike sociological categories, which lend themselves to quantification and to stratification analysis). This is one of the reasons why it often really is difficult to speak about race. The social theorist Michael Apple encapsulates the sociological problem, which is also a policy problem:

> Placing race at the center is less easy than one might expect, for one must do this with due recognition of its complexity. Race is not a stable category. What it means, how it is used, by whom, how it is mobilized in public discourse, and its role in educational and more general social policy – all of this is contingent and historical. Indeed, it would be misleading to talk of race as an 'it'. 'It' is not a thing, a reified object

that can be measured as if it were a simple biological entity. Race is a construction, a set of fully social relationships. (Apple, 2001: 204)

Race resists representation because, as Apple says, 'it' is not a thing. That might seem odd to say because racism exists to be scrawled on walls and doors, screamed from passing cars. Any Black or Brown Briton can tell you this, particularly if they are refugees or wear a hijab or venture into social media – or if, like me, they are just of a certain age and grew up in the 1960s and 1970s. Yet race *as a social relationship* evades exhibition. Its effects are myriad but, particularly in the contemporary postracial turn, we are encouraged to misrecognise those effects, to attribute them to 'anything but' race.

My old PhD supervisor, a working-class Marxist, had a gnomic but incisive saying. It was that most social class research is not about class at all. What he meant was that research on social class and education, for example, was mostly stratification research that presupposed class groups and assumed that that the job of researchers was to rank them in terms of exam attainment or access to Oxbridge. The problem, he said, was twofold. First, this approach treats class only as a category, a variable like height or age – but what Marx taught was that class is not just a category; it is also a living social relationship, shaped by the labour process and its history of effects (Marx, 1883/1976). Research that treats class only as a variable struggles to convey the effects of class *relations* but it tends to be viewed kindly in policy circles because it lends itself to quantification.

Second, there is a circularity to much of this category research, wherein findings tell us, for example, that the most disadvantaged populations have the poorest school outcomes. At this point my supervisor would really tear his hair out. Of course, disadvantaged children have the worst educational outcomes: that is part of what disadvantage is! Much the same can be said about race. Research that treats race only as a sociological category or variable struggles to explain how racialised social relationships are reproduced within and by the institutions through which we move. Schools, workplaces, courts and borders all differentiate and position us in racialised terms.

We can learn useful things from stratification research. It might tell us that British Indian pupils have better attainment at secondary school level than White British pupils and lower attainment at university level. However, that may not reveal much about the actual work that race does. Race, like class, is not a lunch bag that children carry with them into school, fully wrapped. Schools, universities and workplaces are not neutral spaces into which different racial groups enter; they are institutions that do racialising work. A 6 foot, 13-year-old boy of African descent, maybe with dyslexia or adolescent depression, is constituted as 'Black' in particular ways in the classroom. Stratification analysis has its place but when we limit our understanding of race and racism solely to what stratification research tells us or define policy solely in terms of addressing 'race relations' between groups, we run the risk of misrecognising how race is constituted and how it mutates, of misrecognising exactly what it means to say that race is socially constructed.

In contemporary social policy, regression analysis that claims to control for the separate influence of different variables is amenable to government departments building 'evidence bases'. However, regression analyses of this kind rely on statistical models that are often only partially explained in published accounts. Their results are frequently reported as if they directly report reality, rather than belonging to a specific genre of statistical manipulations (Gillborn et al, 2018). Their weakness lies in being unable to account for the ways in which variables mutually constitute each other. For example, explaining racial inequalities by 'controlling for' maternal education or pupils' prior attainment fails to account for the fact that racialisation is already present in and has shaped prior attainment or maternal education. This is the way race works; it may not be 'everywhere' but it saturates too much of social life to be hived off as a discrete variable, as a 'thing'.

Race as sociocultural mediation

In shifting away from the view of race as a 'thing' and towards understanding it as a social relationship, it is useful to think further about race as a mode of social or cultural mediation. In addition to Fanon (1963, 1967), we might turn to concepts developed by the Marxist social psychologist Lev Vygotsky and his followers, such as A.N. Leont'ev and A.R. Luria. Their analyses of sociocultural mediation originated in Marx and Engels's ideas about the role of tool creation and usage in human history (Warmington, 2011; see also Leonardo and Manning, 2017). In particular, Vygotsky drew upon Engels's discussion of the ways in which societies alter the world through the production and appropriation of cultural tools but are themselves altered by using and developing those very artifacts:

> Engels argued that tool use, over evolutionary time, changed not only human environments but human physiology as well. Musculature, cerebral architecture ... were shaped to the tool as effectively as the tool was shaped to human purpose. Vygotsky drew an analogy between tools and signs, suggesting that the use of signs altered not only the social environment but also the very behavioural architecture of the users. (Holland et al, 1998: 35)

One of the analytical disputes that critical race studies have perennially encountered is the crude quasi-Marxist distinction between the subjective and the objective, the cultural and the economic. Treating race as a tool of sociocultural mediation (a tool for structuring social power via a particular politics of difference) is useful because it obviates contrived distinctions between culture and economy. Sociocultural theorist Katie Vann has critiqued the adherence to rigid distinctions between economic (supposedly objective) and cultural (supposedly subjective) domains. She argues that orthodox Marxists make a category error in their oft-expressed suspicion that struggles for political recognition might overwhelm struggles for economic redistribution. In the orthodox paradigm, labour is assigned to the economic realm; race, gender, sexuality and so forth are assigned to the cultural. Vann (2006) reframes these categories, suggesting that the contemporary political world is characterised not by the marginalisation of labour as a site for struggle but by the culturalisation of labour as a site for political struggle. She argues:

> To see that the qualification of social categories as either 'cultural' or 'economic' does not naturally follow from any intrinsic features of the subject identities they cover, one need only imagine a society in which forms of economic compensation are organized with respect to gender. In such a world, 'gender' would emerge as an 'economic' category under the rubric of which distribution struggles were engaged. Indeed, it is not difficult to imagine such a society; and this illustrates that the apparently 'economic' character of 'labor' as a social category is itself a culturally *contingent* assignment. (Vann, 2006: 2)

It hardly needs to be pointed out that the preceding paragraph could be rewritten with race as its key term. Nor, as the histories of slavery and colonialism show, is the culturalisation of labour a new phenomenon. As a mode of sociocultural mediation, race can be understood as real not because it is an essential or scientific category but as a historically specific means of effecting certain forms of social organisation, of mediating human relations.

In short, race is real and has materiality insofar as it is a cultural and political tool: as real as a hammer. In turn, myriad other tools, such as media representations, policy discourses and education systems, are also required to sustain race as a social practice, to make race work as a cultural tool. Once understood as a tool of sociocultural mediation, race can no longer be conceived of as an epiphenomenon; it must, as Apple (2001) urges, be placed at the centre. It must be understood as an invention that over time has reinvented our social architecture and social selves.

Contemporary critical approaches

This chapter explores what it means to be critical about race. So far, it has discussed ways of understanding what is meant by 'race' – as a social construct, a social relationship and in terms of sociocultural mediation. The remainder of the chapter surveys contemporary approaches in critical race studies. We should pause briefly at the use of the word 'critical'. The philosopher Lewis R. Gordon notes that in the most basic terms, being critical about the concept of race might indicate 'a purely negative function – to determine what must be eliminated or rejected' (Gordon, 2011). Indeed, there are some theorists who reject the concept of race outright, precisely because of its constructed character. For those thinkers, it is a fiction that defies proper critical analysis. However, Gordon reminds us that being critical is also about developing critique: determining the 'meaning and limits of concepts, in this case the concept of "race"' (Gordon, 2011). For the most part, those engaged in the field of critical race studies retain a concept of race to some degree, knowing the risks and sensing that race is ambiguous: that it has both real and unreal dimensions. In a minimal sense, social analyses that retain 'race' as a category can be described as *race conscious*.

Discussion in this chapter examines not just CRT, but a range of related and sometimes conflicting approaches within critical race studies. In recent years CRT has gained a public profile as a folk demon in right-wing circles. CRT is, in fact, a very specific approach within critical race studies; it is not a generic term. More often than not, attacks on CRT in mainstream media and politics refer to work that, while it may be valuable, would not be recognised as CRT in the field of Bell, Crenshaw, Delgado and their peers. It should also be noted that the approaches discussed here are not primarily theories of Blackness (even a radical theory such as Afropessimism does not describe itself as a positive theory of Blackness). Black Atlantic thought does, of course, explore Black cultural identities, styles and expression, but this book is not primarily concerned with those dimensions, vital as they are. Instead, this chapter concentrates on approaches to understanding ontologies of race and racism: ways of being critical about the concept of race and racialised social formations.

There is no simple guide to what we might include in the category of critical race studies. There is a strong argument for going back at least as far as the early 20th century writing of W.E.B. Dubois and other pioneers such as Alain Locke. In considering the larger Black Atlantic tradition we might go back to the 19th century, to the work of Frederick Douglass, and perhaps even earlier. Because this book's starting point is in Derrick Bell's concept of permanent racism, the discussion here focuses primarily on recent critical developments, beginning with CRT.

The 'critical' in Critical Race Theory

Chapter 3 examines CRT through the ideas of its founder, Derrick Bell. For the moment, however, we shall consider CRT in terms of the kinds of criticality it offers. CRT inhabits the space that Leonardo (2011) calls race ambivalence, regarding race as simultaneously unreal and unreal, as a social construct with effects that are material and far reaching. What distinguishes CRT is its sense of *realpolitik* – or racial realism (although Hogan's [2018] discussion of the tensions between the realpolitikal and the moral dimensions of Bell's thought is insightful).

One brief but influential unpacking of the critical dimensions of CRT is Gordon's (2011) essay *A Short History of the 'Critical' in Critical Race Theory*. In terms of CRT's critical genealogy, Gordon sees the ideas of W.E.B. Dubois and Frantz Fanon as pervasive influences. CRT's structural and institutional analyses (what Gordon calls its 'policy focus') have their origins in Dubois's rejection of the early 20th-century definition of racism in the US as the 'Negro problem', as a set of antagonisms caused by the very presence of African-American communities in a White majority society. Dubois was the first sociologist to contest the 'failure on the part of the theorists to study the problems of racialized people instead of reducing such peoples to the problems themselves' (Gordon, 2011). In that tradition, CRT emphasises structural analyses of racism and rejects behavioural or cultural deficit accounts: the colourblind, 'anything but' racism explanations of existing social inequalities.

Fanon's influence on CRT, argues Gordon, derives from his refusal to treat the failures of those studying race merely as failures of *method*. In a sense, Fanon's concern was with studying failure in itself: the failure of liberal modernity to realise its promises of equality, democracy and human rights. Fanon's analysis was that the cultural normativity of racist thinking in the west's conceptions of being and humanity produced 'problems where the assumptions and presumptions of the social system and its modes of rationalization break down' (Gordon, 2011). So, for example, in a racialised society, concepts of equality and human rights became so heavily qualified as to be rendered incoherent. However, Fanon argued that in a modern, rationalist culture that was also a racist culture, racist thinking was imbued with both a logic and a rationality: ones that made racism so normal that it was, except in extreme circumstances, invisible. As Gordon has written elsewhere, in a society built upon White supremacy, 'the racist is therefore normal. He has achieved a perfect harmony of economic relations and ideology in his environment' (Gordon, 2015: 86). It was from this starting point that Fanon's work focused on 'the tensions between structural identities and lived identities' (Gordon, 2011), a focus that informs CRT's analysis of the ways in which racialised groups are positioned by and experience state power – and, in particular, CRT's analysis of the ordinariness of such processes.

Put bluntly, from Dubois CRT derives its concern with the structural; from Fanon it gains its social interactionist approach. Gordon's commentary is particularly useful in identifying the origins of CRT's concern with the permanence and ordinariness of racism, its concern with the structural and with the limitations of trying to 'fix' existing systems of law or education.

Above all, CRT comprises an analytical framework that is concerned principally with structural and institutional cultures and practices, not with individuals and their prejudices, which tend merely to be the most extreme and visible manifestations of racism. In CRT even 'microaggressions' have a structural role in stabilising asymmetric racial relations.

CRT also self-evidently follows both Dubois and Fanon in retaining 'race' as an analytical concept. One is reminded of Toni Morrison's sceptical take on postracial approaches: 'It always seemed to me that the people who invented the hierarchy of "race" when it was convenient for them ought not to be the ones to explain it away, now that it does not suit their purposes for it to exist' (2019: 164).

Morrison was not arguing for retaining race in any simple sense but querying why, after centuries in which race was understood as the key social marker, conservatives (in the UK as much as in the US) now so often dismiss race as a lens for understanding social injustice. Any person of colour is entitled to a quizzical response to this turn: to ask whom this kind of postracialism serves. Morrison's response is that race consciousness becomes problematic in White-majority societies only when it ceases to be solely a tool of subordination and instead becomes a language of solidarity among people of colour (see also Hartman, 2021) and, moreover, when it becomes a language of solidarity *and* a mode of social analysis.

CRT's insistence on the social centrality of racism sets up a theoretical challenge for those who are rightly determined to reject hierarchies of racism and victimhood. CRT recognises that there are multiple processes of racialisation and that these are experienced differently by the racialised groups in question; hence, CRT has evolved off-shoots, such as LatCrit, AsianCrit, TribalCrit and HebCrit. However, what CRT has done historically is to take the Black/White or non-White/White polarity as a starting point for understanding the origins and the social reproduction of racism. In this, CRT's method is, as Leonardo (2012) has argued, somewhat akin to Marx's focus on the contradiction between workers and owners as the starting point for understanding capitalism in general. CRT's aim is not to discern which racial group suffers most but to understand racism, and colour racism particularly, by understanding 'which dynamic represents the fundamental racial tension in history' (Leonardo, 2012: 434). With its origins in Critical Legal Studies (CLS) scholarship on civil rights legislation, CRT's original proximity was to the Black/White polarity of the civil rights struggle, just as Marx and Engels's proximity was to the factories of Manchester.

Critical Theory of Race

Leonardo (2012) usefully identifies two broad approaches that sit alongside CRT. These are Critical Theory of Race (CTR) and Race Critical Theory

(RCT). CTR refers to scholarship that has applied critical theory, derived from Marxism, and most particularly the Frankfurt School, to the study of racism. CTR treats race as a dependent concept, an epiphenomenon of class antagonisms within capitalism (see Warmington, 2009, 2011, 2020). Its central argument is that one of the ways in which capitalism sustains itself is by encouraging racialised social divisions. Cruder renditions treat racism as a divide and rule strategy, a false consciousness imposed intentionally by capitalist forces. Marxist CTR rejects race as a primary relationship, regarding it instead as an ideological concept that, precisely because of its 'ideological' nature, is impossible to study critically. Instead, the concept of race must be separated from racism, which *does* merit critical analysis, insofar as it is a function of the primary relationship: the class relations of capitalist production.

Therefore, the 'Marxist inspired version of CTR is not a race conscious analysis of race but a class analysis of racialization' (Leonardo, 2012: 5). Critics of CTR, however, have sometimes argued that it is not entirely clear why a theoretical approach that rejects race as a critical concept, continues to speak in terms of racism at all. Important figures in critical race studies, such as Cedric Robinson and Zeus Leonardo, have encouraged dialogue with Marxist analyses while bearing in mind Stuart Hall's words on the position of European Marxism in relation to the histories of formerly colonised and enslaved peoples. Hall was troubled by what he thought of as the silences and evasions of Marx's historically specific models of exploitation and subordination:

> It is not just a matter of where Marx happened to be born, and of what he talked about, but of the model at the center of the most developed parts of Marxist theory, which suggested that capitalism evolved organically from within its own transformations. Whereas I came from a society where the profound integument of capitalist society, economy, and culture had been imposed by conquest and colonization. This is a theoretical, not a vulgar critique. I don't blame Marx because of where he was born; I'm questioning the theory for the model around which it is articulated: its Eurocentrism. (Hall, 1996: 265)

As noted, there is an atavistic tendency in Marxist CTR to treat class as an objective relationship and race as subjective (Warmington, 2020). The view of race as secondary and subjective has generated tensions over how to think in terms of race and class, not only in academia but in political activism. In *A Note on Race and the Left*, Nikhil Pak Singh critiques the political capital lost by the antagonism to race conscious approaches shown by a subset of the Left:

> a lot of ground was lost, particularly within a certain segment of the left, which in the aftermath of the civil rights era frequently partook of

a mean-spirited universalism that viewed most race talk as a distraction from fundamental and more general inequalities of capitalist society. ... However sympathetic to antiracist struggle, it remains difficult for left analysis and action to resist the political and theoretical reiteration of race's *secondariness*. This stance retains traces of an older socialist presumption – that the race line is 'merely' a class-line in a different and deceptive guise – that any 'left' politics that puts race first risks a descent into parochialism and mystification, leaving foundational issues of capitalist domination and class inequality untouched. (Singh, 2015)

Some of the haughtier responses to CRT in Britain suggest that the view of race as an epiphenomenon of class persists (see Warmington, 2020). Gordon (1995) relates an anecdote about an exchange at a US philosophy conference with a White colleague, a self-defined Marxist and antiracist. The White colleague argued that Black activists of the 1960s had derailed their own liberation struggle because their emphasis on Black identity impeded a unified class struggle. This colleague's view seemed to be that 'Black people's affirmation of their Black identity [was] an impediment to their liberatory goals' (Gordon, 1995: 39). In short, Black identity was a problem for Black people. Gordon reflected that: 'The problem rests within the antiblack racist's response to black presence. The speaker's argument ultimately responds to problems of race by placing the burden of racial tension upon black people; in effect, he demanded their phenomenological disappearance' (Gordon, 1995: 40).

Gordon objected to the mode of thinking in which Blacks were made to bear the responsibility for racial divisions and for tensions between race and class analyses, while (White) class-based movements were largely presumed to act from raceless and genderless positions. The onus to learn and to shift political positions lay with Blacks who deviated from proper political analysis. Insofar as CRT retains race as a critical concept, it contrasts directly with CTR. While understanding that race is a social construct, CRT argues that race-is-unreal fundamentalism fails to acknowledge the racialised assumptions of its own social theory and carries with it the risk of underestimating the continuing effects of racialised thinking and practice.

Race Critical Theory

Leonardo (2012) relates the term 'Race Critical Theory' (RCT) mainly to the writing of Philomena Essed and David Theo Goldberg (see, for instance Essed and Goldberg, 2002 – though others regard Essed and Goldberg as critical race theorists). Thinkers such as Mica Pollock in the US or Clare Alexander in the UK might also conceivably be grouped together under this broad designation. RCT is informed by a cultural studies approach, rejecting essentialist concepts of race and treating race instead as a cultural formation. In the cultural studies approach, race (as a cultural formation) has its own genealogy that does not map on to the history of capitalism in ways that are always readily decipherable. Race is not crudely regarded as an imposed identity and much of RCT's focus is on the myriad ways in which racial identities are lived and claimed. Thus:

> identity is not simply imposed but is also chosen and actively used, albeit within particular social contexts and constraints. Against dominant representations of others there is resistance. Within structures of dominance, there is agency. Analysing resistance and agency re-politicises relations between collectivities and draws attention to the central constituting factor of power in social relations. (Collins and Solomos, 2010: 6)

In RCT social interactionalist analyses of power, culture and identity are to the fore, as per Stuart Hall's famous formulation that 'Race is the modality in which class is lived' (Hall et al, 1978: 394). Exploration of the lived modality of race and its intersections with class, gender and sexuality opens up multiple focuses on identification, fluidity and resistance.

RCT has a marked British influence, since its approaches overlap with British cultural studies, whose institutional home between the 1970s and 1990s was the Centre for Contemporary Cultural Studies (CCCS) at the University of Birmingham. Under Stuart Hall's leadership (1968–79), CCCS's concepts of culture and academic study upset distinctions between 'elite' and 'mass' cultures, and between culture, economy and politics. CCCS pulsated with multi-directional influences: the Frankfurt School of sociology; Lacan's rethinking of Freud; Althusser's Marxism, Foucault's cultural archaeology and Fanon's troubling philosophy of race and being. Among CCCS's alumni were scholars from the first generation of Black British academics, including Hazel Carby, Errol Lawrence and Paul Gilroy.

Black Marxism and racial capitalism

Contemporary dialogue between Black Atlantic thought and Marxism has been invigorated in recent years by a number of scholars returning to the work of Cedric Robinson, who popularised the idea of 'racial capitalism' in his book *Black Marxism* (Robinson, 1983; see also Robinson, 2019). While acknowledging Marxism as the west's most penetrating account of capitalism, Robinson argued that Eurocentric Marxism has significant limitations in enabling understanding of Atlantic slavery and colonialism – and therefore in understanding capitalism's origins and development. Robinson argued that Marx underestimated the extent to which prototypical European racisms (against Jews, Slavs, Roma, the Irish) were embedded in European cultures long before capitalism emerged and that Marx overestimated the extent to which capitalism created a decisive break with those pre-modern racisms. Conventional Marxist analysis holds that the emergence of modern capitalism transformed medieval social relations, producing a universal capitalist relation based on commodity value and wage labour (Marx, 1883/1976; see also Postone, 1996). In contrast, Robinson argued that in large parts of the modern world – particularly the sphere of the Black Atlantic – capitalism did not represent a break with those older social relations but, in fact, deepened pre-modern racism into its modern form.

Robinson's position has subsequently been taken up by Ruth Wilson Gilmore and Robin D.G. Kelley in the US, and by Gargi Bhattacharyya (2018) and Arun Kundnani (2020) in the UK. Their work recognises that modernity and capitalism have never been non-racial projects. Racism and capitalism are coterminous; race is, therefore, neither secondary nor subjective in any distinct sense. As Bhattacharyya observes, racial capitalism is not a particular form of capitalism; it is the *only* form in which capitalism has existed: 'All capitalism emerges from a basis of racialised division ... racial capitalism is the underlying, if unacknowledged, character of capitalism as such' (Bhattacharyya, 2018: 9).

Analyses of racial capitalism are critical of the concept of race, in that they understand race and capitalism as mutually constituting each other. As an analysis of capitalism, it is far more sophisticated than the presumptive model that views capitalism as simply making divisions between racial groups that it dominates. Bhattacharyya, for example, argues that: 'Racial capitalism is not an account of how capitalism treats different "racial groups" but it is a tale of how capitalism makes difference' (Bhattacharyya, 2018: 103).

Racism (or racialisation) is therefore the process of making racial difference *and* making those differences into economic substance. We should note the implications of this understanding of the social reproduction of race for the still dominant idea of race relations, which rests on the uncritical assumption that society comprises competing racial groups and that the primary concern of race equality projects is simply with 'levelling up' and trading off between racial or ethnic groups. Analyses of racial capitalism overlap with CRT in that both question the 'levelling up' model of race equality. For if the social model depends for its stability on racial subordination and disparity, the idea that such disparities can be 'fixed' while retaining that socio-economic model are meaningless. Racism is not a glitch in the system; it is the system.

There is, however, a query about the extent to which Robinson's *Black Marxism* can be regarded as Marxist. For while Bhattacharyya's (2018) development of Robinson's thought is quite squarely Marxist, there is an argument for regarding Robinson's (1983) original analysis not as Marxism per se, but as a radical reimagining of what Marx's historical method might have produced had it taken the Black Atlantic as its analytical point of origin, rather than the European industrial capitalism that the Black Atlantic financed. Nonetheless, Robinson's work is part of an ongoing conversation about the role of Atlantic slavery as central rather than marginal to the emergence of modernity and modern capitalism. It is a conversation that stretches from C.L.R. James and Eric Williams in the first half of the 20th century to contemporary analyses of racial capitalism and to writers on race and modernity, such as Sylvia Wynter and Charles W. Mills.

Racism, modernity and political philosophy

CRT's main focus tends to be on contemporary manifestations of racism. After all, when CRT first emerged from Critical Legal Studies (CLS) in the US, its concern was with the limitations of the civil rights and equalities legislation that had been enacted relatively recently, between the 1950s and 1980s (see Chapter 3). That said, CRT is not exclusively concerned with race problems in the present. Since CRT examines contemporary societies, in which there is 'interest convergence', 'contradiction closure', 'colour-blindness', in which racism is 'ordinary' and 'permanent', some understanding of the historical processes through which those social features have been embedded is also required.

The work of Charles W. Mills examines the historical development of racial formations in western societies from a political philosophy perspective. Mills's writing ranges beyond mainstream CRT but he explicitly framed his landmark book *The Racial Contract* (Mills, 2022, originally published in 1997) as a contribution to CRT's corpus. Critical race scholars are often discouraged from pointing out the fact that the models of liberal democracy delineated by the great political philosophers of early modernity emerged in societies engaged in imperial expansion, societies that were organising concepts of the polity and human rights with reference to visions of civilisation and savagery, 'the people' and 'the other'. Mills, like fellow Jamaican Sylvia Wynter, argued that the invention of race, far from being historically peripheral, played a determining role in constituting the modern social contract and its conceptions of the polity. The social contract tradition in western political theory was not conceived as a universal contract. Mills reminds us:

> The peculiar contract to which I am referring, though based on the social contract tradition that has been central to Western political theory, is not a contract between everybody ('we the people'), but between just the people who count, the people who really are people ('we the white people'). So it is a Racial Contract. (Mills, 2022: 3)

The reference to 'the people who count' is a salient one in understanding racialised (and gendered and classed) conceptions of the national interest, given that one of this current book's concerns is with who really counts within the national interest as being British, rather than provisionally British, or as writer Afua Hirsch (2018) quips Brit(ish).

In the 21st century White supremacy is rarely codified into a formal delineation of the people who count, but then as Malcolmson (2000) has noted, White supremacy is so taken for granted that it is no longer a mode of living to which there is much need to lay claim. It is unsaid and unseen, and many will deny that it exists. Mills considers that the absence of the term 'white supremacy' from mainstream political theory's curricula and textbooks is not accidental but is simply because today White supremacy is not even perceived as a system of domination. It is 'not seen as a political system at all. It is just the background against which other systems, which we *are* to see as political are highlighted' (Mills, 2022: 1–2).

So who counts within this system of domination? Sylvia Wynter has argued that the 'archipelago' of plantation societies maintained by African labour in the Americas was pivotal in the west's 'institutionalization of the first form of its "modern world system"' (Wynter and McKittrick, 2015: 42). For Wynter, the invention of race – predicated on oppositions between civilisation and savagery, between reason and unreason – was, in a profound sense, a project to answer the bourgeois question of what it is to be human in that early modern, early secular period (Wynter, 2003). In her account Wynter prefers the term 'Man' to 'human', since early modern political philosophy was, of course, bounded by gender. She insists that since secular Man could no longer simply be defined within a Christian theological framework, the coloniser/colonised, free/unfree relationship initiated in the Caribbean (and later in the mainland Americas) provided a basis for late Renaissance and Enlightenment thought to reposition Man. This relationship became the basis on which to reimagine human-ness via an epistemological transformation, in the marking of differences that were held to indicate a permanent hierarchy of racial superiority and inferiority – of who counts as Man (Wynter, 2003; Wynter and McKittrick, 2015).

Denise Ferreira da Silva, examining Wynter's contribution to understanding the ways in which European colonial domination institutionalised racial inequality in modern thought, describes the epistemological shift from plantation racism to pseudo-scientific models:

> The post-medieval secularization of Man is followed by a second descriptive statement of man (Man2), framed within the evolution paradigm and put forth in Charles Darwin's insights on natural selection and science. This ideological shift revised humanness, according to Wynter, to differentially categorize 'all the colonized darker-skinned

natives of the world and the darker-skinned poorer European peoples themselves'. The 'new master code', a purely scientific one divided the world into the 'selected' and the 'dysselected'. (Ferreira da Silva, 2015: 94–5)

Wynter argues that the 'universal' figure of Man was, in truth, a front for a very specific racialised, classed and gendered being. As Nigel C. Gibson (2019) reflects in his own consideration of Wynter's work, Wynter's historical analysis explains how with the emergence of modernity, 'being' was colonised and Whiteness came to be regarded as 'being'. Gibson goes on to argue that although European humanism succeeded in presenting itself as universal, in its origins 'Europe's concept of humanism is intimately connected with racism, colonialism, and violence, and the subjugation of others who by definition are not human' (Gibson, 2019: 11). Speaking specifically of anti-Black racism, Gibson adds that: 'Once reified and biologized and made black, black people are overdetermined by the referent of racial inferiority' (Gibson, 2019: 11).

In Wynter's terms, the colonised humanism of early modernity was framed according to a 'principle of non-homogeneity' (Wynters, cited in Ferreira da Silva, 2015: 95). Moving into the 20th century this non-homogeneity, a structuring of power through 'racial' differentiation, was embodied in what Dubois famously called 'the color line' (Dubois, 1903: 3). The color line, notes Ferreira Da Silva, replaced previous codes that distinguished between deserving/undeserving and selected/dysselected because it functioned so effectively not only within colonised territories but also within nation states, wherein fellow nationals could be categorised and ranked into racial-colour hierarchies. Wynter's writing offers a broader historical account of what CRT defines as the stabilising role of racism: its role in structuring the allocation of rights and resources, of delineating boundaries of exclusion and inclusion, in structuring ontologies of being.

In the field of critical race studies, Wynter's interventions are significant also in recognising transnational connections between 'the black U.S. antiapartheid movement cum civil rights movement and what had been my own direct childhood memories of the anticolonial and "native" labour uprisings that had taken place in British imperial Jamaica' (Wynter and McKittrick, 2015: 41). Both, argues Wynter, need to be understood in relation to the legacy of Marcus Garvey's globally influential Pan-Africanism, a legacy that 'was to powerfully fuel the anticolonial and antiapartheid emancipatory struggles as they erupted in separate areas of the overall ex-slave-labor archipelago' (Wynter and McKittrick, 2015: 41). Garvey's influence was felt first in the Caribbean in the 1910s, in the Harlem Renaissance of the 1920s, later across the US in the 1950s and 1960s, spreading also across parts of Central and South America and to Europe. Wynter's transnational analysis is not dissimilar to that of Martiniquan writer Édouard Glissant, who urges us to '*think* like an archipelago' when exploring the transverse relations of the postcolonial world (Wiedorn, 2018: 113).

As Chapter 3 of this book recounts, CRT emerged from the US civil rights struggle, as a revisionist critique of legislation and policy. In Britain a spread of organised Black political activity was evident from the 1930s and 1940s onwards. Garvey was resident in Britain from 1935, dying in London in 1940. Around the same period, Pan-African and anticolonial groupings cohered around African-Caribbean activists in London such as George Padmore, C.L.R. James, Amy Ashwood Garvey and Harold Moody (Warmington, 2014). There were direct links between these pre-war activists and some of those Caribbeans who organised around antiracist struggles in Britain between the 1950s and the 1980s, and who were directly influenced by US civil rights and Black power struggles, such as Claudia Jones, John La Rose and Darcus Howe. Black British politics is, in an important sense, a product of Wynter's ex-slave archipelago.

Afropessimism

Those in Britain who decry CRT without having read a word of it would likely quake at Afropessimism, a body of theory with its origins in the work of Frank B. Wilderson III and Jared Sexton (see Sexton, 2016; Wilderson, 2020). Afropessimism extends Black/White polarity into what is arguably a kind of dystopianism (although, as with Bell's permanence of racism, Sexton has argued that Afropessimism is descriptive, not prescriptive). For Afropessimists, Blackness is coterminous with the *social death* conferred by Atlantic slavery. Social death is a state of (non)being in which the socially dead are exiled from the human relation: from social recognition, agency and subjecthood (Cacho, 2012). The idea of Black slavery as a form of social death is drawn from the writer and sociologist Orlando Patterson (see Chapter 6). For Afropessimists, Africans were not, as Toni Morrison or Cedric Robinson might argue, inserted into western modernity as a new people, but as 'non' people. Blacks and Whites are not asymmetrically positioned racial groups; they are qualitatively different because Black social death is the predicate for White life, subjecthood and humanity. In his pugnacious essay *Afropessimism and the End of Redemption*, Frank Wilderson states:

> Afropessimism is premised on an iconoclastic claim: that Blackness is coterminous with Slaveness. Blackness *is* social death, which is to say that there was never a prior meta-moment of plenitude, never a moment of equilibrium, never a moment of social life. Blackness, as a paradigmatic position (rather than as an ensemble of identities, cultural

practices, or anthropological accoutrement), cannot be disimbricated from slavery. (Wilderson, 2015)

Wilderson is unambiguous about what Blackness means. In his terms it refers to those of African descent, and primarily Africans in the diaspora. Non-Black people of colour experience racialised oppression but can still lay claim to humanity in opposition to Blacks, who are the negative of what it means to be human. There is, say the Afropessimists, no possibility of redemption from this social relationship.

The position of Wilderson and Sexton has a number of critical implications. First, it renders straightforward ideas of struggling for racial equality incoherent. They argue that it is impossible to assimilate the social death of Blackness into humanist narratives and into the humanist imagination. Since the Black negation of being cannot be anything other than an absence, there is no possibility of redemption (see R.L., 2013). Indeed, Wilderson (2015) argues that 'Black emplotment is a catastrophe for narrative at a meta-level rather than a crisis or aporia within a particular narrative'. Moreover, because anti-Blackness is, for Afropessimists, a unique oppression, alliances and forms of intersectionality are rendered suspect, likely becoming what Wilderson dismisses as 'borrowed institutionality', wherein Black 'allies' are encouraged to recognise analogies with other oppressed groups that are not valid, or where Black people become props by which to measure putative racial progress:

> Afropessimism argues that Blacks do not function as political subjects; instead, our flesh and energies are instrumentalized for postcolonial, immigrant, feminist, LGBT, and workers' agendas. These so-called allies are never *authorized* by Black agendas predicated on Black ethical dilemmas. A Black radical agenda is terrifying to most people on the Left because it emanates from a condition of suffering for which there is no imaginable strategy for redress – no narrative of redemption. (Wilderson, 2015)

A number of critics have pointed to theoretical and political difficulties with Wilderson and Sexton's ideas. Olaloku-Teriba (2018) sees exceptionalism and essentialism in Wilderson's definitions of anti-Blackness. She notes that, unlike Fanon, both Wilderson and Sexton seem to regard slavery as *paradigmatically* rather than *contingently* Black. Moten (2008) and Alves (2014) suggest that Afropessimism's opposition between Blackness and humanity is overstretched. Certainly, there is an antagonism between modernity's renderings of human-ness and Blackness, and this has long been recognised in Black Atlantic thought, but should that require us to frame Blackness as non-being, and as death-driven? Nevertheless, as both

Alves and Moten acknowledge, Afropessimism offers a radical interrogation of the universalising claims of redemptive models of equality, freedom and human rights. It is a significant contemporary response to the questions of ontology that emerged first in the work of Fanon and Aimé Césaire and which have subsequently informed the work of, for example, Mills, Wynter and Hartman. Like CRT, Afropessimism is an unfolding body of work (see, for instance Grant et al's [2021] development of Afropessimism in education research). It is one that refuses to frame its thought in terms of policy solutions, which are so often demanded as the price of admission Black thinkers must pay in order to enter conversation.

Conclusion

Those of us working in critical race studies are engaged in a dialogue with the old evil spirit of race: a concept that seduces us to believe in it as being natural and as old as time but which is, in fact, a relatively recent construct. However, although it grew out of both folk myth and discredited race science, racism is not merely a historical remnant; it has a powerful contemporary presence, not static but shifting and mutating. Therein lies its resistance to technical reforms, therein lies its durability. Returning to Bell's ideas about the permanence of racism, Chapter 2 argues that the history and practice of race mean that we cannot shed the category of race at will, as if it were possible to go back to a place where race does not exist, where it had never been invented: an *ante-race* world, as it were (see Leonardo, 2009).

In particular, we should be sceptical about why some of those who long relied on concepts of colour-coded race to rationalise social injustice have become sudden converts to a certain mode of postracialism. Among those converts, CRT is a fly in the postracial ointment. In one respect it has indeed been used by antagonists as an 'an empty signifier for any talk of race and racism at all' (Goldberg, 2021). However, CRT's antagonists also correctly perceive CRT as a rebuttal of vulgar postracialism. Chapter 3 of this book revisits the writing of Derrick Bell and his CRT contemporaries, such as Kimberlé Crenshaw. It endeavours to cut through contemporary disinformation about what CRT is and is not. It explains how CRT's analytical framework emerged and why it represents a challenge to seductive discourses of postracialism. Its starting points are Bell's concepts of racial realism and the permanence of racism.

3

Permanent racism: Derrick Bell's racial realism

CRT's concept of permanent racism is a troubling one, at odds with Britain's current self-image as 'the most successful multiracial democracy on earth'. The concept comes specifically from the work of Derrick Bell, whose *Faces at the Bottom of The Well: The Permanence of Racism* (Bell, 1992) is one of CRT's founding statements. In both the UK and the US, CRT is currently cast as a bête noir. It is a fitting term. Usually translated politely as a 'dislike' or 'bugbear', its literal meaning is, of course, 'Black beast'. But what is CRT and how did it come into being? Among British scholars, Bell is best known as the father of CRT and for the oft-cited though not always well understood concept of interest convergence. It is often considered enough to reference Bell in these terms and move on. This chapter explores more fully Bell's (1992, 1995b) 'racial realism' and what he meant by realist concepts such as the permanence of racism, interest convergence, contradiction closure and racism's 'critically important stabilizing role' (Bell, 1992: 8). It also revisits Bell's dystopian satire 'The Space Traders' (Bell, 1992), which allegorised the stabilising role of racism and the ways in which the interests of communities of colour can be traded away to serve racialised national projects, not least those that take on the guise of postraciality. Chapter 3 ends by discussing the development of CRT in Britain, where in the past 20 years it has emerged as a significant intellectual force among scholars and activists.

Derrick Bell did not create CRT single-handedly, but his work was its point of origin. To understand Bell's place in CRT and in critical race studies more broadly, it is necessary to examine how his ideas grew out of a revisionist critique of US civil rights law, developed by Bell along with colleagues such as Kimberlé Crenshaw, Richard Delgado, Alan Freeman, Cheryl Harris, Mari Matsuda and Patricia Williams. They argued that liberal approaches to race equality were bound up in misrecognition of how racism operates, misconceptions about the limits of legal formalism and a denial of the persistence of institutional racism. As the growth of CRT in Britain and other countries over the past two decades has made clear, those misconceptions are not limited to the US; they find parallels in Britain's own exceptionalism and in our postracial turn.

Derrick Bell

In appearance, Derrick Bell was not poster-boy material. Perhaps that is one of the reasons his legacy took time to transfer across the Atlantic. He was not Malcolm X, in Blue Note suit, posed with M1 carbine. He was not Angela Davis: clenched fist, leather jacket and Afro. He was certainly not the Alberto Korda image of Ché Guevara on the set of coffee coasters gifted to me by my wife (it is, I am sure, what Ché would have wanted). Bell looked like what he was: a middle-aged African-American law professor in conservative suit, with owlish glasses accentuating studious features. Yet, when I first encountered Bell's writing, he unsettled my worldview as much as those more fabled liberation icons. When I first read Malcolm, Angela and even Fanon, my experiences of race and racism in Britain had made me ready for them. I was not ready for Derrick Bell.

Born in Pittsburgh, Pennsylvania in 1930, Bell was the first in his family to attend college. He qualified as a lawyer in 1957, after serving in the US Airforce, including time in Korea. As a serviceman in Louisiana, Bell worked to integrate churches and bus services, and by the late 1950s the young lawyer was active in the US civil rights movement. In 1959 Bell's involvement in civil rights led to him quitting his post in the Department of Justice's Civil Rights Division, after coming under pressure because of his membership of the National Association for the Advancement of Colored People (NAACP) (Bernstein, 2011). It was not the last time Bell would resign over matters of principle. In 1985 he stood down as Dean of the University of Oregon's School of Law when an East Asian woman colleague was denied tenure; in 1992 he took unpaid leave from Harvard Law School (where he had been its first tenured African-American professor) over the lack of African-American women hired by the faculty (Harvard Law Schools News, 2011).

By the time he became known for these public stances Bell's writing had already entered the US legal canon. His 1973 book *Race, Racism and American Law* became a standard text. His scholarship was capable of rattling liberals and conservatives alike, not least because of his decades-long study of the iconic *Brown v. Board of Education* (1954) ruling by the US Supreme Court on school desegregation (Bell, 1973, 1980). His revisionist critique was eventually drawn together in *Silent Covenants: Brown v Board of Education and the Unfulfilled Hopes for Racial Reform* (Bell, 2004). Among the books that popularised CRT beyond the field of legal scholarship were Bell's *And We Are Not Saved: The Elusive Quest for Racial Justice* (Bell, 1987) and, of course, *Faces at The Bottom of The Well* (Bell, 1992). In the latter two books Bell wove together legal analysis, social theory, personal memoir and allegorical fiction into disquisitions on race in the post-civil rights United States.

Bell died in 2011. Despite his distinguished academic career, he was still, as a founder of CRT, considered sufficiently controversial for right-wing US website Breitbart to make his relationship with Barack Obama the subject of a widely shared news story during Obama's 2012 election campaign (Graham, 2012). Breitbart 'revealed' that not only had Bell been one of Obama's Harvard professors but that Obama had introduced Bell as speaker at an event in which the professor protested against Harvard Law School's lack of female faculty of colour. Over the ensuing decade CRT would take on a life of its own as a folk devil in conservative media: a trend that by the early 2020s was being clumsily emulated in Britain.

From Critical Legal Studies to Critical Race Theory

Bell's innovations in CRT were rooted in what he called racial realism (Bell, 1991, 1992, 1995b). How did he get to the racial realist position? It was in the mid-1980s that Bell and a small multiracial group of colleagues pioneered the branch of Critical Legal Studies (CLS) that has become known across disciplines as Critical Race Theory. CRT's key analytical tools – interest convergence, contradiction closure, colourblindness, racial standing and so forth – were crafted out of revisionist critiques of US civil rights law's underpinning assumptions about race equality, justice and reform. The emergence of CRT out of CLS during the 1980s is told fully and eloquently in Crenshaw et al (1995) and more recently in Crenshaw et al (2019). Crenshaw explains CRT's origin story in these terms:

> Critical Race Theory ... represents an attempt to inhabit and expand the space between two very different intellectual and ideological formations. Critical Race Theory sought to stage a simultaneous encounter with the exhausted vision of reformist civil rights scholarship, on the one hand, and the emergent critique of left legal scholarship on the other. (Crenshaw et al, 1995: xix)

CLS was founded as a Left movement in the late 1970s (Unger, 2015). Its focus was to critique legal formalism: that is, uncritical claims to neutrality and objectivity within the US legal system. For CLS's adherents (the 'crits'), the law was 'neither apolitical, neutral, nor determinate' (Crenshaw et al, 1995: xii). They argued that the legal system reproduced capitalist power relations by privileging particular topics within legal training, by enshrining property rights in law and by denying that the cultural practices of legal professionals had any bearing upon the ways in which the law was interpreted and legal decisions reached. The consequence, the 'crits' argued, was that while there was *formal* commitment to justice and equality before US law, the system's failure to acknowledge its own cultural assumptions and the social and economic contexts of wider society meant that legal decisions often compounded the disadvantages of the least powerful in society (Unger, 2015).

In CLS's analysis we can see the seeds of the critical approach to understanding political and institutional dynamics that CRT has brought to multiple fields. Education systems, for example, are formally committed to providing 'good education' to all, but this formal commitment dissolves on exposure to the social world's extremely unlevel playing field, and because the education system's own culture and practices are not themselves neutral. So it is too with the labour market, policing, health provision, housing, news media, social media and academia. In one of CRT's founding statements Crenshaw et al (1995) – speaking in the first instance about the legal system but with clear application to other state institutions – assert that what is critical about CRT is that it views the unequal practices and outcomes of institutions not merely as an instrumental reflection of existing social interests and inequalities but as *constituting* them: 'On this account the law is shown to be thoroughly involved in constructing the rules of the game, in selecting the eligible players, and in choosing the field on which the game must be played' (Crenshaw et al, 1995: xxv).

CRT came about as a partial breakaway by CLS scholars who felt that while its analysis of class and power within the legal system was sophisticated, CLS's critique of race and gender was underdeveloped. Indeed, Crenshaw (2019) has identified dissatisfaction with colourblind readings of the law by both 'formalists' and 'crits' as the primary instigator of CRT. It is also worth noting that one of CRT's principal concerns was with the colourblind content of the legal studies curriculum. Thus, from the beginning CRT focused on both the law and on education. Since the 1980s, CRT has extended its analysis, examining how multiple institutional sites produce racial differentiation and injustice. Here we see again the influence of Fanon's social interactionism and Dubois's policy focus (see Chapter 2).

Racial recognition

In an important sense then, CRT begins with a rejection of colourblindness in law, policy and education. It is not hard to see the rationale behind colourblind approaches. Under regimes of the past in which White supremacy was codified – colonial societies, South African apartheid, US segregation and what Britain once daintily called the 'colour bar' – human rights and social resources were explicitly accorded along racial lines. An obvious response to this deadly history is to insist on expunging references to race from the future practices of law, government, education and so forth: the formal application of colourblindness. However, the underlying assumption of that approach is that racial recognition in itself is the problem, rather than racism. In Crenshaw et al's (2019) *Seeing Race Again: Countering Colorblindness Across the Disciplines*, George Lipsistz offers a compelling restatement of the argument against colourblind discourses: 'Colorblindness pretends that racial recognition rather than racist rule is the problem to be solved. Colorblindness does not do away with color, but rather reinforces whiteness as the unmarked norm against which difference is measured' (Lipsistz, 2019: 24).

CRT's pioneers were well aware that the passing of civil rights law (the *formal* ending of racial discrimination and segregation) had not ended racial inequality. They held that in the absence of a level playing field, formalist colourblind approaches were insufficient to address existing racial injustice. Moreover, colourblind approaches tend to place a burden upon people of colour and on antiracists: the suggestion being that a proper solution to racist rule requires not only a rejection of overt racism but the silence of those who insist that particular attention must be paid to institutionally racist norms and practices.

As Crenshaw has also noted, 'Colorblindness is further entrenched by the fact that opponents and true believers are not easily positioned along conventional liberal/conservative lines' (Crenshaw: 2019: 52). CRT pioneer Richard Delgado explains the liberal/conservative confluence in the voice of his alter-ego Rodrigo, who in Delgado's CRT 'chronicles', helps to narrate contemporary problems in law, legal scholarship and social justice: 'Both liberals and conservatives champion neutrality in antidiscrimination law, as though treating blacks and whites exactly the same will make discrimination go away. But as we have seen, it won't. We fare little better under one regime than the other' (Delgado, 1996: 67).

Liberals will often generally adhere to colourblind principles but argue for exceptions in the cause of diversifying institutions and addressing institutional racism. Conservatives in both the US and Britain who were historically opposed to race equality policies have now often changed their strategies, adopting the colourblind moral high ground as a front for opposing antiracist action. In the US, for instance, the landmark ruling *Brown v. Board of Education* (1954) against school segregation has in several instances been used by conservative policy-makers to 'justify race-blind limits on the scope of race reform' (Crenshaw, 2019: 53).

Lest we fall into the trap of thinking these dynamics are limited to the US ('our racism is better than theirs'), the argument of this book is that contemporary postracial discourses in Britain represent exactly this kind of change in conservative strategies, whereby a society that is 'not racist' is a society whose institutions are colourblind – and a society in which antiracism is held to be as much a culprit as racism. Recent examples include the report by the Commission on Race and Ethnic Disparities (CRED) (March 2021) that sought to erase the concept of institutional racism; the House of Commons Education Committee agonising over the term 'White privilege' (June 2021); and claims that BLM has infiltrated and captured state institutions (see Chapters 4 and 5).

Bell's racial realism

The rejection of colourblindness in law and policy framed Bell's racial realist standpoint. Bell was both a CLS 'crit' and, insofar as he regarded racism as embedded in legal structures, a 'legal realist' too. Legal realists were early 20th-century legal scholars who prefigured aspects of CLS, in that they 'challenged the classical structure of law as a formal group of common law rules that, if properly applied to any given situation, lead to a right – and therefore just – result' (Bell, 1995b: 302–3). In short, legal realists argued that the law, if it were to be truly just, could not be treated as an abstract formula that merely had to be applied correctly. CRT's racial realists later adopted a similar position specifically to critique civil rights and race equality legislation and policy; their interest was in racial realpolitik, not abstract ethics.

For Bell, the problem with cleaving to what he saw as abstract and unworldly principles of law, property and rights was that it took insufficient account of history, power, demographic shifts and social trends. Courts ostensibly acted blindly but in reality were liable to act on premises that best protected the social structures of which they were part. This might sometimes mean making concessions to interests that were antagonistic to existing formations of power (as in the case of rulings on labour law or civil rights) but preservation of state authority and legitimacy was the prevailing principle. Bell referred to the state's ability to make strategic concessions to demands for racial justice in order to defend its fundamental race and class structures as *interest convergence* (Bell, 1980, 2004).

For Bell, state power in the US was a racial project: not just in the explicit terms of racial segregation, but in the everyday structural grind of policing, incarceration, housing, health and employment. Bell did not believe that racial interests remained static (hence the principle of interest convergence) but that the tendency of the state, and the law as a state institution, was towards stability and towards the national interest, as defined in majoritarian terms by White elites. It was therefore an error, Bell argued, to believe that the aim of antiracist struggle should be to ensure justice and equality merely through the proper application of legal formulae:

> What was it about our reliance on racial remedies that may have prevented us recognizing that abstract rights, such as equality, could do little more than bring about the cessation of one form of discriminatory conduct, which soon appeared in a more subtle though no less discriminatory form? I predict that this examination will require us to redefine goals of racial equality and opportunity to which blacks have adhered with far more simple faith than hardheaded reflection. (Bell, 1995b: 306)

Given some conservative critiques of CRT, a point to emphasise is that Bell's arguments about the permanence of racism did not imply that he thought nothing had changed as a result of civil rights action in the US. His overarching critique of civil rights legislation and the changes it had wrought was that, in confronting segregation's history of separate but equal policies, the law had addressed racial separation (at least in theory) but not racial inequality. Formal change had been enacted but the stabilising relationship was maintained. Bell's revisionist critique was not straightforwardly pessimistic because it urged antiracists to find new goals that were not reliant on faith in legal formalism. However, Bell's writing also involved wrestling with the ghosts of the civil rights struggle in which he had been active and a reckoning with its stillborn promises, what Bell called 'the ashes of our expectations' (Bell, 1987: 3).

Bell wrote that 'precedents we thought permanent have been overturned, distinguished or simply ignored' (Bell, 1995b: 306) and that too often campaigners 'worked for substantive reform, then settled for weakly worded and poorly enforced legislation' (Bell, 1992: 13). For precedents that have been overturned recently we need only look to moves in the US to roll back *Roe v. Wade* in the area of abortion rights, and the *Shelby County v. Holder* ruling of 2013 that partially overturned the *Voting Rights Act* of 1965, one of the major gains of the civil rights movement. In many instances, said Bell, civil rights victories served to defuse movements for racial justice. That is, they became *contradiction-closing* cases, held up as proof that racial antagonisms were now resolved. The guise of improvement – of greater opportunity, representation or diversity – too often gave the appearance of striking against racial equality, while, in actuality, maintaining racial inequality at manageable levels (see Gillborn's [2008] similar analysis of race equality policy in Britain).

Bell's four themes

In *Faces at the Bottom of The Well* Bell described his racial realism as comprising four major 'themes'. First, there was the *permanence of racism*, wherein struggles for racial justice were locked into 'a pattern of cyclical progress and cyclical regression' (Bell, 1992: 98). This pattern was not an unfortunate policy failure but an active means of stabilising a society beset by calls for racial reform. Second, there was the *economic theme*, where again Bell challenged civil rights idealism that too often became caught up in 'working towards' deferred goals. Bell cautioned: 'In our battles with racism, we need less discussion of ethics and more discussion of economics – much more. Ideals must not be allowed to obscure the blacks' real position in the socioeconomic realm, which happens to be the real indicator of power in this country' (Bell, 1992: 98).

His third theme was the importance of organising around *ongoing struggle*. Bell spoke in terms not dissimilar to those used by Stuart Hall in the British context: emphasising that the worth of our political actions should not always be measured solely by whether a putative goal or end point was achieved; learning and change also came through the journey itself. Bell spoke of this as 'fulfilment – some might call it salvation – through struggle' (Bell, 1992: 98). Salvation through struggle contrasts with the deferred salvation of race equality. Pessimism might be justified but it should not occlude resistance: 'We reject any philosophy that insists on "measuring life's successes on the achieving of specific goals – overlooking the process of living"' (Bell, 1992: 98).

Finally, Bell's fourth theme was a call for change in *political consciousness*, a rejection both of bureaucratic 'solutions' to racial injustice and of faith in endlessly deferred promises of equality: 'We also insist on the possibility for justice, requiring that we shed reactionary attachments to myths that derive their destructive and legitimating power from our belief in them' (Bell, 1992: 99).

Bell's racial realism was, above all, non-utopian. His long involvement in community activism led him to suggest that, for working-class people of colour, daily struggle was of greater practical importance than the long moral arc. In *Faces at the Bottom of The Well*, he alludes to his conversations, during his time as a civil rights lawyer in the southern states during the early 1960s, with an elderly African-American woman:

> Mrs MacDonald assumed that I knew that not all whites are racist, but that the oppression she was committed to resist was racial and emanated from whites. She did not even hint that her harassment would topple those whites' well entrenched power. Rather her goal was defiance, and its harassing effect was more potent precisely because she did what she did without expecting to topple her oppressors ... (She) avoided discouragement and defeat because at the point that she determined to resist her oppressor, she was triumphant. (Bell, 1992, xii)

Here, Bell depicts CRT as a war of position, its purpose to defy, harass and block White supremacy: to get down and dirty. Bell's insistence on the permanence of racism, as a practice and as a tool for ordering society, was itself a defiance of ahistorical understandings of race and racism.

The permanence of racism

Faces at the Bottom of The Well begins with a reference to Fanon's (1967) *Black Skin, White Masks* and an example of the 'both'/'and' dialectics central to Bell's own view of antiracist struggle:

Fanon argued two seemingly irreconcilable points, and insisted on both. On the one hand, he believed racist structures to be permanently embedded in the psychology, economy, society, and culture of the modern world – so much that he expressed the belief 'that a true culture cannot come to life under present conditions'. But on the other hand, he urged people of color to resist psychologically the inheritance they had come into. (Bell, 1992: x)

In what sense then did Bell regard racism to be a permanent feature of his society? It should be stressed here that while Bell's CRT emerged out of the post-civil rights US, it would require a high degree of exceptionalism to believe that Bell's thought applied to the US but not Brazil, that it applied to the US but not Britain or France (where, at time of writing, five nights of civil unrest, with thousands of arrests, have occurred across the country in response to the police shooting of 17-year-old Nahel Merzouk in Paris). Bell's analysis was of the contemporary legacy of racism in societies that had grown out of slavery and conquest, out of racial capitalism. Moreover, when Bell asked why racial equality continued to elude liberal democracies, he was consciously channelling Fanon's great historical question: that is, why was it that with all the tools of human rights, democratic representation, science, sociology and political philosophy at our disposal, societies have failed to eliminate racism? He wrote:

With the realization that the salvation of racial equality has eluded us again, questions arise from the ashes of our expectations: How have we failed – and why? What does this failure mean – for black people and for whites? Where do we go from here? Should we redirect the quest for racial justice? (Bell, 1987: 3)

The sobering conclusion running through Bell's scholarship was that even after the contested gains of the civil rights movements, racism remained politically necessary in the US as a stabilising force that delineated the distribution of rights and resources, and the boundaries of inclusion and exclusion within the national interest. It was a bonding mechanism with the potential to cut across White class and gender antagonisms: one that, in terms of membership of 'the people', keeps even working-class Whites from the bottom of the well (Bell, 1993). Permanent racism was akin to, or begat by, what Charles W. Mills, writing roughly contemporaneously with Bell, termed the racial contract (see Chapter 2). Mills (2022) made clear that the racial contract was not a legacy limited to the US; it was embedded across the Black Atlantic. Fanon had posed the question in Algeria; Leopold Senghor in Senegal; C.L.R. James, Aimé Césaire and Claudia Jones had posed the question across the Caribbean, and back into Europe.

For Bell, the endemic presence of racism derived in large part from the continuing economic rationale. In this he was not at odds with conventional Left analyses. However, without (racialised) social and political stability, profit is endangered; therefore, racism's role in providing social stability was coterminous with its economic value. However, as per Fanon, racism also provided collective psychic stability, a form of identification that keeps on giving. The stabilising role ensured the permanence of racism. In *Faces at the Bottom of The Well*, Bell wrote: 'The critically important stabilizing role that blacks play in this society constitutes a major barrier in the way of achieving racial equality. Throughout history, politicians have used blacks as scapegoats for failed economic or political policies' (Bell, 1992: 8).

Note here that Bell refers specifically to the role that *Blacks* play in stabilising US society. This is a given, insofar as Bell's analysis of the stabilising role emerged first from his critique of civil rights and that the initial focus of his writing was therefore on African-American communities (see, for example, his satire 'The Space Traders', Bell, 1992). However, in the context of CRT's development it is also a kind of shorthand. The stabilising force to which Bell refers is clearly anti-Black *racism*. While Bell argued that there were unique aspects to anti-Black racism in the US, he was not an Afropessimist in the mould of Frank Wilderson or Jared Sexton (see Chapter 2); Bell's corpus and the subsequent development of CRT into areas such as LatCrit and TribalCrit speak to his concern with structural and institutional racism experienced across multiple minoritised communities.

Writing in the early 1990s, Bell cast his eye over US history but also wrote in terms prescient of our own times:

> And in the 1990s, as through much of the 1980s, millions of Americans – white as well as black – face steadily worsening conditions: unemployment, inaccessible health care, inadequate housing, mediocre education, and pollution of the environment. The gap in national incomes is approaching a crisis as those in the top fifth now earn more than their counterparts in the bottom four fifths combined. (Bell, 1992: 8)

Under such circumstances, how could it be that conservative politics regularly achieved such success? Bell's answer was that, in significant part, 'They rely upon the time-tested formula of getting needy whites to identify on the basis of their shared skin color' (Bell, 1992: 8).

Bell understood that Whiteness and Blackness do not map on to economic status in a deterministic fashion, although they do a good job in this respect. However, their existential force is powerful, not least in the stubbornness of what Lewis R. Gordon has referred to as 'the gnawing feeling that racial justice is not for whites' (Gordon, 1995: 25). It was the stabilising role that rendered racial inequality immune to what policy makers in Britain have called 'levelling up'; racial disparities are the very substance of the social relationship. Far from being a levelling up, patching-up operation, putting an end to racism would indeed impose radical incoherence on our societies. In short, if racism were to cease to make sense, what else in our societies would also cease to make sense? Pull out one Jenga block and the whole edifice is liable to crash.

It hardly requires repeating that the conditions Bell perceived in the 1980s and 1990s have deepened in our own current period, post the financial crash of 2008 and amidst worsening environmental conditions. The Right populist politics that have emerged have often been seen as an expression of political chaos, but their power also lies in their promise of stability and consolation – the dream of 'restoring' economic and social order, the appeal to the values of the past, the offer of protection against the demands of minority groups. John B. Judis's (2016) historical analysis of the global emergence of populist politics over the past century, distinguishes between the ways in which Left populism and Right populism define problems in policy and politics. Judis argues that Left populists encourage a vertical and 'dyadic' worldview, wherein 'the people' are engaged in struggle against 'the elite'. In contrast, Right populism is 'triadic', in that it purports to represent 'the people' against an elite that has neglected the masses by favouring a third group, usually a racialised minority. That third group is cast as a legitimate grievance in triadic populism's schema (see Gillborn et al, 2022).

Interest convergence

Bell's theorisation of the critically important stabilising role of racism is somewhat akin to Judis's (2016) account of triadic populism. However, as a veteran of the civil rights struggle, Bell was well aware that the ruling bloc also had to negotiate, though not on equal terms, with this 'third group' (which in Bell's context comprised people of colour and, given that his analysis drew on civil rights legislation, African-Americans in particular). Racism stabilised relationships between elite and needy Whites but stabilising work also had to be done in order to govern communities of colour. Out of this insight, Bell developed the concept of *interest convergence*.

Bell's principle of interest convergence is not always well understood. It emerged from legal scholars' debates over the landmark *Brown v. Board of Education* (1954) civil rights ruling, which held that racial segregation in public schools violated the Equal Protection clause included in the Fourteenth Amendment of the US Constitution (Bell, 1980, 2004). In particular, Bell developed the concept of interest convergence in response to a contention by legal scholar Herbert Wechsler. Wechsler supported the *Brown* decision but suggested that there might be a question over whether the *Brown* ruling was based on neutral and formal legal principles or whether it was, in fact, predicated upon a particular group interest (that is, opposition to the damage that racial segregation did to Black communities). Wechsler's conclusion was that the *Brown* decision could be argued to rest on a neutral legal principle but that the principle should be regarded not as one of anti-discrimination, but of the right to free association (which, Wechsler argued, transcended the rights of any particular group, such as Whites who did not wish their children to be schooled alongside Blacks) (Bell, 1980, 1987, 2004).

In considering the *Brown* ruling and related cases, however, Bell identified a competing thesis, one that departed from Wechsler's formal analysis. It was a deeply heretical position, based on racial realism and on an understanding of the US as a racialised state. Writing in 1980, Bell argued that in considering civil rights legislation, *political history provided precedents that were as important as strictly legal precedents*. History, said Bell, demonstrated that: 'Whites may agree in the abstract that blacks are citizens and are entitled to constitutional protection against racial discrimination but few are willing to recognize that racial segregation is much more than a series of quaint customs that can be remedied effectively without altering the status of whites' (Bell, 1995a: 22).

Bell's racial realism was, as he saw it, descriptive, being grounded not in how the world should be but the world as it was. For Bell the civil rights activist, it was a world in which racial equality was not accepted as legitimate 'by large segments of the American people, at least to the extent that it threatens to impede the societal status of whites' (Bell, 1995a: 22). For Bell, this was self-evident in relation to *Brown* because African-American communities had campaigned against segregated schooling for decades. At best, these campaigns had been met with legal orders to improve resourcing for segregated Black schools, without ever endangering the status of segregated White schools by authorising integration (Bell, 2004).

However, in *Brown v. Board of Education* (1954) the Supreme Court had eventually ruled against segregated schooling. Bell argued that the decades of frustrated legal struggle preceding (and following) Brown meant that, since the essential demand for desegregation had not changed over that time, Brown's success could only be understood *in relation to shifts in the state's interests* (Bell, 1980, 2004). Paradoxically, it was the necessity of preserving the stability and authority of the state (defined by Bell in terms of middle- and upper-class White positioning) in civil rights legislation that provided the guiding political and legal principle in race relations cases.

> Translated from judicial activity in racial cases both before and after *Brown*, this principle of 'interest convergence' provides: The interest of blacks in achieving racial equality will be accommodated only when it converges with white interests. The Fourteenth Amendment standing alone, will not authorize a judicial remedy providing effective racial

equality for blacks where the remedy sought threatens the superior social status of middle- and upper-class whites. (Bell, 1995a: 22)

The preservation of racial asymmetry was so deeply embedded in the culture as to be regarded, in a racialised society, not so much a principle of group interest, but as an overriding principle of the state.

The state's interest in race equality

So what were the shifts in US interests – as in *state* interests – that by 1954 had made the Brown ruling fit the principle of interest convergence? Why did the demand for desegregation of schools that had been repeatedly rejected as incompatible with the nation's interests become compatible with US interests in 1954? Bell (1995a, 2004) identified three key shifts in the US's national interest in the late 1940s and 1950s. First, in the cold war world the *Brown* decision buffered the US's image among emergent nations in the global south whom the US sought to keep away from communist influence. Second, in the decade following the Second World War, *Brown* offered some reassurance to discontented and politically active African-Americans that the promises of the Just War, of freedom and equality, might be realised at home in the US, not only in Europe. As with the peoples of the global south, it was also essential to stall left-wing influence among African-Americans. Third, at national and federal level, there were industrial stakeholders who regarded continuing formal segregation as a barrier to economic growth in the South, both in terms of the constraints it placed on the mobility of the labour force and because of the divisions it encouraged between the segregated southern states and other parts of the country.

Critics of Bell's concept of interest convergence have focused on its pessimism, implicitly refusing to acknowledge pessimism as a legitimate philosophical position. Bell's work has been treated as overly cynical and as encouraging a fatalistic, conspiratorial mindset that some critics have argued is prevalent in African-American communities (Church, 2022). There is an air of aesthetic objection to Bell's perceived cynicism but also a familiar redirection of attention away from the state and its institutional practices towards a behaviourist view of the shortcomings of African-American communities.

Perhaps a more serious criticism is that Bell's analysis homogenises both Black interests (with, for instance, insufficient attendance to gender) and White interests (Higgins, 1992). However, Bell's work takes pains to distinguish different perspectives within White America: poor White southerners had a different historical relationship to segregation than White industrialists or the US's foreign affairs office had. However, Bell's concern was to identify what he regarded as the most critically important dynamics.

Bell well knew that there were White Americans who genuinely opposed racial injustice but, since there always had been some White opposition to racial injustice, good players in a bad system could not in themselves account for relatively sudden shifts in policy or be relied upon to counter the stabilising role played by racism, with its power to unify fractions of White society that in class terms had objectively opposed interests. Indeed, one very important aspect of Bell's work was its willingness to consider the question of how alliances between White working-class or middle-class people and White elites emerged: a question rarely addressed in the pre-Trump era. What Bell certainly did was to refuse the burden of racial divisions customarily placed on Blacks. That is, Bell did not accept that race consciousness was a barrier to liberatory goals; nor did he accept the onus of managing alliances: of working out when White Americans would or would not place racial identity above egalitarianism (Bell, 1995c).

Bell set the terms of subsequent CRT work in fields such as law, social policy and education by arguing that apparently progressive measures to address racial inequality are initiated at moments of *interest convergence*, when demands for reform converge with the self-interest of White elites. However, as David Gillborn (2010) has noted, interest convergence is sometimes misunderstood and referred to as if it were the outcome of careful managerialist policy negotiation, rather than a crisis response. Gillborn cautions that:

> It is important to note that interest-convergence does not envisage a rational and balanced negotiation, between minoritised groups and White power holders, where change is achieved through the mere force of reason and logic. Rather, history suggests that advances in racial justice must be won, through protest and mobilisation, so that taking action against racism becomes the lesser of two evils for White interests because an even greater loss of privilege might be risked by failure to take action. (Gillborn, 2010: 6)

CRT rejects assumptions that powerful elites in racist societies reform willingly. It is only when racist practices threaten to destabilise rather than secure elite power that it is in the self-interest of elites to address racism through legislation and policy. Resulting measures, usually steeped in liberal self-congratulation, tend to address only the most blatant kinds of discrimination but they often become enshrined as *contradiction-closing cases*, which are assumed to have resolved problems of racism, rendering further action unnecessary and excessive. Postracial ideology is, in a sense, a meta-level contradiction closure because it suggests that that gains in racial equality have been so substantial and irreversible that antiracist action is now unnecessary except in extreme cases; all else is 'antiracism gone-too-far'.

The romance of abolition

Other thinkers have considered the senses in which focusing on formal change has occluded our understanding of race as a fully social relationship. Jamaican sociologist Orlando Patterson and British Jamaican cultural theorist Stuart Hall have both questioned what they called the 'romance of abolition' (Hall, 2017: 77). Hall was referring to the tendency, not least in Britain, to view slavery and its legacy through the prism of Emancipation. The abolition of slavery is viewed in heroic terms, both as a form of historical redemption (Britain may have practiced chattel slavery but it also abolished slavery) and as a decisive historical break: an epochal level of contradiction closure.

Hall argued that the romance of abolition obscured the 'afterlife' of slavery. Reflecting on Patterson's examination of race, slavery and social death (see also Chapter 6 of this book), Hall suggested that it is necessary to understand chattel slavery as only one form of the 'unfreedom' that shaped the societies of the Black Atlantic, just one mode of 'coercive social discipline' (Hall, 2017: 77). Other unfreedoms might include systems of indentured labour, penal servitude and the racial hierarchies and racist violence that were sustained post-slavery. Once the persistence of unfreedoms is acknowledged then Emancipation appears less pivotal, less of a historical break than in the cheering stories offered in our education systems and our Black history months. Hall argued that:

> If our concern is not only slavery itself but also its various continuing afterlives, then recognition of the imposition of different systems of unfree labour, and of the emergence of new systems of coercive, state-sanctioned disciplines, unsettles the received story of both Emancipation and its aftermath. It's not that there had once been plantation terror, which on 1st August 1834 turned into the beneficent world of free labour. (Hall, 2017: 77)

This position is a rejection of formalist understandings of freedom and unfreedom, and a refusal of contradiction closure. Bell's insistence on the continuing role of racism as a stabilising force can also be understood as an analysis of the afterlife of slavery, the persistence of unfreedom. Bell's work was a rejection of the postracial idea that there was a definitive break between slavery and abolition, a definitive break between segregation and desegregation, or a definitive break between the pre- and post-civil rights worlds.

In this sense, Bell's work suggests an epistemological break with the civil rights narrative that some find daunting. Most of us are well aware of the important organisational role of the church in the civil rights movement, but the influence of Christian theology is profound too. The civil rights movement was rooted in a Christian philosophy of redemption and a Christian eschatology that produced the horizontal, progressive view of history. The horizontal understanding of history is rooted in Judaeo-Christian apocalyptic belief, or millenarianism. Humanity progresses across epochs towards a conclusive break in history, wherein our imperfect world, dominated by forces of corruption is overturned, ushering in the kingdom of God (see Ehrman, 1999; Fredricksen, 2018). How this new, redeemed world is to be ushered in has been subject to myriad interpretations across Judaeo-Christian history. Some have tended towards divine intervention, others have emphasised the role of human agency, wherein particular groups become the agents of history. The common trace is a view of history predicated upon the break between old and new worlds. The cultural remnants of this view of history are endemic in western culture: in the French Revolution, in Hegel, in variants of Marxism, and certainly in neoliberalism, as well as in contemporary niche ideas, such as accelerationism. In social justice struggles rooted in the civil rights movement, to take a position that is sceptical of redemption is not just revisionist but iconoclastic.

Space trading: stability and disposability

Bell combined legal scholarship, policy sociology, memoir and allegorical fiction in his writing. Particularly notable were his 'chronicles': allegories and satires through which he explored racial themes. These were often voiced through dialogues between his fictional civil rights lawyer Geneva Crenshaw and a professor, who is never named (Bell, 1987, 1992). Bell's careful critique of idealism and formalism in law was genuine but there was also an element of the provocateur. By this, I do not mean that he courted heresy for its own sake, but that like all good satirists he was a moralist who urged those who did not like the reality he presented to change that reality, rather than griping at the messenger.

The most famous of the chronicles appears in *Faces at the Bottom of The Well* (Bell, 1992). 'The Space Traders' takes a cue from the great African-American science fiction authors and political satirists, such as Octavia E. Butler, Samuel R. Delany and Ishmael Reed. It explores four of the perennials of Bell's work. First, there is the critically important stabilising role of racism (African-Americans once again secure the US's stability and prosperity through their sacrifices). Second, it depicts the disposability of African-American communities (CRT has a relationship with other 'dystopian' social analyses that view racialised capitalism as pricing in large degrees of social waste – see Blacker, 2013; Mbembe, 2019; Feagin, 2020). Third, Bell points to the limits of economic growth as a solution to racism (prosperity does not guarantee economic redistribution or status for Black people). Lastly, we perceive the threat of radical incoherence (what the removal of the Black/White polarity might mean for societal integration).

How is this plotted out? The titular Space Traders are alien beings who arrive in the US, offering a package of resources that will revive and secure the country's ailing economy. What they ask for in return is to take all African-Americans back in their spaceships to their alien planet. Splits immediately emerge between African-American communities, their liberal allies and the US government. The state must specify the boundaries of the national interest, with all the political and economic trade-offs implied. Eventually, the government – all too aware of White public opinion at a time of economic decline – comes to its 'inevitable' decision: that the (racialised) national interest will best served by the trade-off. In short, African-Americans are to be placed outside the national interest; the health of the nation is dependent (as in 1776) on defining the bonds of rights, citizenship and nation in racial terms. The trade is depicted by the President as African-Americans' collective opportunity to do one final service to the nation.

Within this satire, there are nuances in the definition of 'national interest'. Business leaders, for instance, recognise a potential threat to capital from those non-Black Americans who will now fall to the bottom of the well, to the bottom of the socio-economic scale. How will class antagonisms be muted and managed without the US's historical scapegoats? What of other minority ethnic groups? Will they take the place of African-Americans at the bottom of the well? A conservative African-American leader suggests that the government might portray the aliens' planet as a utopia. If White Americans believe that the trade will benefit African-Americans over them, then perhaps the tide of public opinion in favour of the trade will turn. However, this attempt to manufacture a rational form of interest convergence is judged to be unrealistic when measured against the moment of crisis and the immediate material benefits of the trade-off. In the end, we are left with a final image: 'On the dunes above the beaches, guns at the ready, stood U.S. guards. There was no escape, no alternative. Heads bowed, arms now linked by slender chains, black people left the New World as their forebears had arrived' (Bell, 1992: 194).

It is not only the chains on the arms of the prisoners that carry historical resonance. Pervading 'The Space Traders' is a historical understanding of Black disposability, which may comprise the trading away of interests, or literal bodily elimination. The disposability of Black bodies is a recurring theme in classic and contemporary Black Atlantic thought, but also in neo-Marxist analyses of terminal capitalism (see Warmington, 2015a). Bell maps a landscape defined by a racialised national interest: one that places African-Americans outside the legitimate national interest and largely excludes them from its decision-making. At the end of the chronicle, one despairing character reflects on the predicament of 'no escape, no alternative', knowing that if the space trade had failed, then African-Americans would have been blamed for the resulting economic and environmental decline. The trading of African-Americans stabilises the US in economic terms but not to the benefit of those whose bodies have generated the wealth. Yet there is also a concerted effort by government to mask the trade-off in postracial rhetoric; it is 'not about race' but about national economic wellbeing and stability.

Critiquing Bell

Bell does not pretend to offer us a theory of everything. Bell's specific aim was to explain the failure of formalist efforts to address racial injustice and to consider the implications of those failures, principal among them the need to redefine the direction of antiracist struggle in terms of racial realism. His theory of change focuses on the necessity of shifting away from the limits of 'official' definitions of racial justice towards Black radical imaginaries. CRT as a whole has been dismissed by some of those who still seek global theories and by those for whom critical race theories will always, by definition, be theories of 'nothing'. Critiques of CRT offered by commentators who take issue with antiracism in general are considered in Chapter 5, but it is more fruitful first to consider critiques of Bell and CRT that have come from within critical race studies.

Leonardo comments that while it is wrong to cast Bell's racial realism simply as cynicism, 'Where Bell may be criticized is in his apparent lack of a utopian discourse that imagines an alternative state of affair, whether or not it may be realized' (Leonardo, 2009: 187). It is true that Bell's position is firmly non-utopian. In a sense, Bell argues that realism is as much part of the African-American heritage of struggle and resistance as the utopian visions with which the world is more familiar (whether Garvey's or King's). In this respect, his position is similar to Robin D.G. Kelley's (2022) current focus on antiracist struggle without the promise of final liberation or utopia. That said, in urging that we should 'seek new goals for our struggles' (Bell, 1992: 14), Bell suggests that racial realism does not imply a closed future.

One set of criticisms of Bell's model of struggle is that there is a tension between CRT's realpolitik, which is apparent in the concept of interest convergence, wherein it might be argued that political blocs act amorally, and Bell's insistence on the moral dimensions of Black struggle (see Hogan, 2018). Critics such as Hogan (2018) regard the tension between moral and amoral behavioural motives as a significant theoretical dilemma in Bell's work but nevertheless maintain that Bell's pessimism contains within it an appeal to Black and antiracist struggle. While it is true that Bell offers no 'Blackprint' for the future, others have taken Bell's pessimism about the current state of affairs as the cue to imagine new goals, working in fields such as Afrofuturism (see Zamalin, 2019).

It might also be argued that, particularly in his most widely-read books, Bell depicts African-American communities in broad strokes: perhaps not entirely homogeneous but bracketing some of the fissures of class, gender and age (Higgins, 1992). It has been the job of Bell's diverse successors to apply his insights to gender, sexuality and disability, and to other social settings. Dixson et al's (2018) edited collection of work from CRT's off-shoots in the field of education is an essential map of key writings in DisCrit, QueerCrit, LatCrit, TribalCrit and AsianCrit.

Among Afropessimists, there has been ambivalence towards Bell's work. Henry and Powell (2021), for instance, have found affinities between Bell's ideas and Afropessimism's analyses of anti-Blackness. They focus directly on intersections between racial realism and the concept of social death (drawn from Orlando Patterson's writing) that is central to Afropessimism: 'The perpetual pattern of white violence is what connects the social death concept to a Bellian racial realist perspective. A racial realist perspective moves us away from pollyannaish views of a society structured in dominance to one which sees how deeply entrenched and pervasive racism actually is' (Henry and Powell, 2021: 82).

However, Afropessimists have in general not regarded CRT as providing a critical theory of anti-Blackness in the sense that it is understood in Afropessimism. Michael Dumas and kihana ross comment that:

> CRT, as a general theory of racism, is limited in its ability to adequately interrogate what we call 'the specificity of the Black' (Wynter, 1989). That is, CRT is not intended to pointedly address how antiblackness – which is something different than White supremacy – informs and facilitates racist ideology and institutional practice. More, it cannot fully employ the counterstories of Black experiences of structural and cultural racisms, because it does not, on its own, have language to richly capture how antiblackness constructs Black subjects, and positions them in and against law, policy, and everyday (civic) life. (Dumas and ross, 2016: 417)

Thus while Dumas and ross (2016: 416) acknowledge CRT as a 'decidedly *Black* theorization of race', they define it correctly as a theory of racism not Blackness, and argue that there is a need to take Bell's insights and to use them to develop a specifically Black CRT: a *BlackCrit*, in the same way that we have LatCrit or QueerCrit. Interestingly, Dumas and ross (2016) suggest that 'The Space Traders' is an instance in which Bell *does* tend towards exploring anti-Blackness.

It is instructive to note Dumas and ross's (2016) critique of CRT as having an insufficient grasp of the specificity of Blackness/anti-Blackness, given that critics of antiracism often misrepresent CRT as a theory of Black identity. The critiques of Bell advanced by Leonardo, Hogan, and Dumas and ross are also important in showing up, by comparison, the banality of mainstream attacks on CRT as cynical, as anti-White and so forth; such attacks have not in any way addressed the complexities and tensions within CRT's framework.

Two kinds of realism

It is interesting that while CRT's racial realism has been problematic for some academics in Britain, social theorist Mark Fisher's (2009) concept of *capitalist realism* has rightly been heralded as an incisive analysis of 'permanence'. Fisher (2009) used the phrase capitalist realism to refer to the power of 21st-century capitalism to depict itself as the only realistically attainable mode of social organisation. For Fisher, capitalist realism is 'a pervasive atmosphere, conditioning not only the production of culture but also the regulation of work and education, and acting as a kind of invisible barrier, constraining thought and action' (Fisher, 2009: 16). Arguments persist over the extent to which Fisher believed that capitalism really had become the only available system and the extent to which he regarded capitalist realism as an ideological front that forestalled but could not eliminate resistance (his views may have changed over time). Debates over Bell's writing are not dissimilar. Was the 'permanence of racism' absolute and non-negotiable, or did Bell provoke us to reject the belief in a racialised society as the only realistic one, and urge us instead towards the possibility of new imaginaries that would render the state's racial project incoherent?

In his critique of the failures of civil rights legislation, Bell's work bears comparison both with Fanon's study of the failures of modernity and Fisher's fascination with lost futures, potential avenues of human progress that were never realised but which continue to haunt the present. In *Ghosts of My Life*, his collection of writings on truncated social and cultural progress, Fisher contended that 21st-century culture is afflicted by 'anachronism and inertia' but that this social stasis 'has been buried behind a superficial frenzy of "newness", of perpetual movement' (Fisher, 2014: 6). Fisher argued that the perception of progress halted is not born out of the simple failure of old folks (an example might be the veterans of civil rights struggle!) to grasp new social arrangements; on the contrary, it is symptomatic of frustration among progressives with 'the sheer persistence of recognisable forms' (Fisher, 2014: 7). What Bell recognised, after decades of civil rights legislation and equalities policies, was the sheer persistence of racial injustice.

Fisher describes late capitalism as having birthed a kind of 'market Stalinism' (Fisher, 2009: 44), wherein symbolic achievements and reputation management have become more important than real achievements (see Chapter 1 of this book). Bell was keenly aware that the post-civil rights US had produced an official culture that too often defined progress in terms of symbolic achievements ('There is, for some, improvement that is substantive and impressive. But we often define as progress, change that is more symbolic than real' [Bell, 1991: 83]).

In *Faces at the Bottom of The Well*, Bell's encounter with Mrs MacDonald is emblematic of experiences of 'really existing post-civil rights society', or 'really existing postracialism'. Mrs MacDonald distinguishes only too well between the vision of the US put forward in its political (and postracial) rhetoric and her living struggle; she is not distracted by the symbols of salvation. Bell's project, sceptical rather than cynical, was to harass the 'really existing' post-civil rights world. He encouraged us to see where legislation and policy were symbolic rather than actual achievements. In Fisher's (2009) terms, Bell's project was to hasten the crisis of symbolic efficiency.

Critical Race Theory in Britain

As indicated in Chapter 1, CRT did not enter mainstream (as distinct from academic) consciousness in Britain until 2020 when it was lined up alongside BLM as an example of a dangerous new antiracism. However, CRT was not a new presence. Its arrival in British scholarship can be dated to the period 2003–6. CRT had from its beginnings been concerned with education, in the form of legal training and scholarship; in the US during the 1990s CRT was taken up in the wider field of educational research. The paper that signalled the transfer was Ladson-Billings and Tate's (1995) 'Towards a Critical Race Theory of education'. Their insights were subsequently developed in the work of, among others, Adrienne Dixson, Zeus Leonardo, Laurence Parker, Daniel Solórzano, Edward Taylor and Tara Yosso (for overviews of CRT in education, see Dixson et al, 2018; Parker and Gillborn, 2020; Taylor et al, 2023).

In Britain it was educational researchers, rather than legal scholars, who first adopted CRT. The reasons for this are not hard to fathom. From the 1950s onwards, as Britain's post-Windrush migrants became settled, activists and intellectuals had waged antiracist struggles that tended to focus on schooling, policing, immigration, health and employment – on policy rather than legislation per se. Among these fields, education was very prominent (Warmington, 2014). Given its vitality in the US, it was unsurprising that CRT's influence was felt among educators and sociologists of education. It was another part of the long history of Black Atlantic intellectual exchange.

CRT's 'foreignness' and its 'Blackness' have made it the object of censure, with British critics on the Left and Right fixating on the idea of CRT as an 'import'. While its antagonists have suggested that CRT is entirely predicated on African-American experiences, in fact, CRT has generated a whole series of distinctive and international off-shoots (Chapter 1, see also Dixson et al, 2018). In 2003, English educational researcher David Gillborn gave the first CRT paper to be presented at the British Educational Research Association Conference (published as Gillborn, 2005). Other early adopters included Kevin Hylton, Lorna Roberts, Namita Chakrabarty, John Preston, Shirin Housee and the current author. Importantly, their development of CRT came about, in part, through direct collaboration with a range of US theorists, including Adrienne Dixson, Zeus Leonardo, Laurence Parker, Marvin Lynn and Devon Carbado. In terms of published work, the first book-length explorations of CRT, education and sociology included Gillborn's (2008) *Racism and Education: Coincidence or Conspiracy*; Preston's (2008) *Whiteness and Class in Education*; and Hylton et al's (2011) *Atlantic Crossings: International Dialogues on Critical Race Theory*. Recent additions to 'BritCrit' have included work by Veronica Poku (2022), Sriprakash et al (2022) and Christopher Vieler-Porter (2022).

'BritCrit' has been applied to a range of issues in education and social policy, and has been used to reinterrogate concerns that have persisted in policy, professional practice and scholarship at least since the 1960s. These have included inequalities in educational attainment; the marginalisation of race equality in education policy and wider social policy; barriers to and within academia; school-to-prison pipelines; discourses around national security. CRT has also overlapped with emergent critical Whiteness studies in the UK and has become a regular feature in British-based social science journals and conferences (see Warmington, 2020).

Almost as soon as CRT emerged in Britain, it became the object of academic antipathy, not least from a subset of White Left scholars, who showed an atavistic suspicion of race conscious social analyses (Warmington, 2020). For a short period, this race-is-not real fundamentalism spawned a mini-industry in British academic journals. Given the routine marginalisation of Black Atlantic scholarship in British academia, such antagonism raised perennial questions about academia's reproduction of wider racialised assumptions about who has legitimate voice in Britain. In the US, CRT has certainly been seen as a conceptual interloper, unwelcome in fields such as law and education. Indeed, one of the seminal CRT education research papers was Gloria Ladson-Billings's article, 'Just what is critical race theory and what's it doing in a nice field like education?' (Ladson-Billings, 1998). However, among its British critics, CRT's alienness seemed to be a very literal problem. This nativism and a nostalgic longing for unchallenged White masculinist conceptions of class has tended to reproduce rather than critique Britain's post-imperial melancholy. However, in recent years academic spats of this kind have resembled soft play. In both the US and Britain, CRT has now been inserted into mainstream media and political consciousness, becoming a prop in conservative culture war strategies. Chapters 4 and 5 of this book look at why CRT is inimical to Britain's postracial turn.

Conclusion

Throughout his writing, Derrick Bell acknowledged the work of Frantz Fanon, whose spectre haunts postcolonial and antiracist scholarship. Fanon had opened up space to consider the failure of liberalism to overcome its historical demons and propose solutions to one of humanity's great problems, that being racism:

> All the elements of a solution to the great problems of humanity have, at different times, existed in European thought. But Europeans have not carried out in practice the mission which fell to them, which consisted of bringing their whole weight to bear violently upon these elements, of modifying their arrangements and their nature, of changing them and, finally, of bringing the problem of mankind to an infinitely higher plain. (Fanon, 1963: 253)

Fanon in Algeria wrote at a moment of global existential crisis, as the colonial structures that had for centuries scaffolded Western thought and action fell away. There is no doubt that Bell, writing as 'a veteran of a civil rights era that is now over' (Bell, 1995b: 307), regarded the US in his time as being in existential crisis. Amidst the anticolonial struggles of the mid-20th century Fanon engaged with Enlightenment understandings of being and humanity – not through the lens of abstract ethics but as things embedded in empire, colonialism, racism and nation state. Bell engaged with similar themes in his immediate context of US law, policy and society. Much the same can be said of Derrick Bell as Nigel C. Gibson has said of Fanon: that his critique 'is neither a simple embrace nor a rejection of European thought but a radical engagement' (Gibson, 2019: 397). This radical engagement is where CRT begins and it is why it remains alive in our own time of crisis: post-2008 financial crash, post-COVID-19 pandemic, amidst environmental threat, distracted by culture wars.

Bell argued that one of the reasons why we have failed is that too often our antiracist energies have been directed to the goals, ethics and aspirations suggested to us in legislation, policy and mission statements on race equality. Bell instead urged a 'hard eyed view of racism as it is' (Bell, 1995b: 308). Notions of linear racial progress were neither here nor there. We should always remain alert to bogus claims that issues of race and racism had simply been dealt with, contradiction closed. This knowledge would free us from investing our hopes in institutions that were less interested in countering racial inequalities than in maintaining them as a stabilising force. Bell was, if you like, a pessimist with benefits. He saw little to be gained by wasting time and energy in the belief that liberal society would, through formal mechanisms, deliver us from racial injustice – but he believed that a kind of targeted pessimism might free us to explore new futures.

The initial chapters of this book have offered a standpoint from which to examine Britain's postracial turn without being crunched into its current self-image as a uniquely successful, uniquely innocent multiracial democracy. Having retreated from significant policy gains made at the turn of the century, most particularly the *Macpherson Report* (1999) and the *Race Relations (Amendment) Act 2000*, Britain has come to stake a great deal on symbolic achievements, on weakly worded and poorly enforced race equality measures. Chapter 4 considers Britain's state postracialism.

4

Postracial Britain

What might it mean to describe a society as postracial? It is a term that has been used to denote very different, sometimes conflicting, views of the world. For some commentators, postracial thinking requires a revolutionary shift. A postracial world of this kind would bring radical incoherence to the narratives of modernity, overturning our ideas about what it is to be human. For others, a postracial world implies, more modestly, a *postracist* world: a world in which racial inequalities have been removed. Both are aspirational views; no one seriously believes that we have reached either situation, in Britain or elsewhere.

However, there is another putative postracialism in the air. It rests upon an assumption that we have moved into a new phase in British society, wherein Britain's approach to race equality stands as a model for the world. This facile mode of postracialism does not assert that racism no longer exists; it is not that bold. Instead, it holds that racism has declined as a feature of social life: that it has lost much of its social salience and that consequently race is no longer a useful lens through which to understand social inequalities. In particular, its racial grammar eliminates concepts of structural and institutional racism and presents colourblind accounts of why racial inequalities persist. In fact, *anything but racism* is preferred as an explanation for disparities in unemployment, health outcomes, incarceration, police harassment or school exclusions.

The facile mode of postracialism has particular purchase in 21st-century Britain, where it informs much current discourse and policy, underpinning what this chapter calls *state postracialism*. In the early 2000s commentators such as Gilroy (2004), Bourne (2007) and Kundnani (2007) argued that Britain had shifted away from the models of state or municipal multiculturalism that had been a feature of social policy in the 1980s and 1990s (as in, for instance, the work of the Greater London Council, the Inner London Education Authority and the Macpherson Inquiry). That shift, Gilroy argued, was backed by a 'growing sense that it is now illegitimate to believe that multiculture can and should be orchestrated by government in the public interest' (Gilroy, 2004: 1). Despite making liberal claims, the postracial shift tends to be antagonistic to antiracist social movements and to critical race analyses. Might it not be better if we all joined together to agree not to 'see' race? Would not racism then disappear through natural decay? It is, to return to Bell, a postracialism that is comforting to many White people but largely illusory to people of colour.

This chapter argues that state postracialism is the approach that has superseded the old state multiculturalism; it is Britain's attempt to turn the page on the policies of the past in the hope of a 'conclusive end' to matters of race and racism. In actuality, the postracial turn speaks both to the permanence and the mutability of racism. As Goldberg (2015) has argued, postraciality of this kind creates discursive space for the disavowal of explicit appeals to racism while, at the same, offering ways of rearticulating the old racism, offering new racist expression. Chapter 4 begins by comparing different definitions of postracialism. Insofar as postracialism denotes moving on from race thinking and practice, what exactly is it that we might wish to transcend? Sticking with the present, what are the features of Britain's 'really existing postracialism' and who benefits from its colourblind discourse? Discussion then turns to the delegitimisation of the concept of institutional racism within current politics and policy. In particular, it examines the role of the report by the Commission on Race and Ethnic Disparities (CRED), published by the UK's Conservative government in March 2021. The *CRED Report* (2021) was presented as a landmark that explicitly sought to change the narrative about institutional racism put in place by the *Macpherson Report* (1999) into police handling of the murder of London teenager Stephen Lawrence; it is considered in the context of a decade of rolling back on *Macpherson*. The current chapter also points to the symbiosis between British postracialism and the forms of 'contra-' antiracism explored in Chapter 5.

Racial identities, postracial identities

Chapter 2 of this book discussed race as a social construct. The rejection of pseudo-scientific racial categories might be regarded, in itself, as a kind of postracialism. However, as Chapter 2 also noted, understanding race as a social construct, as unreal, has not in itself led either to the abandonment of racial identities or to the negation of racial hierarchies. Race thinking and practice continue, and race remains a powerful ideological framework. The stubborn persistence of these old forms begs another postracial question. Assuming we desire a postracial world (which is a big assumption and relies on a generous definition of 'we'), what is it that we wish to dispense with and what, if anything, might we wish to retain from our racialised pasts?

Radical postracialism, as opposed to the facile, policy-led version, would by definition denote a world freed from racial injustice and inequalities. Would it also, though, comprise a world in which race ceased altogether to be an organising principle in society: a world in which racial identities as we have understood them over the past half millennium were dissolved? The struggle to counter racial inequality is clearly the minimum irreducible framework of antiracism. However, desire for the dismantling of racial identity is, at present, less fundamental to most antiracist movements. CRT, for example, has been concerned with addressing racial injustice, with less attention paid to abolishing racial identity. The same would apply to most antiracist movements, in all their diversity, from Martin Luther King's campaigns to today's BLM movement. One reason for this is the power and agency that subordinated communities have discovered in reclaiming scorned identities. In other words, racial identification is not just a top-down exercise of power. As Yasmin Gunaratnam reminds us: 'These very categories, when mobilized by socially marginalised individuals and groups in asserting claims to personhood, can be less about a preservation of oppressive racial hierarchies and can be more about ambivalent, situated and strategic moves to transform such hierarchies … and to invent new positions within them' (Gunaratnam, 2003: 28).

Reclaiming subaltern identities is a means of rejecting colourblindness, or gender-blindness or queer-blindness. It is a refusal, in our case, of the erasure implicit in the phrase, 'I don't see race', which is so often used to signal not being racist, and is tied into personal exoneration, to being regarded as a good person. As a teacher, my response to well-meaning students taking this line was always that the point is not whether we claim to see or not see race in any given instance; the point is whether or not we *can* see race whenever we choose – which, in our current world, we can. Not seeing race can all too easily conflate with choosing not to see racism: that is not seeing those directly affected by racism.

Multiculturalism, which we might define as the political life of cultural diversity, is by definition at odds with colourblindness and other erasures of identity. For Tariq Modood (2005), this tension rests on how the relationship between public and private identity is understood. Colourblindness rests on non-racism, in that it proposes ostensibly that no social group should be either advantaged or discriminated against on the basis of ascriptive categories over which they have no choice; we were all, in the words of Lady Gaga, 'born this way'. Private identities should be no concern of the state, institutions or other individuals. Non-racism deplores overt displays of racial bigotry but tends to define racism in terms of individual intentional acts and, therefore, mistrusts both state-led approaches to tackling racism and grassroots antiracist movements, since both of these focus on structural and institutional racism.

Some would argue that the distinction between non-racism and antiracism is almost aesthetic: that when antiracists regard approaches to tackling racism as inadequate, they dismiss them as merely non-racist. In fact, non-racism or colourblindness is something more specific; it rests upon a particular liberal tradition that insists on the non-significance of race. While there are surely instances in which any of us would wish our racial, gendered, dis/abled, faith or class identities to be without significance, antiracists argue that since non-racism is ahistorical, it gives little clue as to how to rectify or make reparation for social inequalities that exist and are deeply embedded. In policy terms, its approach tends to be what the sociologist David Kirp (1979) once described as 'doing good by doing little'. In contrast, multiculturalism proposes a society in which diverse identities are visible and celebrated, and may become the bases of social movements demanding public resources and representation. Black, feminist, queer or disabled identities become public, rather than merely being private categories. As Modood wrote, we do not choose our ascriptive category 'but we choose how to politically live with it' (Modood, 2005: 65).

Insisting on the absolute non-significance of racial identities would be an extreme definition of postracialism. However, there are daily instances in which we are urged, sometimes out of sincere motives, to see ourselves as 'just people' and there are certainly many instances in which activists are called upon to tone down their supposedly divisive racial or gender politics for the common good. In Britain today to accuse someone of practicing 'identity politics' is pretty much to dismiss them outright. However, to call for subaltern communities to relinquish political identities in a world in which discrimination still exists risks disregarding decades or centuries of struggle. Reflecting on the tensions between postracialism and antiracism, Ernest Allen (1997) surmises that eliminating racism would be more likely to bring about a raceless world than utopian declarations about the evils of race-thinking.

Radical postracialism

Radical 'abolitionist' approaches to postracialism are not at all the same as simply claiming not to see race. Radical postracialism has been explored (although not uncritically accepted) in a variety of ways by scholars and activists such as Ruth Wilson Gilmore, Paul Gilroy, and Stefano Harney and Fred Moten, as well as some within both Afropessimist and Afrofuturist circles (see, for example, Gilroy, 2000; Harney and Moten, 2013). What their takes have in common is an insistence that race and racism cannot simply be unseen, abolished at the wave of a hand. Gilroy states:

> For many racialized populations, 'race' and the hard-won, oppositional identities it supports are not to be lightly or prematurely given up … These groups will need to be persuaded very carefully that there is something worthwhile to be gained from a deliberate renunciation of 'race' as the basis for belonging to one another and acting in concert. They will have to be reassured that the dramatic gestures involved in turning against racial observance can be accomplished without violating the precious forms of solidarity and community that have been created by their protracted subordination along racial lines. (Gilroy, 2004: 12–13)

For Gilroy, the only forms of postracialism worth contemplating are unruly, avant-garde forms that would disorder modern narratives of race and identity. Gilroy, for example, speaks of exploiting the crisis of race thinking produced by the social construct thesis, by Fanon and his successors, by the DNA revolution, and by centuries of Black resistance, in order to 'free ourselves from the bonds of all raciology in a novel and ambitious abolitionist project' (Gilroy, 2004: 15). Contemporary state postracialism is neither novel nor ambitious.

Stefano Harney and Fred Moten (2013) argue that the ending of racism requires not simply banishment, but overturning the very standpoint from which racism – the social relationship that binds racialised subjects – makes sense. Harney and Moten's new society is aspirational, visionary and utopian:

> What is, so to speak, the object of abolition? Not so much the abolition of prisons but the abolition of a society that could have prisons, that could have slavery, that could have the wage, and therefore not abolition as the elimination of anything but abolition as the founding of a new society. (Harney and Moten, 2013: 42)

Reflecting on these radical takes on racial abolitionism helps illustrate the diversity of postracial imaginaries. What Harney and Moten have in common with, say, the emergent Afrofuturists is their fascination with the possibility of a new society: one that would necessitate a programme of disorder, of destabilising the racial narratives of the past half millennium. As noted, this possibility is something to which CRT, with its non-utopian stance, has a more ambivalent relationship.

Facile postracialism

The modes of postracialism that have emerged in Britain, and which might be roughly dated to the pushback against *Macpherson* (1999) that began early in the 2000s, are clearly very far removed from radical abolitionism. Facile forms of postracialism often employ the rhetoric of newness, of 'moving on' from old multicultural policies. However, to paraphrase Fisher (2009), these flurries of novelty are designed to allow the persistence of recognisable forms of racial hierarchy. Brazilian sociologist Alexandre Emboaba Da Costa (2016) offers a helpful definition of the ways in which 'post-' can conceal 'permanence':

> I define as 'post-racial ideologies' those forms of thought, discourse, and action that evade, delegitimize, and seek to eliminate racial differences and their effects from the focus of academic scholarship, activist struggle, public debate, and state policy. Post-racial ideologies operate

through racialized forms of power while simultaneously claiming the non-significance of race. They generate fraught understandings of belonging and inclusion that elide racial difference and structural racism in ways that allow the re-articulation rather than the transformation of racial inequalities within national and global developments. (Da Costa, 2016: 496)

Da Costa (2016) focuses directly on the political project of state postracialism, which is, through persistent claims about the non-significance of race, to erase matters of race and racism as legitimate parts of political, policy and academic discourse. The elimination of concepts of structural and institutional racism (and some modes of cultural diversity) creates space to rearticulate explanations of racial inequality in cultural behaviouralist terms: that is, as being due to cultural deficits within Black and Brown communities. In several instances this eliminationism has indeed become a state project, backed by the machinery of government. In Britain since 2020, researchers and educators have been warned by government bodies against employing concepts such as institutional racism 'as fact' and against using materials from campaigns such as BLM. In the US, legislation has been enacted in multiple states to constrain teaching about racism and the histories of slavery and segregation. Da Costa (2016) also points to Brazil's long-established usage of its multiracial and mixed heritage character to claim exoneration. This is noteworthy given that in Britain the increase in the mixed heritage population is often exploited in postracial discourse as evidence of the non-significance of racism, despite the disadvantages that Black and Brown people of mixed heritage experience.

British educator Kalwant Bhopal argues that state postracialism is embedded in neoliberal realism: the myth that neoliberalism is of universal benefit across lines of race, class and gender and that, therefore, the only relevant policy questions are about how to *manage* these essentially beneficent structures. Questions of race and social justice are, in discursive terms, rendered non-significant, even though:

Neoliberalism does not benefit *all* members of society equally. We do not live in a post-racial society. Instead race remains central to the judgements and values made about who is *deserving* and who is *undeserving*: who belongs and who does not. Race acts as a marker of difference in a society poisoned by fear, insecurity and instability. (Bhopal, 2018: 164)

These forms of state postracialism, or 'really existing postracialism', rearticulate racism and are, because of their appeals to cultural deficit models, profoundly racialising.

Racism and bad faith

In short, vulgar postracialism is Iago's 'I am not what I am'. For, insofar as its claims allow recognisable social arrangements to persist, we are left not merely with hypocrisy or tactical trickery but with social relationships that are predicated upon bad faith. Gordon (1995, 2022) notes that the concept of bad faith has particular meaning within both legal and philosophical worlds. In law, to act in bad faith is to enter knowingly into a contract with false intentions. It may be, then, that postracial or non-racial claims are proffered in bad faith, insofar as they are designed not to eliminate racism but to maintain racial inequalities at manageable levels. However, Gordon adds that:

> The philosophical meaning rests on the peculiar fact that people are capable of lying to themselves. In his defence, the signatory to the agreement could claim that he did not sign the contract in bad faith; he did so sincerely. Sincerity, however, from the philosophical perspective, can be in bad faith. Many racists are sincere. (Gordon, 2022: 59)

In this sense, the weakly worded, poorly enforced policies to which Derrick Bell referred may also be the product of a misrecognition of how racism operates: sincere but utterly missing the mark. One way of understanding racism is indeed as a form of bad faith: 'A form of lying about oneself and others that is nurtured and encouraged by the very institutions of racist society' (Gordon, 1995: 38). In policy terms, we are left with an institutional bad faith wherein, invoking the horizontal view of history, a definitive break has been declared between the bad old world in which we confess that racism did unfortunately exist and the brave new postracial world, in which things have changed (even if they have not always changed as much as we would like). 'Really existing postracialism' insists that the world as understood by the 'woke' and the antiracists has reached its end of days and even though racial inequalities persist they are not the effects of racism; in fact, you can rest assured that they are produced by anything but racism.

The *Commission on Race and Ethnic Disparities Report* (2021)

In March 2021 the UK's then Prime Minister Boris Johnson (2019–22) welcomed the publication of a report by the Commission on Race and Ethnic Disparities (CRED), led by Professor Tony Sewell, examining the state of race relations in Britain. The much-heralded report had been commissioned, in part, as a response to the BLM protests of the previous summer. It announced that: 'The country has come a long way in 50 years and the success of much of the ethnic minority population in education and, to a lesser extent, the economy, should be regarded as a model for other White-majority countries' (CRED, 2021: 9).

The *CRED Report*'s tone was part state of the nation address and part post-imperial plea for exoneration. Its portrayal of Britain as a 'model' and a 'beacon' was quickly picked up in press releases and trailed in news media. The report provided stark contrast with the Joint Parliamentary Committee on Human Rights (JCHR)'s report *Black People, Racism and Human Rights*, which had appeared with little fanfare the previous November. It reported that 85 per cent of Black people in the UK were 'not confident that they would be treated the same as a white person by the police'; that post-COVID-19, over 60 per cent of Black people did not 'believe their health is as equally protected by the NHS compared to white people' and that the death rate for Black women in childbirth was five times higher than for White women (JCHR, 2020: 3).

The *CRED Report* was determined to tell a less grim story. Prefiguring the *CRED Report*, Prime Minister Johnson had declared that changing the narrative on race was one of his government's priorities (Oluwole, 2020). In truth, there was nothing particularly new in his call. A decade earlier Johnson's predecessor David Cameron (UK Prime Minister, 2010–16) commented on multiculturalism and race equality in Britain, stating that it was time to 'turn the page on the failed policies of the past' (Bunting, 2011: 25). The authors of the *CRED Report* were, it should be said, careful to state that they did not believe that Britain had yet 'completed the long journey to equality of opportunity' (CRED, 2021: 9). Its authors readily acknowledged the existence of individual and deplorable acts of race hate: 'And we know, too many of us from personal experience, that prejudice and discrimination can still cast a shadow over lives. Outright racism still exists in the UK, whether it surfaces as graffiti on someone's business, violence in the street, or prejudice in the labour market' (CRED, 2021: 9).

However, the report was keen to stress that this accumulation of personal experience and instances of overt racism should be understood as exceptional, as aberrant: 'But we have ensured our analysis has gone beyond these individual instances, to carefully examine the evidence and data, and the evidence reveals that ours is nevertheless a relatively open society' (CRED, 2021: 9)

In its framing of racism in terms of overt racial prejudice rather than institutional racism, in its emphasis on the deplorable act, rather than the ordinary, and in its return to conservative behavioural explanations of racial disparities (family structures, defeatist attitudes) the report reproduced a colourblind racial grammar. Its provisos and qualifications notwithstanding, the *CRED Report* (2021) sat squarely as a postracial artefact: a depiction of an 'open' Britain in which problems of race and racism had largely evaporated, in which race was primarily a private identity, and in which institutional racism was no longer a valid policy concept.

On publication, the new narrative was questioned even by some of those who had contributed to the Commission (Mohdin and Walker, 2021). Nevertheless, the *CRED Report* laid down a marker as to where official discourse on racism was now located. The 'new' narrative, in fact, reproduced some of Britain's old policy tropes, aimed particularly at delegitimising the concept of institutional racism that had been central to the *Macpherson Report* (1999).

Unseeing institutional racism

The *CRED Report* (2021) is a significant reference point in understanding contemporary Britain's 'really existing postracialism'. It is significant not because its failings were unique but because it combined so many postracial tropes. These were far more than mere decorative motifs; their purpose was precisely to rearticulate racialised relationships:

> Put simply we no longer see a Britain where the system is deliberately rigged against ethnic minorities. The impediments and disparities do exist, they are varied, and ironically very few of them are directly to do with racism. Too often 'racism' is the catch-all explanation, and can be simply implicitly accepted rather than explicitly examined.
>
> The evidence shows that geography, family influence, socio-economic background, culture and religion have more significant impact on life chances than the existence of racism. That said, we take the reality of racism seriously and we do not deny that it is a real force in the UK.
>
> The Commission was keen to gain a more forensic and rigorous understanding of underlying causes of disparities. However, we have argued for the use of the term 'institutional racism' to be applied only when deep-seated racism can be proven on a systemic level and not be used as a general catch-all phrase for any microaggression, witting or unwitting. (CRED, 2021: 8)

In seeking to circumscribe the concept of institutional racism, the report deployed a misrecognition of the way that racism works. It utilised a particular methodology that sought to identify variables such as geography, family influence and socio-economic background as both distinct from and equivalent to racism. It was as if the geographical spread of communities and their socio-economic backgrounds were not already racialised. This way of ascribing particular domains of social life as 'non-racial' is a powerful aspect of postracial grammar. In my own area of education research this 'anything but racism' methodological approach is frequently used. There is nothing inherently wrong with correlating the educational achievements of Somali,

Pakistani or African-Caribbean children with parents' levels of education, but to argue that the parental education is a factor that exists prior to racism and that might 'control for' the role of racism is misleading (see Gillborn et al, 2018). In its submission to the Commission, the University of Birmingham's Centre for Research on Race and Education (CRRE) (with the current author as a contributor) explained that the 'anything but racism' methodology includes both technical error and conceptual misrecognition:

> Essentially the problem is that many factors that are treated by statisticians as discrete drivers of inequality are themselves shaped by discrimination and unfairness (e.g., socio-economic status, poverty, home ownership, level of parental education, pre-existing health issues). Unfortunately, many statistical models assume that 'racism' can only account for discrepancies that remain *after* they have tested for every other conceivable issue – as if each issue were a separate layer in a cake. But racism and other forms of discrimination cross-contaminate other factors through race discrimination in the economy, in the housing and labour markets. Fundamentally, this is a question of understanding how racism operates; not as a minimal thing to be measured as what is 'left over' when everything else has been accounted for; but as a complex, dynamic set of processes working through each aspect of society. (CRRE, 2020: 4)

The *CRED Report*, like much social stratification research, had no way of conceptualising race as a social relationship, as a mediator of experiences of housing, health or education. The aim of CRT has been to refuse this kind of unseeing: to counter institutional claims to race neutrality and to make racialised social relationships visible. Conversely, bad-faith postracial discourses unsee racialised social relationships: not by denying the existence of racism as such, but by depicting racism as aberrant, as extraordinary.

The violent or abusive acts of far-right racists can, of course, be treated as extraordinary because, in a sense, they are. One of the contributions of the *Macpherson Report* (1999) was to put the concept of institutional racism back into play in UK policy, by emphasising that while racist thuggery was exceptional, ordinary operations in policing, education, housing, healthcare and so forth were where racial injustices were most commonly enacted. The rolling back of *Macpherson* that began very shortly after its publication (Gillborn, 2008; Warmington et al, 2018) sought to depict institutional racism too as exceptional. It should be noted that this post-*Macpherson* drive has not yet completely excised the concept of institutional racism from policy spaces. Eighteen months after the *CRED Report*, a review of the London Fire Brigade described the service as 'institutionally misogynist and racist' (Afzal, 2022: 78). A report by Heriot-Watt University into the housing needs of Black and minority ethnic families concluded that 'the planning system continues to perpetuate socially conservative outcomes with regards to racial equality' (Bristow, 2021: 1) and that its failures were often the result of 'a view within the planning profession that *formal equality* of treatment is sufficient in pursuit of social justice, meaning that planners and housing specialists can be reluctant to take steps to address the specific needs of BAME groups in policy and practice' (Bristow, 2021: 1, emphasis added). Such colourblind formalism is, of course, precisely the kind of policy approach that CRT has critiqued.

However, the residual impact of the *CRED Report* has also been evident. In March 2023 Baroness Louise Casey published her *Independent Review into the Standards of Behaviour and Internal Culture of The Metropolitan Police Service* (Casey, 2023). The report had been commissioned in response to widespread public concern over serial scandals involving misconduct and lawbreaking within the Metropolitan Police, not least the recent murder of 33-year-old Sarah Everard by a serving Met officer, myriad incidents of racist police behaviour and perennial issues relating to the over-policing of Black communities. Casey (2023) concluded that there was extensive evidence of institutional racism, sexism and homophobia across the force. However, adopting the new, post-*CRED* racial grammar, the Met's Commissioner, the Prime Minister and the Opposition all publicly distanced themselves from Casey's charge of *institutional* discrimination.

Changing the narrative

In the *CRED Report* there was a mix of the somewhat novel (the claim both to acknowledge the importance of the *Macpherson Report* and to 'correct' it) and the antique (the emphasis on racism as mere prejudice). In addition, it claimed extravagantly to be 'the first government-commissioned study on race that seriously engages with the family' (CRED, 2021: 6). 'Family structure' with all its scope for misogynoir, remains one of the tropes of conservative cultural analyses of Black poverty and marginalisation. The *CRED Report* was not beyond utilising discourses akin to those belonging to the US 'conservative behaviourists' described by Cornel West, 'who stress the behavioral impediments to black upward mobility … the waning of the Protestant ethic – hard work, deferred gratification' (West, 1992: 37). In the perennial tension between structural and behavioural analyses of racial inequalities, the authors of the *CRED Report*, if sometimes coy about their cultural deficit thesis, urged skepticism about structural analyses, instead conferring attention on family structures, aspirations and model minorities.

What then was the purpose of the *CRED Report*? It was, in Prime Minister Boris Johnson's terms, to change the narrative: to redraw the boundaries of legitimate debate on race in Britain. This involved the long-term aim of delegitimising the concept of institutional racism in policy, as well as the immediate job of pushing back against the resurgent BLM movement. The authors stated that:

> The purpose of this report is to provide the UK with a road map for racial fairness. There are still real obstacles and there are also practical ways to surmount them, but that becomes much harder if people from ethnic minority backgrounds absorb a fatalistic narrative that says the deck is permanently stacked against them. Armed with the rich data from the RDU [Race Disparity Unit], we have aimed to dispel some myths and reach a more nuanced view. (CRED, 2021: 8)

This paragraph is illustrative in a number of ways. It avoids the term 'social justice', which had become the target of conservatives in the US, replacing it with 'social fairness'. The authors prioritise the managerial over the political, with their emphasis on 'practical ways' to surmount 'obstacles', and their reference to big data. One of the obstacles identified is the behaviour of people from minority ethnic backgrounds who absorb 'fatalistic' narratives and who have bought into 'myths' that the report, as a source of truth, will dispel.

The Commission's barely disguised hostility to the term 'institutional racism' led critics to suggest that CRED's aim was to signal in official terms that institutional racism was a concept now out of bounds. At least one proponent of the *CRED Report*, the Policy Exchange think tank's David Goodhart, was explicit about this:

> The [CRED] report pays proper homage to that other great report on race, the Macpherson report of 1999, on the Metropolitan Police's failures over the Stephen Lawrence murder. But it also draws a line under it, not least in its scepticism about the casual use of the term institutional racism, that was popularised by Macpherson, and in its rejection of the subjectivism about race that was also legitimised by that report. (Goodhart, 2021)

BLM activists who dipped into the report would, he suggested, 'find their most cherished beliefs gently shredded by an older generation of accomplished ethnic minority professionals' (Goodhart, 2021).

In defence of the concept of institutional racism

However, the *CRED Report* did not speak for much of that older generation. A fortnight after publication, *The Guardian* newspaper reported that 'At least 20 organisations and individuals who were listed as stakeholders in the government's race disparity commission have distanced themselves from the report and its findings' (Mohdin and Walker, 2021). Simon Woolley, former director of Operation Black Vote, described the *CRED Report* as a 'monumental denial of structural racial inequality in the UK' (John, 2021). Professor Kalwant Bhopal, whose scholarship has long informed UK educational policy and practice, criticised the cultural deficit model inherent in the report's belief in what she called 'an illusory meritocracy' (Bhopal, 2021). She concluded that 'The result of refusing to acknowledge institutional racism is that the government will refuse to act upon it. Instead, Black and minority ethnic children will be blamed for their failings' (Bhopal, 2021).

Critics of the report identified examples of its tendency to avoid structural issues. The Director of the Runnymede Trust think tank Halima Begum queried the basis of the claim that Britain was a beacon for other White majority nations, pointing out that only two other European countries (Finland and Ireland) produced adequate data with which to track trends in race equality (John, 2021). Begum also criticised the lack of attention paid to disproportionate minority ethnic deaths during the COVID-19 pandemic, particularly among NHS workers (BBC News, 2021). In addition, it was later revealed that the Commission had omitted from its report evidence from a study on the education sector that CRED had itself commissioned. The study found that Black and South Asian students in majority White schools and colleges felt prone to low expectations from teachers and had experienced racism, discrimination and limited post-16 opportunities (Mansell, 2021).

A researcher who had extensively studied racism and antiracism across western Europe was Alana Lentin (see Lentin, 2004, 2020). She commented:

> The publication of the commission's report is the culmination of a long campaign to discredit antiracism. It is part of a general strategy, not confined to the UK, to blame those who speak out against racism for the very social divisions that they're identifying. From this perverse point of view, people who experience, study and challenge racism – not those responsible for maintaining and reproducing it – keep it alive. Every factor can be used to explain racism but race itself.
>
> To claim that an event, policy, or action is 'not racist' has become so common that, contrary to the claims of the report, it is rare to see an official acknowledgment that racism ever occurs. 'Not racism' goes beyond the mere denial of racism; rather racism is redefined in ways that contradict the experiences of those affected by it – experiences that are discounted as not objective enough to provide a trustworthy definition. Years of scholarship and activism are thrown out and replaced by an interpretation of racism that separates it from social class, geography and other factors, as though it were impossible to be affected by race, economic and place-based inequalities at the same time. (Lentin, 2021)

Lentin rejected the *CRED Report*'s insistence that the concept of institutional racism had been inflated, and argued that, in fact, policy-makers had long rolled back on the use of the term (see also Warmington et al, 2018). Lentin also pointed to the report's reliance on model minority tropes to 'disprove' instances of institutional racism; the absence of any focus on the experiences of migrants and asylum seekers; and the report's failure to grasp racism's mutability:

> However, the report has an understanding of racism as frozen in the past and never changing. So, it seems that if racism today does not precisely mirror the experiences of the report's middle-aged authors, it is not racism. In particular, their understanding of racism is narrowly based on individual economic advancement. (Lentin, 2021)

The response, particularly from those who had made contributions to the Commission, cast a pall over the report. Moreover, there was arguably another inbuilt limitation to the *CRED Report*'s impact, which was simply the fact that it was a report on race in Britain. The years since the *Macpherson Report* have seen a series of reports on areas of race equality; their recommendations have largely lain dormant. In June 2020 the BBC reported on some six government reviews related to racial inequality conducted over the previous decade whose recommendations had not been implemented (Aitken and Butcher, 2020). These included *The Lammy Review* (2017) on the treatment of and outcomes for minority ethnic people within the criminal justice system; *The McGregor-Smith Review* (Department for Business and Trade, 2017) on under-employment and lack of promotion in the workplace; the *Angiolini Review 2017* (Angiolini, 2017) into serious incidents and deaths in police custody. In addition to these, there was the Race Disparity Audit initiated in 2016 by then Conservative Prime Minister Theresa May (2016–19) as a broad review of racial inequalities in relation to local authority services and the public sector workforce. These frozen reviews join earlier examples, such as the report on rates of school exclusion among Black children, conducted by the Department for Education and Skills in 2006. Such reports remained largely symbolic achievements.

There is also a sense in which the *CRED Report* was something of a feint in the project to delegitimise antiracism. The report was heralded as a response to the BLM protests of 2020. However, in spring 2022 the *Police, Crime, Sentencing and Courts Crime Act 2022*, which gave the police new powers to restrict protest activities, became law. The Act was, in part, a response to BLM protests, as well as to Extinction Rebellion protests and demonstrations in the aftermath of the murder of Sarah Everard. One of the Act's provisions was in relation to damaging public memorials: a direct response to BLM protestors' toppling of the statue of slave trader Edward Colston in Bristol in

2020. The delegitimisation of antiracist activity in Britain was a culture war fought on multiple fronts. Chapter 5 of this book explains the emergence in Britain of an aggressive 'contra-' antiracism.

Postracialism versus institutional racism

Gillborn (2008) has argued that the public sector duties deriving from the *Macpherson Report* (1999) and initiated in the *Race Relations (Amendment) Act 2000* comprised the most powerful race equality policy yet seen in Britain. One of the reasons that *Macpherson* resonated with many of those working in the field of race equality was its willingness to name institutional racism. They recognised the value of *Macpherson*'s interrogation of organisational cultures, practices and structures, as opposed merely to condemning individual prejudice. *Macpherson*'s much quoted definition of institutional racism was:

> The collective failure of an organisation to provide an appropriate and professional service to people because of their colour, culture, or ethnic origin. It can be seen or detected in processes, attitudes and behaviour which amount to discrimination through unwitting prejudice, ignorance, thoughtlessness and racist stereotyping which disadvantage minority ethnic people. (Macpherson, 1999: 49)

Why is the idea of institutional racism incompatible with state postracialism and its colourblind approaches? After all, the postracialism in play in contemporary British policy and debate does not deny the existence of racism per se. What is it about the concept of *institutional* racism that now requires its strict containment? In their book *Seeing Race Again: Countering Colorblindness Across the Disciplines*, Crenshaw et al (2019) examine the hegemonic position of colorblindness in academic institutions and in wider society: 'Most institutions are now formally organised around the untested assumption that colorblindness is the exclusive measure of a fair and just organizational practice, an assumption that is predicated upon and enabled by the privileging of colorblind solutions to colorbound problems within the scholarly disciplines' (Crenshaw et al, 2019: 2).

In Crenshaw et al's definition, colourblind racism constitutes both the 'construction and disavowal' (Crenshaw et al, 2019: 2) of institutional racism. Their argument is that institutions, primarily concerned with reputation management, emphasise the fairness of their *formally* non-racist, colourblind policies which, so they insist, ensure that no group is either advantaged or disadvantaged. The appeal to abstract ethics, such as fairness and justice, ensures that colourbound problems are not addressed directly and simultaneously ensures that where racial inequalities persist they cannot be attributed to the practices of the institutions, which are assumed to be fair.

As Chapters 2 and 3 of this book have explained, CRT has addressed the construction/disavowal dynamic by emphasising the ordinariness of racism. CRT has always argued that racism is so ordinary, so business-as-usual within institutions, that its existence is routinely denied (Delgado and Stefancic, 2001). The *Macpherson Report* grasped something of this ordinariness in its problematising of culture and practice in public services. Gloria Ladson-Billings, a pioneer of the use of CRT in education research, has emphasised CRT's analysis of racism as ordinary, as the normal order:

> The first tenet of CRT is the notion that racism is not some random, isolated act of individuals behaving badly. Rather, to a CRT scholar racism is the normal order of things in US society. This is the thing that distinguishes CRT scholars from others who investigate race. Some focus on specific instances of racism or might admit to institutional racism. However, few outside of CRT would declare that racism is normal. Most argue that racism resides in individual (and sometimes corporate) beliefs and behaviors regarding the inferiority of people of another race. (Ladson-Billings, 2013: 37)

Ladson-Billings's argument is that neither individual nor institutional racism should be seen as anomalies that intrude into an otherwise healthy body politic. However, equating racism solely with intentional discrimination (either on the part of individuals or organisations) renders structural and institutional racism invisible. This unseeing of institutional racism is what Stokely Carmichael and Charles Hamilton pointed to in their classic definition of the distinction between personal prejudice and institutional racism:

> Racism is both overt and covert. It takes two, closely related forms: individual whites acting against individual blacks, and acts by the total white community against the total black community. We call these individual racism and institutional racism. ... When a black family moves into a ... white neighbourhood and is ... routed out, they are victims of an overt act of individual racism, which many will condemn – at least in words. But it is institutional racism that keeps black people locked in dilapidated slum tenements ... society either pretends it does not know of this latter situation, or is in fact incapable of doing anything meaningful about it. (Carmichael and Hamilton, 1967: 20–21)

In fact, Bell, Crenshaw and their CRT contemporaries argued that contemporary social conditions provided a double whammy; policy and legislation were often built equally on pretense and impotence. However, Carmichael and Hamilton's famous quote is arguably less useful as a fully theorised definition of institutional racism than as a depiction of how the different modes of racism are *received* in the public discourse. To most, extreme bigotry and racist violence are intelligible but, as Eddo-Lodge (2017) has said, many still refuse to treat institutional racism as a legitimate concept.

This kind of compartmentalisation is revealed in two frequently employed postracial tics. The first is the tendency to overgeneralise the implications of public disgust at crude, ugly racism. This is the 'no place in our society' thesis. The willingness to deplore overt individual acts of racism is read as proof that society has 'moved on'. The second is to use anachronistic questions as evidence that racism has declined in significance, rather than just mutating. There can be little doubt that in 1972 Britain would have baulked at the prospect of a British Indian Prime Minister or Home Secretary and that many would have objected to their child choosing a partner 'of another race'. In 2022 fewer might strongly object but framing a debate around changed individual social attitudes gives little purchase when it comes to understanding the persistence of racism in government policy and social provision. Social attitudes studies give little insight into why Black rates of unemployment have, over the past 30 years, normally remained double that of White Britons or why job applicants from Pakistani backgrounds face discrimination 'at levels unchanged since the late 1960s and 1970s' (Heath and Di Stasio, 2019). They simply tell us that we are not living 50 years previous. In 21st-century Britain, crude expressions of race hate are normally met with public expressions of disgust. Much of this disgust is no doubt genuine, although performative reputation management also comes into play (witness the rush of organisational statements of sympathy with BLM after the killing of George Floyd was broadcast worldwide). However, forms of racism that require transformational change receive less news media support and less policy attention and they may, as in the case of the *Macpherson Report*, prompt stubborn organisational resistance after initial displays of being on board.

The prejudice problematic

CRT's primary concern has never been with individual prejudice. This has always been a problem for those who suggest mischievously that CRT claims all White people are 'racist'; in CRT even micro-aggressions are regarded as systemic, serving to reinforce social norms, identities and relationships. Bonilla-Silva (2015) argues that seeing racism principally as an expression of personal prejudice is a powerful aspect of postracialism, and of colourblind racism. Among the problems Bonilla-Silva identifies with 'racism as prejudice' are that it treats racism as external to the social structure (depicting it as the domain of bigots and extremists) and that it prioritises the psychological over the historical, the cultural and the social (with racism depicted both as irrational and as a static quality). Moreover, it represents racism as something divorced from contemporary political logic, as 'an aftereffect of the past' (Crenshaw, 2019: 137).

Within critical race studies Bonilla-Silva's most influential work has been his analysis of postraciality and, in particular, its relationship to colourblind racism (see his influence on, for example, Crenshaw et al, 2019). Bonilla-Silva (2015) argues that in the 21st century, postracialism is the globally dominant mode of racialised social systems. He begins from the position that racialisation persists as a material structure, wherein:

> racialized groups are hierarchically ordered and 'social relations' and 'practices' emerge that fit the position of the groups in the racial regime. Those at the top of the order develop views and practices that support the racial status quo and those at the bottom develop views and practices that challenge it. (Bonilla-Silva, 2015: 77)

Crucially, colourblind framing ensures that the political and historical perspectives that normalise racism remain unseen; they are understood simply as 'human', 'logical' or 'rational' points of view, with no relation to racialisation. Bonilla-Silva and Dietrich state that: 'Dominant racial frames are not "false consciousness" but rather unacknowledged, contextual standpoints that provide the intellectual (and moral) building blocks whites use to explain racial matters' (Bonilla-Silva and Dietrich, 2011: 192).

Bonilla-Silva and Dietrich (2011) identify three constituent elements in the colourblind framework: elements that enable racism to persist without being acknowledged. First, there is an *abstract liberalism*, whereby racial injustices are justified by incorporating 'tenets associated with political and economic liberalism in an abstract and de-contextualized manner' (Bonilla-Silva and Dietrich, 2011: 192). For instance, equality policies can be decried because they 'favour' minority ethnic groups. Antagonism towards equalities policies, we are assured, has nothing to do with racism; it is simply a matter of liberal principles that insist no social group should be treated differently to any other. Second, there is *cultural racism*, wherein Whites distance themselves from biological racism, the idea that Black and Brown people are inherently inferior, but also deny the effects of structural racism, so that racialised social inequalities are implied to be the consequence of cultural or behavioural deficits. Third, there is the *minimisation of racism*, the 'anything but racism' account which holds that racial inequalities are rarely caused by racism but by a roll call of variables assumed to be distinct from race and racism, such as social class and family background (Bonilla-Silva and Dietrich, 2011: 194; see also CRRE, 2013, 2020).

We are left with a phenomenological disappearance. Each of these strands of colourblind racism occludes understanding of structural and institutional racism, directing our gaze elsewhere. Racism itself disappears as a social feature; the causes and effects of racism evade reflection; and those who insist on the continuing need to tackle racism are depicted as bogus, as what one English daily newspaper likes to call 'race grifters'. Yet, as Crenshaw et al (2019) argue, this apparent disavowal of (institutional) racism constructs another set of racialised discourses, wherein cultural failure accounts for racial inequalities, and mutterings about freeing oneself of fatalism and pulling oneself up by the bootstraps become policy.

State multiculturalism: lost futures

Chapter 3 of this book discussed Derrick Bell's racial realism, suggesting that it was haunted both by the lost futures of the civil rights movement and by the sheer persistence of recognisable forms of racism. Britain lives with its own lost futures. Postracial ideology constantly urges us to 'move on' and to 'move beyond' difficult debates about racism: to frame social inequalities within a postracial lens without doing the hard work of naming and owning the racism it purports to have transcended. What British postracialism does name are the *policy* approaches that it wishes to consign to the past, those rooted in the state multiculturalism and state antiracism that had uneven and contested purchase in Britain, particularly between the 1980s and early 2000s.

Britain's history of state multiculturalism should not be idealised but in western Europe it was distinctive and few would argue with the claim that it wrought gains against racism (see Parekh, 2006; Rattansi, 2011; Warmington, 2014). In the decades following the Second World War and the arrival of migrants from the Commonwealth, Britain took three broad policy routes. First, it tended to prioritise integration over assimilationism; second, it passed legislation against racial discrimination; third, over time Britain developed mechanisms for monitoring racial demographics and inequalities. A fourth important feature of Britain's racial politics was the absence of a strong far-right party in its Parliamentary system. It is important not to privilege the role of the state as an antiracist actor; Britain's policy direction and cultural shifts were driven also by communities and by grassroots antiracist movements, and by interest convergence between those movements and the state. Histories of Britain's Black and antiracist movements are documented in, for example, Sivanandan (1982); Fryer (1984); Bryan et al (1985); Warmington (2014); Olusoga (2021). However, the focus of this chapter is on critical race analyses of state action and the shift from state multiculturalism to state postracialism.

The first UK legislation to address racial discrimination directly was the *Race Relations Act 1965*. The Act exemplified the confluence of top-down Parliamentary activity, grassroots antiracist activism and social instability. In Parliament the socialist, anticolonialist MP Fenner Brockway made successive attempts to introduce some form of race relations bill from the mid-1950s onwards, to counter the 'colour bar' experienced by post-Second World War arrivals from the Caribbean, India and other parts of the Black and Brown 'New Commonwealth'. Increased community activity, such as 1963's Bristol bus boycott protesting discriminatory employment practices, was also instrumental in creating a sense of the need to act in government. The original Act evolved through successive amendments, notably in 1968, 1976 and in 2000 (following the *Macpherson Report*). Legislation was introduced and amended to cover areas such as racial harassment, workplace discrimination in housing and employment, and direct and indirect discrimination. The *Equality Act 2010* superseded the *Race Relations Acts*, conflating them with equalities provision covering gender, sexuality, disability and other protected characteristics.

Alongside overarching race relations legislation, there has, since the 1960s, been a series of landmark policy papers and reports that have shaped and responded to changes in race relations in Britain. Among them are reports as diverse in focus as the *Scarman Report* (1981), produced in response to the Brixton riots; the *Swann Report* (1985) on multicultural education; the *Cantle Report* (2001) on community cohesion; and the work of Labour Prime Minister Gordon Brown (2007–10) on 'British values' (Ministry of Justice, 2007). To these, we can add specific legislation and policy in areas such as immigration, criminal justice, health and education that have impinged acutely on the lives of Black and Brown communities.

Authors such as Parekh (2000), and Malik (2009) have pointed to the duality of the term 'multiculturalism' as understood in Britain, where it denotes the growth of a culturally diverse society (factual multiculturalism) but also denotes approaches to managing that diversity (state multiculturalism). Late 20th-century politics across the world were informed by 'multiculturalism' in the broadest sense. New forms of pluralist social activism included feminism, LGBTQIA+ rights, disability rights, indigenous peoples' movements and minority faith, ethnic and linguistic struggles. Contests over multiculturalism in Britain have played out in a global context of post-war population shifts and social reconfiguration.

Britain's state multiculturalism has been concerned with how institutions, and public services in particular, should recognise and manage cultural diversity, ensuring legal fairness and equality but also addressing cultural pluralism. As such, it exists within the overlap between politics of recognition and the politics of redistribution. Both factual and state multiculturalism were – and continue to be – contested spaces. Between the 1950s and 1980s opposition to the fact of multiculturalism was expressed across the political spectrum, though most often on the Right. However, by the 1980s the belief that Britain could, in a literal sense, be 'kept White' was largely the province of the extreme right. Even among those proponents of the 'Great Replacement Theory' who have today edged into the mainstream, and who prophesy the death of White Europe, melancholy tends to prevail over political proposals to 'repatriate' Black and Brown communities en masse. Instead, preserving Britain's 'Whiteness' has shifted increasingly to what we now often term 'culture wars'.

Nor has antagonism towards multiculturalism divided readily along Left/Right lines. On the Right there has often been opposition to efforts to diversify educational curricula, national symbols and readings of British history. However, such opposition shifts over time and in specifics. The opponent of the National Trust's recent project to uncover historical links between its properties and the profits of slavery and colonialism might be happy enough to tout chicken korma as the national dish. Recent Conservative governments have been keen to promenade the diversity of their top ranks, while maintaining hostile policies on immigration, policing and public protest. On the Left, there has often been suspicion of the perceived tendency of state multiculturalism to promote symbolic achievements at the expense of tackling structural inequalities. In the 1970s and 1980s antiracist activists were sceptical about superficial models of cultural diversity (what they referred to as 'samosas, steelpans and saris') that implied racism was principally a form of ignorance that could be educated away by exposure to diverse cultures. However, in the 21st-century, as government commitment to state multiculturalism waned and conservative attacks increased, former critics of liberal multiculturalism frequently found themselves defending the remnants of multicultural practice (see Bourne, 2007).

Multiculturalism and antiracism are not necessarily opposed to one another. However, in conceptual terms we can say that multiculturalism operates on a horizontal axis, being primarily concerned with relations across communities; antiracism's principal concern is with the vertical axis of social hierarchies and inequalities. Conservative discourses, particularly in their voguish 'anti-woke' incarnation, tend to conflate multiculturalism and antiracism. A host of phenomena from revision of the school curriculum to unconscious bias training, cross-racial casting or taking the knee in solidarity with BLM are all seen as part of the same liberal mission creep. However, it should be acknowledged that the spaces around race equality policy and legislation have also been vigorously contested by those sympathetic to antiracist aims. Complex settlements between state provision and community demands (and between the diverse stakeholders and tendencies within those broad blocs) have often produced dynamics of 'rolling back', whereby, as Bell observed in the US context, decades of community struggle and protest lead to ineffectual government policies, and over time even those policies are partially reversed. Thus we have instances of interest convergence ossifying into contradiction closure, then fading as state and community interests again diverge.

The *Macpherson Report*: interest convergence and contradiction closure

The concept of contradiction-closing cases has been influential in CRT analyses of legislation and policy in both the UK and the US. In the UK Gillborn (2008) has written on the Stephen Lawrence case, in which the investigation of the racist murder of the South London teenager was hampered by institutional racism within the Metropolitan Police. It led, after years of family campaigning, to the Macpherson Inquiry, which for Gillborn was an example both of interest convergence and contradiction closure. The Lawrence family's initial questions about police handling of Stephen's murder in 1993 were rebuffed but as the campaign gained widespread attention and was supported by the popular conservative newspaper *The Daily Mail* (whose editor had employed Stephen's father Neville in building work), Tony Blair's New Labour government initiated the Macpherson Inquiry into the murder investigation and eventually into wider police culture and practice. The *Macpherson Report* (1999) extended its coverage to address institutional racism across state sectors and informed both the *RRAA 2000* and the later *Equality Act 2010*.

In 2021 government papers relating to the New Labour and Macpherson period revealed that then Prime Minister Tony Blair (1997–2007) had, in fact, initially resisted broadening the Macpherson Inquiry to cover wider relations between the Metropolitan Police and London's Black communities, preferring to examine Lawrence's murder as a singular case (Rawlinson and Davies, 2021). Investigating police failures in the broader context of historically poor police–community relations might, argued Blair and his senior advisors, raise unrealistic expectations of change among London's Black communities. Moreover, government archives showed a particular concern that a wider investigation might be viewed as an attack on the police and become a cause célèbre across the UK's influential right-wing media, an interest group that Blair's New Labour party had taken pains not to antagonise.

The details of the Lawrence case and, in particular, of initial state attempts to limit the Macpherson Inquiry's scope illustrate that accusations about CRT's supposed cynicism should probably be tempered. Journalist and author Nesrine Malik commented on the Blair story, comparing it with contemporary government antipathy to antiracism:

> There is a sort of sickening relief in seeing those sentiments – expressed behind closed doors – spelled out so matter of factly; in knowing for certain that concerns about racial injustice aren't taken seriously not because they're not believed but because they rock the boat. Indeed, the smothering of a broad, progressive race policy 20 years ago tells us much about where we are today, with a government proudly hostile to interrogating the true state of race relations. (Malik, 2022a)

The light shed on behind closed doors conversations about racial injustice reveals the nature of 'really existing postracialism'. For Malik, UK governments, both Labour and Conservative, have tended to view issues of race and racism as 'merely a government liability' (Malik, 2022a) and have instead prioritised reputation management (which is, of course, an essential part of interest convergence and contradiction closure). The Lawrence case shows contradiction-closing cases to exist in a space between interest convergence and interest divergence. They are enacted in instances where interest convergence exists: we have addressed the issue; let's move on. They are also used to defer interest divergence: that is, when the gap between the professed values of the state and its actual practice again become large enough to begin provoking discontent, communities of colour are encouraged to take consolation in the legacy of measures enacted long ago. So it was that the *CRED Report* (2021) claimed to honour the legacy of Macpherson, and so it is that we are often encouraged to balance in our minds cruel immigration policies of the present with the proud record of past race relations acts. Contradiction-closing cases are a salient feature of state postracialism.

Britain's comfort zone

In 2017 British journalist Reni Eddo-Lodge published *Why I'm No Longer Talking to White People About Race*, a disquisition on race and racism in Britain. Her opening sentences expressed frustration with Britain's colourblind racism. What the book made clear was that in important respects the distance between her world and the colourblind US described by Bell, Crenshaw and Bonilla-Silva was not as great as British exceptionalist commentators often suggest:

> I'm no longer engaging with white people on the topic of race. Not all white people, just the vast majority who refuse to accept the legitimacy of structural racism and its symptoms. I can no longer engage with the gulf of an emotional disconnect that white people display when a person of colour articulates their experience. You can see their eyes shut down and harden. (Eddo-Lodge, 2017: ix)

Eddo-Lodge wrote of the unseeing of racism in contemporary Britain and the bad faith that underpinned much public debate. Around the time that Eddo-Lodge was writing *Why I'm No Longer Talking to White People About Race*, the University of Birmingham's Centre for Research on Race and Education, of which I was a founding member, conducted an extensive research project examining race and education in England between 1993 and 2013: that is in the 20 years following the murder of Stephen Lawrence (see

Gillborn et al, 2016; Warmington et al, 2018). An important strand of the research was a series of interviews with a range of stakeholders, exploring their personal reflections on the shifting status of race equality in education and social policy. They included some of the most notable figures active in race equality work in England. Those interviewed included educators, community activists, third sector workers, trade unionists, politicians and civil servants. Across the course of their professional lives, these actors had moved between the margins and the centre of the policy world, depending on the wider political mood.

Their personal perspectives and political positions were as diverse as that implies but what was surprising was how often their reflections converged in a pessimistic meta-narrative. Their stories depicted race equality concerns as having a precarious place in education policy in England. It was taken as read that moments of apparent progress in policy and legislation would fall short when it came to implementation and that governments – Conservative or Labour – would often regress when issues of racial inequality were deemed to be outside the central policy drive. Those reversals would be accelerated at moments when multiculturalism and antiracism became politically toxic. It was the 'pattern of cyclical progress and cyclical regression' described by Bell (1992: 98). Gus John, the veteran educator and activist whose work stretches back to the late 1960s, summed up the fickleness of successive British governments and the dynamics of interest convergence: 'Governments throughout the decades have had one eye on what they consider to be the responsible and moral thing to do and one eye on making sure that the rest of the population didn't feel that they were being taken out of their comfort zone' (John, quoted in Warmington et al, 2018).

The interviewees focused on the ebb and flow around three particular policy moments. These were: the measures aimed at closing ethnic achievement gaps that began in the early 1990s; the diversity and citizenship agenda that featured in New Labour's first term (1997–2001); the *Macpherson Report* (1999) and the subsequent *RRAA 2000*. Participants' narratives converged in a view of 1993–2013 as a period in which race equality policy had gained momentum, touched the policy mainstream but then been reversed. So, for instance, the diversity and citizenship agenda was arguably rolled back by the *Cantle Report* (2001) which, in the wake of urban unrest in Bradford and Oldham and other northern towns, warned against the danger of communities living 'parallel lives'. The specific focus on ethnic achievement gaps was diminished as New Labour and subsequent Conservative governments focused education policy on regulatory systems aimed at increasing average attainment and standards (see Ball, 2017). These were embedded in colourblind discourses of 'quality', 'standards' and 'accountability'.

By the end of the New Labour administration (1997–2010) and the start of the subsequent Conservative-Liberal Democrat Coalition government

(2010–15) explicit focus on race equality in education policy had, in the views of the participants, been severely diminished. The five-year education strategy issued by New Labour in 2005 mentioned Black and minority ethnic pupils just once. By the 2010s, White working-class pupils had become the political concern of education policy makers (CRRE, 2013, 2020). Chapters 5 and 6 of this book expand on the ways in which the policy focus on White working-class underachievement in education became bound up with a triadic populism that had long been seeking a 'legitimate' focus for antipathy to multiculturalism.

Rolling back *Macpherson*

The initial pushback against the *Macpherson Report* (1999) began long before the *CRED Report* (2021). Macpherson's emphasis on institutional racism was not easily sustained. National events subsequent to the *Macpherson Report* included 2001's northern unrest (which news media sensationalised as 'race riots') and the London 7/7 bombings of July 2005, both of which heightened Islamophobia. In the summer of 2011, the police killing of Mark Duggan was the catalyst for widespread civil unrest, lasting five nights and spreading over many major cities. Alongside all of this was persistent media focus on UK immigration levels and 'bogus' asylum-seekers. Present also was the gnawing idea that the White working class had become Britain's most neglected group, 'left behind' in multicultural Britain.

By the end of the decade that had begun with the *RRAA 2000*, the limits of *Macpherson*'s impact had become apparent. Rob Berkeley, Director of the Runnymede Trust between 2009 and 2014 reflected:

> there's an important moment ten years on from the Lawrence enquiry … in 2009, just a realisation that despite a lot of talk and a lot of effort from some, actually the outcomes hadn't changed. So, the stickiness of the political system and the institutions towards change, I think, is instructive. (Berkeley, quoted in Warmington et al, 2018)

Was *Macpherson* hobbled because of inherent flaws, principally a tendency to bureaucratic inertia, or was it, in fact, that *Macpherson* and the *RRAA 2000* threatened to become all too effective in surfacing racial inequalities? In going where its predecessors *Swann* and *Scarman* had not and naming institutional racism, did *Macpherson* become a political liability? By the time of CRRE's study, government had, several interviewees suggested, retreated to a pre-*Macpherson* position. One (anonymous) former advisor to the Department for Education and Skills said simply: 'You know, if you raise that issue [of institutional racism] you're again thought of as a mad person, which you probably were prior to Macpherson' (quoted in Warmington et al, 2018).

Pertinently, several interviewees explicitly raised the idea of postracialism, viewing Britain's postracial turn in policy as providing rhetorical cover for a period in which race equality matters were being marginalised. Like many of the interviewees, Maxie Hayles truly was part of an older generation of accomplished ethnic minority professionals, founder of the Birmingham Race Action Monitoring Group. He was also a community elder, part of the Windrush generation and he had lived through multiple shifts in social attitudes and government strategy. He reflected: 'There's a fallacy that we live in a postracial era and that's dangerous. It's dangerous because racism is not "*if* or *but*"; it's an inevitable process and we're not going to get utopia' (Maxie Hayles, quoted in Warmington et al, 2018). For Maxie, postracial claims were a dangerous fallacy because they concealed the persistence of racialised forms that he recognised only too well.

Conclusion

The postracial turn is not unique to Britain but it has become pervasive across Britain's political lines. Recent events suggest it is near to being an official state position. In a country still uncomfortable, at the political level, with race and difference, there is a clear logic to postracial ideology. State postracialism, our 'really existing postracialism', offers contradiction closure at a meta level: insistence on a conclusive end to the demands and complications of multiculturalism, antiracism, BLM, CRT and the rest. It is a postracialism in bad faith, in that it seeks a postracial domain without the discomfort of naming and owning the racialised social relationships that it claims to transcend – without the discomfort of going 'through' racism to get to the postracial. It is postracialism on the cheap: a kind of political scrounging. However, this facile postracialism also requires a parallel discourse. For if race and racism are no longer valid sociological or policy lenses then antiracists must be treated as illegitimate political actors. Chapter 5 of this book explores the symbiosis between postracial ideology and the demonisation of antiracism.

5

Against antiracism

Facile postracialism presumes the non-significance of race. However, its political expression (what this book terms state postracialism) requires a parallel discourse, a burly minder. In contemporary Britain our postracial turn has been paralleled by political antagonism to antiracist movements: an 'anti-' or 'contra-' antiracism. Postracialism and 'contra-' antiracism are symbiotic because if race and racism are supposed to have declined in social salience, then those who continue to campaign against racial injustice must be treated with suspicion, as divisive voices, even as 'reverse racists'. Chapter 5 of this book explores this symbiosis. It examines the ways in which the overtly racist discourses of past decades have been superseded, in mainstream political debate, by discursive modes that are less overtly racist but which aim instead to delegitimise contemporary antiracist movements, to harry the discursive space available for critical race voices.

For the most part, these new racist expressions shy away from taking issue with the presence per se of Black and Brown communities in Britain; instead they rest on the insistence that Black political demands, multicultural identification and calls for racial justice have gone too far. In short, Britain may or may not be 'full' in terms of minority ethnic population but it has reached full capacity as regards addressing matters of race and racism. This chapter's discussion focuses on the 'contra-' backlash evident since the BLM summer of 2020, when there was a brief window in which BLM seemed state adjacent, a moment of interest convergence. That moment was brief. After 2020, critics of multiculturalism and antiracism gone-too-far sought renewed discursive spaces, urging moral panics around BLM, CRT and the trial and acquittal of protestors who toppled the statue of slave trader Edward Colston in Bristol in June 2020. Chapter 5 traces the emergence of those 'contra-' discourses, including the transatlantic targeting of CRT, which has been cast as a particular trope.

Anything but antiracism

The first step in delegitimising antiracism is declaring it no longer necessary. Under 'really existing postracialism' racism exists elsewhere: in other places and other historical periods. It is never made entirely clear how British society reached its postracial phase. By discursive sleight, racial progress is abstracted from political struggle and vaguely attributed to historically inevitable forces: the triumph of liberalism, the marketplace of ideas, demographic change or fundamental British values. The decades of work by groups such as New Beacon, Southall Black Sisters, the Grunwick strikers, the New Cross Fire Campaign or Tottenham Rights rarely feature in the postracial narrative. BLM, CRT and the Rhodes Must Fall campaign are often portrayed as active impediments to racial harmony.

The writer Olivia Laing refers to playwright Sarah Schulman's use of the phrase 'the gentrification of the mind' to describe the decades after the trauma of the 1980s AIDS pandemic. Schulman was aware of the subsequent erasure from history of the political struggle for change 'by people who were profoundly disenfranchised – by queers, drug addicts and sex workers, many of them now dead' (Laing, 2020: 251). This erasure, she believed, had left us without either a history or a theory of change, those being lost to what Laing calls 'This process of banalisation, this insidious forgetfulness' (Laing, 2020: 251). The symbiosis between postracialism and 'contra-' antiracism produces a similar banalisation. The changes we have seen in matters of race in Britain are, so we are told, attributable to anything but antiracism.

At best, 'really existing postracialism' enacts what author Philip Hensher, writing about LGBTQIA+ politics in contemporary Britain, has termed 'the performance of sympathy' (Hensher, 2017: 33), wherein evidence of social progress becomes a basis for regulating minority voices:

> The current situation feels as if an exasperated majority is telling us that we have been given a generous legal framework. We used to insist on your silence; these days, we've kindly ensured that there is no reason for you to speak up. That's an improvement, isn't it? Now go away. Shut up. Listen to our explanations of your existence. (Hensher, 2017: 33)

Campaigners for racial justice are frequently met with stern reminders of the legal generosity of race relations acts and of the kinds of improvements evidenced in social attitudes surveys. Moreover, a more strident 'contra-' antiracism is readily available. It aims to delegitimise radical antiracism, not merely through a hopeful 'moving on' narrative but through a discourse of derision and, more seriously, through the machinery of the state.

Seeking 'contra-' spaces

The combination of postracialism and 'contra-' antiracism seeks particular kinds of discursive space. In contemporary Britain, overtly racist public statements are, at least in theory, deplored. The claim that 'You're not allowed to say anything these days' because of 'political correctness gone mad' is so clichéd that it has become a comedy standby. As a claim, it is also demonstrably untrue – as a glance at popular press headlines on migrants, asylum seekers and Muslim communities still show. Describing refugees crossing the channel in small boats as an 'invasion' does not disqualify a politician from becoming Home Secretary (Dearden, 2022) and using questionable language to describe Muslim women or African children does not bar one from becoming Prime Minister (Clegg, 2019). However, recent decades have seen a shrinkage in mainstream discursive space for the crudest kind of racism and for direct attacks on Britain's multiracial presence.

One of the effects of postracial ideology has been to reinforce the discursive divide between factual multiculturalism and state multiculturalism. Even by the late 1970s calls to reverse Britain's demographic multiculturalism by 'repatriating' Black and Brown communities had largely become the domain of the far-right. That said, it is worth noting as recently as the 2010 general election the far-right British National Party fielded 300 candidates, securing over half a million votes, though failing to win a single seat (BBC News, 2010). However, decades of political action at both community and state levels, and cultural and demographic change has meant that calls to 'keep Britain White' have long been off the table. At least in a general sense, the presence of Black and Brown communities in Britain is not disputed.

This has meant that those who are antagonistic to multiculturalism have tended to cede the issue of Black and Brown presence and shifted increasingly to the statist terrains of policy and culture. While it is certainly the case that the cultural impacts of the presence of Black and Brown communities were a political issue from the Windrush era onwards (Warmington, 2014), 'contras' in the present day have had to sever as best they can their professed concerns about culture from their concerns about presence per se. This is why it is an error to regard Britain's 'culture wars' as merely decorative, as manufactured controversy. The terrain of culture provides discursive space for reactionary conversations about race, while conferring plausible deniability: that is, we are told that these conversations are not about race but about culture, British values, the speed of change and a whole range of 'legitimate concerns'.

However, the 'contra-' space constantly needs to be renewed and reopened. Antiracist movements such as BLM, CRT and the Colston protests have been used to populate 'contra-' spaces. This is not to argue that critiques of any form of antiracism are inherently racist. However, attacks on BLM, CRT and so forth have been used for racist ends, carrying as they do greater legitimacy than direct attacks on multiracialism. Depictions of antiracism gone-too-far, of antiracism being anti-White or anti-British, have become an integral part of triadic populism in Britain.

The *bête noir*

For most of its 40-year history, CRT's home was in academia. In recent years, however, discussion of CRT has moved well beyond the universities. Since the resurgence of the BLM movement in 2020, CRT has become a folk demon in both the US and the UK. For instance, journalist Adam Harris calculated that between summer 2020 and spring of 2021, US conservative broadcaster Fox News had referred to CRT in 150 broadcasts (Harris, 2021). In the US there have been attempts in multiple states to introduce bills to ban the teaching of 'divisive concepts' in schools and in anti-discrimination training, the political headline often being that such legislation will 'ban' CRT (Schuessler, 2021).

CRT has become conservative shorthand, used to conflate a disparate collection of ideas and professional practices: teaching Black history, diversity training, equalities monitoring, decolonisation debates and so forth. In the UK conservative politicians have made efforts to replicate the US line on 'divisive concepts'. In historical terms this is not new ground. In England, in particular, the first two decades of the 21st century saw a persistent backlash against multiculturalism and a rise of nativist politics, all long before the international resurgence of BLM (see Tomlinson, 2019).

Before and after 'the end of tolerance'

The 1980s and 1990s were arguably the high watermarks of state multiculturalism in Britain. Multicultural policies were uneven and sometimes contradictory but, in alignment with grassroots antiracism and demographic changes, their effects were to make overtly racist discourses in media and politics less acceptable than they had been in the 1960s or 1970s (see Warmington, 2014). Today's gentrified postracial discourses, however, are predicated upon the assumption of a kind of historical inevitability: that progress against racism is the natural result of generational change, has little to do with political struggle, and is irreversible.

Indeed, one tension between postracialism and CRT is the degree to which the potential for reversal of apparent progress is accepted. CRT is not alone in regarding progress against racism as provisional but CRT goes further than most antiracist thought, in that much of its theory is, in fact, *a theory of reversal* in legislation and policy (Bell, 1987, 1992).

Sally Tomlinson, whose scholarship on race and education dates back to her pioneering research with John Rex in the 1970s, has argued that, while multiculturalism and antiracism have always been contested in British politics, by the early 21st century, issues of race equality had become, in her words, 'toxic' (Warmington et al, 2018; see also Tomlinson, 2018, 2019). This pivot, this point of reversal, was the 'end of tolerance' described by Kundnani (2007), wherein retreat from the state multiculturalism of previous decades became programmatic. In the UK policy context these anxieties over multiculturalism and antiracism coalesced around the war on terror; disturbances in northern British towns in 2001; media hostility to new migration; and political rhetoric depicting Britain as a broken society. News media obsessed over Islam and emblems such as the wearing of the veil (an obsession reflected, in particular, in the Conservative Party conference of 2008). Critiques of state multiculturalism emerged also from ostensibly liberal circles, including the New Labour government in its latter stages (see Warmington, 2015b).

The strength of this 'contra-' flow was such that by 2007 the Institute of Race Relations' Jenny Bourne, by no means an uncritical observer of state multicultural policy, was moved to write:

> Multiculturalism, a term generally accepted across the political spectrum for some three decades, has suddenly become a term to be scoffed at, rather like 'Political Correctness'. Spokespeople, from faith leaders and race relations commissars to politicians, are pointing to the dangers of multicultural policies in the UK. For the Chief Rabbi, 'Multiculturalism encourages people not to integrate, it creates social exclusion'. For Trevor Phillips, head of the Commission for Racial Equality, we are in danger of 'sleep-walking into segregation' and for David Blunkett our over-tolerance has allowed groups, especially of Asians, to 'self-segregate'. And now under Ruth Kelly, appointed to the new post of Communities Minister, we have a Commission on Integration and Cohesion to help usher in an 'honest', national debate about multiculturalism. (Bourne, 2007: 2)

Bourne's article effectively captured the overlapping strands of what we might think of as the pre-George Floyd, pre-BLM backlash against multiculturalism and antiracism in Britain. The pervasive Islamophobia she identifies has often been linked to the transatlantic construction of the war on terror but it should be remembered that in Britain political anxieties over 'self-segregating' Muslim communities, particularly in the north of England, can also be traced back, at least, to protests over Salman Rushdie's novel *The Satanic Verses* in 1988 (Kundnani, 2015). It is difficult now to recall that prior to the late 1980s 'Muslim communities' occupied little space in Britain's national imagination, which had preferred ethnic and national categories to religious ones. In the 21st century, headlines such as 'Muslim schools ban our culture' (*Express*, 20 February 2009 [Hall, 2009]) or 'Warning on 'UK Muslim ghettoes'" (*Daily Mail*, 10 April 2016 [Dolan, 2016]) could be presented as being about values and culture, not race, and anxieties about self-segregation and radicalisation were readily depicted as legitimate concerns for the majority.

Moreover, as Bourne also noted, the focus on British values that had begun to supersede policy focus on cultural diversity in the latter part of the New Labour administration constructed a quietly nationalistic representation of values such as equality, tolerance and fairness, which were now somehow characteristically British (see also Lander, 2016). This widened the space for anti-Muslim racism. If Muslim communities could be depicted as bigoted or intolerant, then they were also by definition un-British, and this un-Britishness had apparently been allowed to flourish by decades of municipal multiculturalism. Anxieties over the supposed erosion of British values and culture also opened up discursive space for a zero-sum analysis wherein multicultural gains equalled White losses. In particular, political bodies and media outlets not known for their social class analyses began to focus on the fate of the White working class, constructing a thesis in which concerns with race equality and multiculturalism had led to the neglect of White Britons (see Chapter 6).

Brexit's space

There is only room for a brief reference to another space that was opened for racist discourse pre-2020, which is Brexit. The extent to which the campaign to leave the European Union was predicated on anxieties over immigration and driven by an exemplary triadic populism has been extensively discussed by, for example, O'Toole (2019) and Tomlinson (2019). Not all those who voted for Brexit were motivated by racism or xenophobia, by any means. However, in Brexit's hauntology concerns about free movement within the EU – in crude terms, 'White' immigration – were also shaped by decades of panic over non-EU 'Black and Brown' immigration.

In Britain antiracists are regularly admonished with the reminder that it is not necessarily racist to be concerned about immigration. That is true in abstract terms but it is also the case that in Britain it is difficult to avoid the elision between concerns about immigration and racism because since the 1940s Black and Brown people have been emblematic of the figure of 'the immigrant'. Moreover, there is credible evidence to suggest that the Brexit campaign increased hostility (in media coverage, in harassment and physical attacks) to minority ethnic communities in Britain in general (Virdee and McGeever, 2018). Depictions of Britain as struggling to preserve its national identity (and its *imperial* identity – with profuse references to Britain standing alone in the dark days of the Second World War) were prevalent in pro-Brexit rhetoric. In July 2019, three years after the UK voted by a four percentage point margin to leave the European Union, Boris Johnson, effectively leader of the pro-Brexit campaign within the Conservative Party, became Prime Minister. The beginning of the following year saw the signing of Britain's treaty of withdrawal from the EU. Johnson had used Churchillian rhetoric to help forge a populist alliance but by the early 2020s antagonism to the EU had begun to fade as a credible unifier of the disparate class and regional elements of Conservative support. New unifiers would need to be put in play, no matter how unlikely.

Unequivocally against Critical Race Theory

In October 2020 during a House of Commons debate on Black History Month there was an unlikely contribution by Equalities Minister Kemi Badenoch, who declared:

> I want to speak about a dangerous trend in race relations that has come far too close to home in my life, which is the promotion of critical race theory, an ideology that sees my blackness as victimhood and their whiteness as oppression. I want to be absolutely clear that the Government stand unequivocally against critical race theory. Some schools have decided to openly support the anti-capitalist Black Lives Matter group, often fully aware that they have a statutory duty to be politically impartial. Of course black lives matter, but we know that the Black Lives Matter movement is political. … That is why we do not endorse that movement on this side of the House. It is a political movement. (Badenoch, 2020: 1011–12)

It was an unlikely intervention because according to Hansard, CRT had never previously been discussed in the House. Why then did the UK government now treat CRT as deserving of official opprobrium? Badenoch's words were perhaps less puzzling when one examined the context of this Black History Month debate. In summer 2020 the UK, like many parts of the world, had witnessed demonstrations in support of BLM, following the killing of George Floyd in Minneapolis in May of that year (see Joseph-Salisbury et al, 2021). The British government could not entirely ignore the strength of feeling shown in these protests. In the midst of the COVID-19 pandemic thousands of people congregated in BLM protests. Multiple institutions responded to the mood, from Twitter to universities to England's national football team (the latter began taking the knee before matches). As recounted in Chapter 4, the UK government would soon commission a major report into racial inequalities in response to that summer's protests.

The Minister's express concern was that BLM was 'a political movement', and a political movement with which, she claimed, some schools had aligned themselves. These associations were carefully chosen and, as discussed later in this chapter, they drew upon rhetoric that had been used successfully to attack CRT, BLM and other antiracist efforts in the US. Despite the fact that CRT had existed in the UK since around 2003, it was important to portray CRT as something novel, posing new and immediate dangers. Elsewhere the Minister's speech depicted CRT as something foreign and imported. CRT was out of its lane in that it had come from the US to British shores and, so it was claimed, entered British schools. The association with schools was crucial. CRT and BLM were a threat to our children and our schools but the education system itself was also suspect; in Britain, as in the US, education had long been scrutinised by conservatives and neo-liberals as a last bastion of liberal-left thought (Apple, 2018).

In the wake of the Equalities Minister's intervention, CRT entered mainstream media consciousness in Britain for the first time. This created a certain double-think. CRT entered the mainstream framed largely *by its critics* – pieces knowledgeable about CRT were few and far between – but was depicted by its critics as being somehow hegemonic.

> Beware Critical Race Theory – the divisive ideology infiltrating school history lessons. (*The Telegraph*, 1 October 2020 [Robinson, 2020a])

> Time to end the teaching of divisive critical race theory in British schools. (*The Telegraph*, 21 October 2020 [Robinson, 2020b])

> UK minister: teaching white privilege and Critical Race Theory in schools is illegal. (*The Federalist*, 21 October 2020 [Boyd, 2020])

> Is teaching anti-discrimination actually discriminatory? Woke culture has become ingrained in our schools, workplaces, and the NHS. As critical race theory has become more prevalent, some are leading a cultural war against these institutions to ensure their rights are protected. (*Institute of Economic Affairs*, October 2020 [IEA, 2020])

> Nearly half of Britain's young people are too frightened of being ostracised to challenge beliefs in 'white privilege', a poll shows. It reveals that 59 per cent of school leavers have been taught critical race theory, the premise by American academics that racism shapes Western life and white people enjoy advantages because of their colour. (*Mail Online*, 20 November 2022 [Charters, 2022])

Also in October 2022, *The Spectator* magazine published an interview with the Equalities Minister that inserted CRT as a headline. Titled 'Kemi Badenoch: the problem with critical race theory' (Nelson, 2020), the piece depicted Badenoch (who was formerly employed by the magazine) as an authentic Black voice suppressed by a liberal consensus that had coalesced around BLM and CRT. It claimed that Badenoch's opponents had not forgiven her for saying that 'Britain is one of the best countries in the world in which to be black' (Nelson, 2020), although the article did not stop to reflect on what was implied about a world in which it was valid to debate which was the best country to live in while Black. The interview itself, conducted shortly *before* the Black History Month debate, contained a number of motifs that drew on the US 'contra-' playbook. There was the use of CRT as a catch-all to encompass miscellaneous aspects of antiracism; insistence that CRT and BLM's influence on public sector institutions was now pervasive; and a claimed affinity with Martin Luther King (though in a domesticated form that overlooked the difficult bits, such as King's willingness to mobilise the streets, his defiance of the law, his support for unionised workers and his unpopularity among White Americans). The interview also included condemnation of popular books on antiracism, in this case Robin DiAngelo's *White Fragility* and Reni Eddo-Lodge's *Why I'm No Longer Talking to White People About Race*. Neither of these books could be described as CRT texts; nevertheless, they were useful props, as debates in the US had already shown.

The politics of respectability

The claim that Black conservative voices were marginalised by liberal media had become a motif during the 2010s (Warmington, 2014, 2015b). In 2010–11 *Prospect* magazine began to provide a platform for Black British commentators who were publicly critical of state multiculturalism. In autumn 2010 it produced the cover story, 'Rethinking race: has multiculturalism had its day?' Encompassing views on education, mental health, the arts and social policy, the thematic thrust was against what the authors perceived as Britain's attachment to outdated models of multiculturalism. The following year, *Prospect's* editor David Goodhart reconvened some of the contributors to the 2010 special issue for a BBC Radio 4 broadcast, titled *A New Black Politics*. The programme expanded upon *Prospect's* themes and levelled criticism at the antiracist alliances built in Britain in the late 20th century. A central claim was that, in the 1970s and 1980s, state multiculturalism and alliances between Black radicals and the British Left produced misrecognition of the authentic values of Black British communities (reliance on the 'authenticity' of Black conservative voices sat oddly with the professed distaste for identity politics). The consequences were an atrophied Black politics, ossified in discourses of oppression and rebellion, and generations locked into patterns of low expectation. Britain's Black politics, old and shabby, were fit to be bulldozed and realigned.

As in the US, the politics of respectability were a persistent feature of the putative 'new Black politics' (see critiques by West, 1992; Gay, 2014). Always an integral part of social conservatism's prescription for working-class people, respectability politics propose rugged individual striving as the behavioural solution to racial inequalities. Embedded in cultural deficit thinking, their rhetoric often relies on misogynoir tropes, wherein Black single mothers are targeted as mythic welfare queens, who have failed to inculcate their children with the work ethic that has enabled other 'model' minorities to overcome social disadvantage. As such, the politics of respectability are pitched in opposition to structural analyses of racism; the roots of disadvantage are presumed to lie within deviant social behaviour. The call for behavioural solutions also rests on a type of contradiction closure: properly behaved Black and Brown communities have the potential, and perhaps the sole responsibility, to erase racism. Author Roxanne Gay has identified the chimeric quality of respectability politics:

> It's a nice idea that we could simply follow a prescribed set of rules and make the world a better place for all. It's a nice idea that racism is a finite problem for which there is a finite solution, and that respectability, perhaps, could have saved all the people who have lost their lives to the effects of racism. (Gay, 2014: 259)

The premise of the politics of respectability, whether in the US or Britain, is that our social structures and institutions have no more give in them, so we must instead remould Black and Brown families and communities.

In the decade following their coverage in *Prospect* and by the BBC, several Black British social conservatives garnered significant media space and forged links with government. Indeed, the claim that these 'authentic' voices were routinely suppressed turned out to be self-refuting. Munira Mirza followed Boris Johnson (whom she had advised as Mayor of London) to Downing Street as one of the Prime Minister's key special advisors. In 2021 conservative educator Katharine Birbalsingh was appointed Chair of the UK's Social Mobility Commission. Tony Sewell, as discussed in Chapter 4, went on to chair the Commission on Race and Ethnic Disparities (CRED). Britain's Black social conservatives did not lack sponsorship. In retrospect, it might be argued that *Prospect's* 'Rethinking Race' special issue was the single most influential publication on race in Britain of its period.

Understanding the culture wars

CRT's conscription to the culture wars was unlikely but not accidental. In 2020 the UK's governing Conservative Party was quick to declare its scepticism about BLM, and its outright hostility to taking the knee and the removal of statues. While sticking to the 'racism has no place in our society' script, the Right was astute enough to recognise that the BLM protests of summer 2020 had opened up discursive space for forms of race talk that could be constructed not as being indifferent to extreme racism, but as being firmly opposed to 'divisive concepts', 'the rewriting of British history', 'bogus accusations of racism', 'vandalism' and, above all, anti-British feeling or lack of patriotism. Journalist Nesrine Malik warned that, even if Britain's culture wars often seemed a half-hearted imitation of those in the US, their political significance should not be minimised:

the right is creating its own new stories. Because culture war is not about winning a debate about what constitutes England through factual disputes about its character, its statues, its football team or its history of empire. It is not a peripheral indulgence, or a mere confection. Culture war is an aggressive political act with the purpose of creating new dividing lines and therefore new and bigger electoral majorities. (Malik, 2021)

Malik (2021) argued that the Right outpaced 'optimistic progressives' and 'polite incrementalists' in understanding that the culture wars were not a quaint grumble in which retired colonels sought to defend the reputations of Cecil Rhodes and Edward Colston, or in which a government minister might quip that he only took the knee for the Queen or when proposing to 'the missus'. Britain's Right had learned more from Gramsci than their opposite numbers, grasping that the culture wars comprised 'a battle between manufactured narratives that seek to mould an England in their own image' (Malik, 2021). In the world of realpolitik, contests over BLM and CRT were not battles over good sense but over what Gramsci termed common sense (see also Toscano, 2023).

How Critical Race Theory became a trope

Gillborn et al (2022) have explored the development of US-influenced conservative think tanks and intellectual networks in Britain during the past decade. A number of these 'contra-' networks promote fairly extreme positions on areas such as race, intelligence, education and crime, and in recent years have had some influence on the governing Conservative Party's social policy thinking. It is therefore not surprising that the British Right's deployment of BLM and CRT as 'anti-woke' tropes has closely resembled conservative 'contra-' tactics in the US.

In June 2021 Benjamin Wallace-Wells published an article in the *New Yorker* titled, 'How a conservative activist invented the conflict over Critical Race Theory' (Wallace-Wells, 2021). It detailed how, far from being a response to the actual presence of CRT in schools and other institutions, much of the recent controversy over CRT in the US had emerged as a journalistic and political opportunity. A key influence in the manufacture of CRT as an existential threat to US institutions was Christopher F. Rufo, a journalist with links to right-wing thinktanks, who in 2020 had begun by accumulating materials sent to him by mainly public sector workers, complaining about anti-bias training in their workplaces (see, for example, Rufo, 2021; see also Harris, 2021). The materials acquired were drawn from diverse types of antiracist training and sources such as popular books by Robin DiAngelo and Ibram X. Kendi. What Rufo did was to suggest that antiracist training and educational projects of various types taking place in different parts of the US were, in fact, part of a unified ideological programme designed to critique US capitalism, embed White guilt, unfairly advantage racial minorities and reshape US institutions by infiltrating federal government.

> When I say that critical race theory is becoming the operating ideology of our public institutions, I am not exaggerating – from the universities to bureaucracies to K-12 school systems, critical race theory has permeated the collective intelligence and decision-making process of American government, with no sign of slowing down. (Rufo, 2021)

Rufo played on the US's atavistic fear of the red menace or 'cultural Marxism'. In actuality, CRT's relationship to conventional Marxism has been complex (Warmington, 2020) but Rufo's narrative excised this history in order to portray CRT as a Marxist project in racial guise. Rufo offered an analysis that had purchase because while its focus on CRT was novel, its depiction of racial politics was essentially one that had long held among US conservatives. Its thesis was that the New Left of the 1960s had recognised the failure of 'really existing' revolutionary projects and 'Abandoning Marx's economic dialectic of capitalists and workers, they substituted race for class and sought to create a revolutionary coalition of the dispossessed based on racial and ethnic categories' (Rufo, 2021). The 'bad' Black radicals of the 1960s had been defeated temporarily by the 'good' civil rights coalition (to sustain this argument, CRT's origins in the civil rights struggle also had to be excised from the narrative). However, in CRT the revolutionary Left had regrouped and produced a new guise in which 'identity is the means; Marxism is the end' (Rufo, 2021).

In summer 2020 Rufo did the rounds of US conservative media channels and did much to put CRT on the agenda for President Donald Trump and other conservative political and media figures (Wallace-Wells, 2021). This media choreography had clearly discernible models in the US. For example, journalist Moira Weigel has traced the emergence of the term 'political correctness' as a conservative trope in US politics, noting that the phrase had rarely appeared in mainstream news media before 1990 when it was used in a wave of US newspaper and magazine articles (Weigel, 2016). Like CRT, 'political correctness' became, for conservatives in both the US and Britain, an emblem to suggest that radical social politics had come to dominate state institutions, arts and media, producing intolerance and silencing legitimate concerns in public debate. Like CRT it became a powerful trope through sheer repetition and, as with CRT, the origins of the discourse lay in links between Right-leaning news media and conservative think tanks.

Drawing partly from personal correspondence with Rufo, Wallace-Wells (2021) describes how Rufo picked on 'Critical Race Theory' as the perfect collective term to describe the anti-American ideology that he wished to portray. Terms such as 'political correctness' and 'woke' were deemed outdated or too vague but CRT, which Rufo discovered by perusing Kendi and DiAngelo's footnotes, fit the bill: 'Strung together, the phrase "critical race theory" connotes hostile, academic, divisive, race-obsessed, poisonous, elitist, anti-American' (Rufo, quoted in Wallace-Wells, 2021).

In the US, the negative framing of CRT began as a marginal and subcultural effort but became a mainstream reactionary political presence, coming to influence legislation over the teaching of history and social studies implemented in 2021 and 2022.

Any talk of race and racism

The popular 2020s construction of CRT had its origins in journalistic motifs and this made it readily reproducible as a story. In 2021 *The Economist* produced a series of pieces on race in America. These focused on 'wokeness' in general and CRT in particular. John McWhorter's May 2021 article contained a motif since repeated: of CRT as a quasi-religious movement. This sits very oddly with Derrick Bell's determinedly non-utopian position (see Chapter 3). McWhorter's article depicted CRT as having a Manichean worldview but itself relied on Manichean thinking: CRT's critics were liberal, while CRT was illiberal; CRT's critics prized free speech, while CRT silenced opponents; CRT's critics were aligned with the vision of Martin Luther King, while CRT blemished his legacy. Like Rufo, McWhorter depicted CRT as hegemonic and as a Black problem, describing it as 'The triumph of an antiracist movement that harms black people' (McWhorter, 2021). McWhorter's textual references were to the same two non-CRT books that Rufo had made emblems: 'Robin DiAngelo's *White Fragility* is a tinny extended pamphlet replete with circular reasoning. Ibram X. Kendi's *How to Be an Antiracist* is founded on dichotomous aphorisms typical of the street preacher, its facile and slipshod reasoning rendering Coleman Hughes's book review title "How to Be an Anti-Intellectual" sadly accurate' (McWhorter, 2021).

McWhorter's rhetoric made interesting use of Black stereotypes. CRT was not a legitimate intellectual position but the outpouring of rabble-rousing holy rollers and/or angry Black power anti-Americans. The misidentification of DiAngelo and Kendi as exemplars of CRT, while keeping a distance from any specific scholarly text, stymied possibilities for insights into what CRT comprised in reality. No matter. These were popular books whose titles might be recognised by a wider public and their titles contained effective triggers. It is worth noting that Rufo warned CRT's antagonists away from engaging in academic discussion, as that is where, he said, critical race scholars had an advantage (see Rufo, 2021).

Interviewed by Wallace-Wells, Kimberlé Crenshaw perceived the emerging anti-CRT discourse as based on a 'a selective, "red-baiting" account of critical race theory's origins, which overlooked less divisive influences such as Martin Luther King, Jr.' (Wallace-Wells, 2021). However, in some respects the opposition between these articles and aspects of CRT was evident. Simple trust in inevitable liberal progress, in social marketplaces and colourblind ethics had indeed been critiqued by CRT scholars, but that is not to say that CRT had not engaged with and was not partially born out of liberal ideas. CRT's critics rarely if ever acknowledge that the civil rights movement was one of CRT's influences, as much as were Fanon and Dubois. For Goldberg, the reactionary discourse that emerged post-George Floyd, post-BLM was a reiteration of old antagonisms against antiracism and minority rights, in which CRT was a convenient stand-in. In May 2021 he wrote:

> The exact targets of CRT's critics vary wildly, but it is obvious that most critics simply do not know what they are talking about. Instead, CRT functions for the right today primarily as an empty signifier for any talk of race and racism at all, a catch-all specter lumping together 'multiculturalism', 'wokeism', 'antiracism', and 'identity politics' – or indeed any suggestion that racial inequities in the United States are anything but fair outcomes, the result of choices made by equally positioned individuals in a free society. They are simply against any talk, discussion, mention, analysis, or intimation of race – except to say we shouldn't talk about it. (Goldberg, 2021)

The depiction of the US as a country whose key institutions had been captured by Left antiracists was audacious. The resurgence of BLM and the supposed spread of CRT had clearly not occurred at a moment of liberal dominance but in the latter part of Donald Trump's Right populist presidency. What also often went unsaid was that the machinery of the US state was in 2020–21 organising a severe clampdown on the funding of any form of antiracist training that was deemed to be 'CRT' and on the teaching of 'divisive concepts' in schools and universities. In September 2020 President Trump issued an executive order 'to ensure that Federal agencies cease and desist from using tax payer dollars to fund these divisive, un-American propaganda training sessions … all agencies are directed to begin to identify all contracts or other agency spending related to any spending on "critical race theory"' (Vought, 2020). In early 2022 journalists Cathryn Stout and Thomas Wilburn reported that 36 US states had 'adopted or introduced laws or policies that restrict teaching about race and racism' (Stout and Wilburn, 2022), often with the intent of 'banning' CRT and other 'divisive concepts' (see Gillborn's [2024] extensive account of the introduction of these restrictive measures).

Post-Black Lives Matter Britain

It is important to have a sense of US conservative discourse because while CRT has often been traduced as a US import, the post-BLM reaction against antiracism has certainly been a transatlantic movement (see Lentin, 2021). It is also instructive because in both Britain and the US the particular usage of CRT within the 'contra-' discourse has very much been a *post hoc* construction. In Britain, as in the US, political and media attacks on CRT followed a period in which there was a search for discursive space in which to express discontent with multiculturalism and antiracism, a search for a unifying and novel theme that could reinvigorate old complaints about multiculturalism and political correctness.

Hughey's (2014) examination of the 21st-century backlash against antiracism in the US identifies many of the 'contra-' features discussed earlier in this chapter. These include resistance to potential gains by communities of colour, whether perceived or real, and to the design and implementation of new race equalities policies (Hughey, 2014). Importantly, Hughey argues that while such backlashes may arise out of very particular moments and events, their political effects are cumulative and durable in terms of producing a collective sense on the Right of what is at stake in contests over race equality: a sense of the resources and identity that need to be protected, hence an enduring narrative of 'non-white success (being) purposefully engineered at the expense of white sacrifice' (Hughey, 2014: 721).

The initial breadth of support and positive media profile afforded to BLM in Britain was short-lived. By November 2020 *The Guardian* reported that 55 per cent of UK adults believed that the summer's BLM protests had increased racial tensions, a figure rising to 78 per cent among Conservative voters (Booth, 2020). Events such as the toppling of the statue of slave trader Edward Colston by BLM protestors in Bristol in June 2020 provided space in which to depict British history and culture as being under attack. Prime Minister Boris Johnson's extrapolation made the Colston case part of the war over culture:

> What you can't do is go around seeking retrospectively to change our history or to bowdlerise it or edit it in retrospect. It's like some person trying to edit their Wikipedia entry – it's wrong. If people democratically want to remove a statue or whatever, that's fine. But I think that, in general, we should preserve our cultural, artistic, historical legacy. (Johnson, quoted in Barrett and Ellicott, 2022)

Four of the Colston protestors were charged with criminal damage, tried and acquitted. The release of the 'Colston Four' was condemned in strong terms by former Justice Secretary Robert Buckland, who urged the Crown Prosecution

Service to refer the acquittal to the Court of Appeal. Subsequently, Attorney General Suella Braverman (later to become Britain's Home Secretary) used the Colston Case in the Court of Appeal to test the ways in which human rights defences were used in trials of protestors. In April 2022, the Johnson government created the *Police, Crime, Sentencing and Courts Act 2022*, described by Katy Watts of human rights body Liberty as 'a draconian piece of legislation which expands police powers and limits our right to protest' (Watts, 2020). Part of the rationale given for the introduction of the Act was that 'Over the summer of 2020, 172 Metropolitan Police Service officers were assaulted by a violent minority during the BLM protests' (Home Office, 2022).

The passion for preserving history was selective. It was rarely commented in coverage of the Colston case that, in fact, there had been a longstanding community campaign to remove the statue and others of the many memorials to Colston in Bristol. The campaign long predated the BLM protests of 2020, but saw little response from Bristol City Council. Historian David Olusoga was among those who had supported calls for the removal of memorials to Colston. Referring to the port city's huge involvement in the Atlantic slave trade, Olusoga commented that 'no British city is more wilfully blind to its history than Bristol' (Olusoga, 2017: 33). Both pre- and post-2020 the Colston campaign exemplified the ways in which antiracist efforts are depicted in 'contra-' discourses as a contest between politically-motivated activism and neutral, disinterested accounts of history and identity.

A very British backlash

In conservative sections of news media the response to the BLM protests of 2020 followed a pattern of escalation modelled on the US conservative play book. Initial condemnation of public disorder was widened to support the claim that Britain's heritage and history were being erased, and the focus of conservative ire broadened from street protestors to a putative liberal hegemony. The idea that radical Left forces had infiltrated Britain's great institutions was voiced in terms not dissimilar to Rufo's in the US. British Journalist Melanie Phillips insisted that taking the knee in sympathy with BLM was a gesture of 'contempt for white society' (Phillips, 2020). The kneeling gesture was, Phillips claimed, being forced upon the capitulating institutions of law and government in Britain by BLM: 'A racist, anti-white, anti-west violent revolutionary movement whose aim is the overthrow of white western society' (Phillips, 2020). Moreover, 'instead of resisting this ignorant and wicked movement, its appeasers have been literally abasing themselves before the mob' (Phillips, 2020).

The depiction of Britain as under attack both from the external forces of antiracism and from liberals within who deferred to BLM's mob agenda was an eccentric conflation of images: plucky little Britain combined with a clash of civilisations thesis. Phillips's essay included a dismissal of the concept of institutional racism, focus on a perceived alliance between Black activists and liberals in positions of power and an insistence that BLM was an attack on western civilisation itself. Embedded in a particular racial grammar, the article was explicit in its attempt to regulate ways of speaking about racism. The refusal to countenance the existence of institutional racism comprised both a rejection of Britain's antiracist traditions and refused any option other than reducing racism to the personal, so that when BLM and those who took the knee referred to structural and institutional discrimination, it could only be read as a cover for anti-White sentiments.

Such rhetoric was not merely a tactical response to the momentum of BLM; it was to become a characteristic feature of ongoing dialogue between right-wing think tanks and the hard Right of the UK's governing Conservative Party, the latter repositioning itself in response to falling government popularity, poor election results and party infighting in 2022–3. In May 2023 a National Conservatism Conference convened in London, promoting itself as a new intellectual hub. Its attendees comprised prominent right-wing thinkers and activists, but also Conservative MPs and senior politicians, including the serving Home Secretary. As such, this new grouping was a public marker of the admission into mainstream Conservative thought of ideas about 'cultural Marxism' and 'majority rights'. Its webpage prominently announced that: 'We see the rich tradition of national conservative thought as an intellectually serious alternative to the excesses of purist libertarianism, and in stark opposition to political theories grounded in race' (NatCon UK, 2023).

In their paper 'An anatomy of the British war on woke' Huw Davis and Sheena Macrae (2023) traced the US-British genealogy of such 'anti-woke' currents. They argued that a central strategy of British hard Right networks was to police and discredit social justice movements through 'an intensive ideological campaign ... mobilising far-right tropes and conspiracy theories within mainstream British political discourse' (Davis and Macrae, 2023: 1). CRT and BLM were key tropes in British 'anti-woke' rhetoric, as was the insistence that antiracism was a fringe phenomenon being mobilised against the majority, and particularly against the authentic/indigenous 'White working class'.

The Black Lives Matter tide turns

Nesrine Malik reflected on shifts in public perceptions of BLM between the summer of 2020 and the acquittal of the Colston Four in early 2022. For Malik, the culture war contests were not about representation of Britain's history in the abstract but about a 'glorification of a past that reinforces and legitimises all the injustices of the present' (Malik, 2022b). Commenting on the ways in which the interests of BLM and British institutions rapidly diverged, Malik wrote:

> There is no better example of how quickly history is rewritten to suit the establishment than the aftermath of the Black Lives Matter protests in the summer of 2020. What seemed like a moment of profound change was quickly miscast as the opposite, a marker in the sand for what happens when demands for racial equality are taken too far, when they become violent, militant and vandalistic. (Malik, 2022b)

The gears of interest convergence, contradiction closure and reversal continued to grind. In the aftermath of 2020's BLM protests the claim that antiracist activists had been overindulged by the state was made frequently (in response, for instance, to some BLM marches taking place during the COVID-19 lockdown period and, later, in response to the acquittal of the Colston Four). However, the claim that a too liberal state had capitulated to radical antiracism was peculiar, given many of the responses by the Conservative government, which had been in power for a decade at the time of the BLM protests.

For instance, in June 2021, a year after the BLM summer, the House of Commons Education Committee published its report on social disadvantage and educational underachievement among White working-class pupils. One of the findings widely discussed in news media in the days following was the Education Committee's claim that the concept of 'white privilege' was prevalent in schools and was an aspect of the 'muddled thinking' (House of Commons Education Committee, 2021: 22) that had led to the neglect of White working-class pupils in England's schools. The report's usage of data was queried, as was the Committee's apparent emphasis on antiracist training as a cause of White working-class disadvantage (opposition Labour Party MPs on the Committee ultimately refused to back the report's conclusions). It is worth noting that the ruling Conservative government had only a few months previously voted against extending free school meals provision for the poorest children. The latter point was emphasised by those who suggested that poverty and hunger might be greater contributors to White working-class disadvantage than a 30-year-old phrase coined by the feminist educator Peggy Mcintosh.

While the Education Committee did not establish how widespread the concept of 'White privilege' was among policy makers or education practitioners, or provide evidence of a correlation between the term and White disadvantaged pupils' school performance, it devoted an entire section to discussing the term, warning that:

Schools should consider whether the promotion of politically controversial terminology, including White Privilege, is consistent with their duties under the Equality Act 2010. The Department should take steps to ensure that young people are not inadvertently being inducted into political movements. ... The Department should issue clear guidance for schools and other Department-affiliated organisations receiving grants from the Department on how to deliver teaching on these complex issues in a balanced, impartial and age-appropriate way. (House of Commons Education Committee, 2021: 17)

In this instance the Education Committee had imported something of the US government's campaign against 'divisive concepts' and an eye for the kinds of language that would cut through, contributing to moral panic. It was highly unlikely that the term White privilege was in common circulation in schools but that was irrelevant; as an emblem of antiracism gone-too-far, it had political value. What the Education Committee had also drawn from the US context was the willingness to threaten state intervention in contests over antiracist education in schools. It was a notable irony that British politicians urged a US style response, while relying frequently on the claim that, in their view, Britain was utterly unlike the US.

The Colston campaign, Rhodes Must Fall, BLM and the general spectre of radicals threatening the teaching of British history continued to have resonance. In summer 2022 Prime Minister Boris Johnson resigned amidst scandal. In the campaign to succeed Johnson, former Chancellor of the Exchequer Rishi Sunak appealed to the Conservative Party membership, whose vote would decide Johnson's successor, by drawing on the language of culture wars and directly on images of statues toppled and schools promoting 'anti-British' histories:

But I have another pledge to you. My government will also safeguard our shared cultural, historical and philosophical heritage. Because what's the point in stopping the bulldozers in the green belt if we allow Left-wing agitators to take a bulldozer to our history, our traditions and our fundamental values? Whether it's pulling down statues of historic figures, replacing the school curriculum with anti-British propaganda or rewriting the English language so we can't even use words like 'man', 'woman' or 'mother' without being told we're offending someone. (Sunak, quoted in Brown, 2022)

Sunak's pledge was also restated in a more authoritarian register. His office explained that a Sunak-led government would scrutinise 'anti-British propaganda', with potentially serious legal consequences, under a proposed plan: 'The news of Sunak's suggested plan was shared by Home Affairs Editor for *The Telegraph*, Charles Hymas, who tweeted: "People who vilify Britain will be treated as extremists and referred to the Government's deradicalisation Prevent programme under plans by Rishi Sunak'" (Abraham, 2022).

A number of historians and educators whose work focused on the British Empire and on histories of slavery and colonialism were sufficiently perturbed to enquire what would be the boundaries of this deradicalisation plan (Nicholson, 2022). Sunak did not immediately succeed in his bid to follow Boris Johnson as Prime Minister. However, in autumn 2022 when Johnson's successor Liz Truss resigned only weeks after taking office, Sunak became Britain's first British Asian Prime Minister, its first Prime Minister of colour.

'If you don't like it here, leave'

'*Why do you stay in this country?*' The question is as familiar to me as that other nativist trump, '*Where are you really from?*' Directed at Black and Brown people, both questions serve a similar function: as a reminder of the provisional nature of our Britishness, even in the 2020s. The 'why do you stay' question is frequently asked of Black or Brown critics who dare to debate the state of the nation in ways that might reframe the stories that Britain tells about itself and its past. The implication it carries is '*How dare you?*' In fact, the 'why do you stay' question is so normal that in one quite public instance it went mostly unremarked until it was retweeted during 2020's BLM summer, two years after its original broadcast.

It was 2018, and on a Sky News current affairs show called *The Pledge* a veteran British broadcaster challenged journalist Afua Hirsch about a comment piece she had written on Britain's monuments to 'problematic figures', such as Nelson and Churchill. The interviewer Nick Ferrari's measured, even genial, tone indicated that the question he was about to pose to Hirsch was to be regarded as entirely legitimate:

> Why do you stay in this country? If you take such offence when you see Nelson's Column, if you take such offence when you hear Winston Churchill's name? I would argue in the unlikely event that anybody wanted to have a poll, probably 80 to 90 per cent of people would say Winston Churchill did a good thing. I'm delighted that I see you each Thursday … but if it offends you so much, how do you manage to stay here? (Quoted in Lothian-McLean, 2020)

In the brief twitterstorm that followed 2 years after the TV broadcast, fellow journalists Krishnan Guru-Murthy and Ayesha Hazarika both commented on this exchange. 'This should be shocking,' wrote Guru-Murthy, 'but it isn't'. Hazarika was less restrained. On national television Afua Hirsch had, Hazarika noted, 'effectively been told to piss off to another country, even though she's British'. It was, Hazarika added 'No biggie' (Lothian-Mclean, 2020).

Hirsch is Norwegian-born, with a British father, Ghanaian mother and a Jewish grandfather who fled Germany in the 1930s. Raised in Wimbledon, she is Oxford-educated and thoroughly middle-class. However, as she explains eloquently in her book *Brit(ish)*, the complex details of her background are, in Britain's public space, displaced details; she is a Black woman. On screen, Hirsch's immediate response to her colleague was poised: 'I find that a really strange thing to say.' Reflecting two years later, Hirsch said that the TV clip belonged to a time 'when I thought you could politely persuade people not to be racist. Their response? "If you don't like it here, LEAVE." Which I'm yet to hear said to a white British person. Racism is telling black people who have a critique of their own country, they should leave' (Lothian-McLean, 2020).

But in a society in which racism is ordinary, it really is 'no biggie'. Why refer to the Hirsch/Ferrari story? You can rest assured that it is not an effort to 'cancel' the broadcaster. Nor do I suggest that a majority of White British people secretly desire the expulsion of Black and Brown neighbours from their midst (although considerable numbers wished that when I was growing up in the 1960s and 1970s). The broadcaster's query was, in all probability, a kind of rhetorical question. That, however, is telling. This kind of rhetorical question only makes sense when it carries the force of pervasive discourse, when it represents a recognisable logic, even though it may not be the questioner's. The speaker who asks, 'Why don't we bring back hanging?' is not necessarily arguing for the restoration of capital punishment but a rhetorical question of that sort only works because we know that there is a long established constituency that favours the rope and the drop. The exchange between Hirsch and Ferrari takes us back to Lipsistz's (2019) argument that in a postracial, colourblind society it is the recognition of racism that is held to be the greater problem, the cause of division in a society otherwise at ease with itself. It is an example too of what Nesrine Malik has called 'racial gravity – for every claim of a racist action there is a wildly unequal and disproportionate reaction' (Malik, 2023). Journalist, activists, academics suggesting that we might not quite be postracial yet have become all too used to the 'How dare you' reaction being followed by symbolic violence: punishment that is often endorsed by media and by government.

Conclusion

In Brandon Taylor's novel *Real Life*, protagonist Wallace contemplates responding to a friend's casual racism. He is aware of the burden he will take on if he names that racism and also that he, Wallace, will not be the one who determines whether his naming is legitimate:

> The most unfair part of it, Wallace thinks, is that when you tell white people that something is racist, they hold it up to the light and try to discern if you are telling the truth. As if they can tell by the grain if something is racist or not, and they always trust their own judgement. It's unfair because white people have a vested interest in underestimating racism, its amount, its intensity, its effects. (Taylor, 2020: 97)

This chapter has explored the symbiosis between Britain's postracial self-image and its 'contra-' discourses. Instances such as Hirsch's experience suggest that critical antiracist voices, particularly Black voices, are mistrusted. But they say more than that; they suggest that within the postracial frame, antiracism is made unintelligible. Antiracism (as distinct from non-racism) is increasingly placed outside the range of possible speech that our racial grammar allows. Phenomenological disappearance is required. After all, why would antiracist efforts be required in a world confident that racism has largely been expunged? Both postracialism and 'contra-' antiracism are profoundly racialising, in terms of where they place the burden of racial tension (with communities of colour and those demanding racial justice) and in their appropriation of the power to determine what constitutes racism and what constitutes legitimate opposition to racism.

What else is erased under Britain's 'really existing postracialism'? Another means of making demands for racial justice unintelligible has been the construction of a zero-sum populism, wherein perceived gains for Black and Brown communities are portrayed as losses for White Britons, specifically the 'White working class'. Chapter 6 of this book explores the discursive erasure of communities of colour from the 'cultural' definition of the working class. This removal is a significant dimension of our state postracialism. It has political expediency but its implications are also existential; for in Britain to be absent from the imagined social class matrix is to experience a kind of non-being. Chapter 6 therefore asks, *Whatever happened to the Black working class?*

6

Whatever happened to the Black working class?

Introduction

Whatever happened to the Black working class? In the 1980s the historian Ron Ramdin could, with a nod to E.P. Thompson's *The Making of the English Working Class*, publish his own classic, *The Making of the Black Working Class in Britain* (Ramdin, 1987). In the same period A. Sivanandan's (1982) *A Different Hunger*, Peter Fryer's (1984) *Staying Power* and Beverley Bryan et al's (1985) *The Heart of the Race* all portrayed histories of Black working-class formation and political organisation in Britain. Yet today the working class is depicted, both by default and by design, as White, as though, in the words of journalist Lynsey Hanley, 'being black or Asian automatically disqualifies you from membership of a social class' (Hanley, 2017: 7). Since the beginning of the 2000s, much has been said about Britain's (and specifically England's) 'White working class', both by those who have constructed the current discourse and by those who have critiqued it. Less has been said about what this exclusionary reimagining of working-class identity means for those in Black and Brown communities who, for the purposes of policy and public debate, have been disqualified from it, and are now positioned outside Britain's social class matrix. Black working-class identity has dropped out of Britain's racial grammar to the extent that, in the words of historian David Olusoga:

> When black and mixed race people claim their working class identities, they now have to confront a strain of political thinking that asserts that only white people can be working class and that the 'white working class' is a group that has been assailed by minorities and betrayed by a 'metropolitan liberal elite' that cares only about minorities and race. (Olusoga, 2019)

Chapters 4 and 5 of this book argued that the key features of Britain's state postracialism include denial of the persistence of institutional racism and an often virulent antipathy to antiracism. Both of these features play into Britain's longing for a conclusive end to the complications of race and racism within the political settlement. Up until the 1970s or 1980s there was still a stubborn fraction of British society clinging on to the fancy that communities of colour could literally be erased en masse from British society. Today those dreams of closure by 'repatriation' have been replaced by the discursive erasures contained in our 'really existing postracialism', one powerful aspect of which is the disqualification of Black and Brown people from Britain's class matrix. Chapter 6 explores the implications of this erasure: one that speaks to the postracial desire to eliminate demands for racial justice, while also rearticulating old ideas about authentic British identity, alien presence and legitimate grievances.

Classbound

Britain is often described as a peculiarly classbound society. It is, of course, no more and no less classbound than any other society built on capitalist production. However, we are all familiar with the tendency of observers to derive humour from what they see as Britain's attachment to the codes and symbols of social class. It would be hard to deny that there is something particular about Britain's historical make-up that makes it prone to invest in class as a cultural identity, rather than as a descriptor of one's place in the labour process. That said, class is, of course, a form of identity. Given this, what might it mean to be placed outside the bounds of social class identity in Britain?

Not all people of colour in Britain are working class. However, the majority of Black and Brown Britons – like the majority of White Britons – are working class in terms of income and occupation. Moreover, Black and Brown Britons are disproportionately more likely to live in relative poverty and in deep poverty, and are more prone to unemployment (Timms and Caddick, 2022). Despite this being the case, from the Windrush era onwards, political discourse in Britain has often placed communities of colour in ambiguous relationship to class identity. To explain this, Chapter 6 pays particular attention to Commonwealth migration and settlement in the latter half of the 20th century, not because 'nothing has changed' since that period, but because it is illustrative of the contradictions that existed between, on one hand, social policies aimed at promoting integration and, on the other, political discourses that periodically constructed communities of colour as alien, with interests materially opposed to those of their White working-class counterparts. The period between the late 1940s and the 1980s (what the Windrush generation calls 'the earlies') was a period in which fractions of the imperial working class that had existed 'there' in South Asia, the Caribbean and (to a lesser extent at that point) West Africa were inserted 'here'. Britain often responded inadequately to this reconfiguration of its working class, in ways that set the tone for future race relations.

In 21st-century Britain there is little space to talk about class, except through a narrow set of ideas about the 'White working class'. Moreover, there is little space to talk about White working-class people, except as the 'left behind': supposedly always socially conservative, bewildered by cultural change and bereft at the loss of old social forms. This depiction of Britain's working class is very current but it is not new; it includes a repurposing of discursive elements that have long been present in the politics of race and class. In fact, it is impossible to understand these repurposed elements without acknowledging them as a form of neo-Powellism. This is an argument from which some will recoil. They will, quite correctly, respond that Britain rejected Enoch Powell's vision of 'the River Tiber flowing with much blood' (Powell, 1968) and his subsequent calls for 'repatriation' of Black and Brown people. However, in considering Powell's impact on racial politics in Britain, we are too often distracted by his nightmare fantasia, and fail to acknowledge the residual influence of his framing arguments. The term Powellism is not used casually here, nor does it apply only to debates on immigration; it comprises a particular mode of triadic populism.

What has this neo-Powellism meant to Black and Brown working-class communities? It has meant that they have not only been discursively positioned as *outside* of working-class identity, but often as the *cause* of White working-class loss and disorientation. At the beginning of the 20th century, W.E.B. Dubois famously asked of African-Americans, 'How does it feel to be a problem?' (Dubois, 1903: 43). In 21st-century Britain we well might ask, 'How does it feel to be a *legitimate grievance?*' For one thing, it imposes a conditional Britishness on Black and Brown people, who too often become props in national conversations on post-imperial and post-industrial decline (just as in other instances they are props in self-congratulatory conversations about postracial progress). The influence in contemporary British politics of the *idea* of the White working class (which is a very different thing from saying that *actual* working-class Whites have influence) speaks to the continuing importance of class identity in Britain, and to the continuing significance of racial identity. Indeed, this chapter suggests that to be outside the imagined class formation is, in Britain, tantamount to a kind of 'social death' (see also Hall, 2017 and Patterson, 1982/2018).

Who belongs to the working class?

> 'In di earlies you work in a factory and di work you do, dem call it semi-skilled. It mean you haffi get train fi do job. So dem train you up and you is doing that job long time and you know fi do it. And den one day foreman bring a lickle white bwoy and say you fi train him up. And yu friend-dem laugh after you and say "Bwoy, you soon get di broom!" Ca' you know after you train di bwoy up, him will do your job and now you is just sweeping di shop floor.' (Bull, Windrush generation Jamaican)

In post-Windrush decades South Asian, African-Caribbean and African migrants were ambiguously inserted into Britain's working class. Were they a reserve army of labour? Were they guest workers? As communities became settled, was assimilation or integration the policy goal? Where were their descendants to be positioned? The location of Black and Brown workers within the working class has often been ambiguous and provisional. Bull's anecdote (in conversation with the current author) about his experiences in 'the earlies' recalls the asymmetric relationships that often existed between Black and White workers on the shop floor. He is clearly not referring to an exceptional experience. Being treated as a reserve in the labour force, replaceable as and when White labour becomes available, is so ordinary that it has its own term: 'getting the broom'.

The reference to semi-skilled labour is in itself noteworthy, since it was not unknown for Black and White workers doing the same jobs to be classified as skilled (White) and semi-skilled (Black) along racialised lines that maintained differentials in pay and status (there was often, of course, similar differentiation by gender). In accounts of 'the earlies' there are many local examples of racist practices that differentiated White working-class labour from their Black and Brown counterparts, and of community resistance: including the Bristol bus boycott (1963) and the Grunwick strike (1976–8). Union support for 'coloured' members was uneven and even after the first *Race Relations Acts* were passed in 1965, 1968 and 1976, protection could not be guaranteed (see Fryer, 1984; Ramdin, 1987; Olusoga, 2021). These were everyday examples of the culturalisation of labour, referred to by Vann (2006) (see Chapter 2).

Maya Goodfellow, author of *Hostile Environment: How Immigrants Became Scapegoats* (Goodfellow, 2019) has spoken of her mother's generation being 'welcome' to work in the NHS but 'expected to disappear' in the evenings, during out of work hours (Goodfellow, 2022). In short, the social mood was very much a case of 'we want what you got but we don't want you – and we do not want your dependents'. For the labour force recruited from the Commonwealth between the 1940s and 1970s, there was a powerful sense that it was only their labour power that was required. However, the recruitment of Commonwealth labour produced new communities, and that was a problem for British politicians seeking ways to translate the 'popular' interests of the working class into the mechanisms of political representation. Hazel Carby was part of the Centre for Contemporary Cultural Studies at the University of Birmingham, which under Stuart Hall's leadership became a rare space for emerging Black British scholars. She wrote of the triadic populism of the 1960s and 1970s, with particular relation to schooling:

> Social-democratic initiatives in the field of education have always displayed profound contradictions, notably in the attempt to balance the

perceived needs of the working class and the demands of capital. One attempt at a resolution of these conflicting interests is the construction of a 'national interest'. This resolution is apparent only, disguising conflict in its attempt to win consent. However, this consent has been won through the creation of a 'national interest' that has been mobilized against and which excludes the black community. (Carby, 1982: 184)

Carby's analysis of the state project had implications beyond the field of education. Importantly, her description of the securing of popular consent via the construction of a racialised national interest does not refer to right-wing populist strategies but to the social democratic settlement that preceded Thatcherism. It is a reminder of the ordinariness of state racism across the political spectrum. Nor is Carby's analysis peculiar to Britain. Building on the 'Black Marxism' of Cedric Robinson, US theorist Robin D.G. Kelley has argued two related points. The first is that under racial capitalism, race is not merely an identity but a structure of power, a means of structuring power through difference. The second is that racial capitalism relies on its ability to incorporate working-class Whites via racialised identification and alliance. For Kelley, that capture is the principal way in which, under capitalism, political power is structured through race (Kelley, 1996).

Nevertheless, the years since have shown that the boundaries of national interest are perhaps more mutable and permeable than Carby, writing in the early 1980s, suggested. There are moments (in, for instance, the promotion of 'urban' culture or sporting endeavour) when Britain's political and media classes are keen to include Black and Brown Britons within national interest and identity. However, (permanent) racism still remains available as a tool for reconstituting national interest in opposition to Black and Brown communities. One way of understanding the precariousness of Black and Brown communities in the construction of a national interest is in terms of the creation of borders (see Goodfellow, 2019).

Governments of Left and Right police external borders; they play tactically on immigration statistics and construct 'crises' around refugees and asylum seekers. However, as generations of migrants and their descendants have discovered, the construction of borders is also an internal project, determining who has the right to remain, who has irrevocable citizenship and who is regarded as authentically British, and in what contexts (El-Enany, 2021).

Numbers and culture

The politics of race in Britain (and the racial grammar in which they are embedded) have historically focused both on numbers (the literal presence of Black and Brown communities) and culture (resultant shifts in national identity). As discussed in Chapters 4 and 5, since the Commonwealth migration of the late 1940s, racial politics in Britain have always focused, in part, on factual multiculturalism, reduced in crude terms to numbers: the numbers of migrants entering Britain; the numbers of Black and Brown people in major cities; numbers in the school population and in the labour market. It is barely necessary to reprise histories of immigration policy and debates in Britain since the Second World War (see extensive histories in, for instance, Winder, 2013, Goodfellow, 2019). Immigration has been the perennial 'political football' across decades and across party lines, with neither Conservative nor Labour governments risking the cardinal sin of being seen as soft on immigration.

Britain today likes to date its post-Second World War history of race and migration to the arrival of the troopship Empire Windrush at Tilbury Docks in June 1948, carrying 500 or so workers from the Caribbean. However, it might be more truthful to use the *British Nationality Act 1948* as a date stamp. The 1948 Act was steeped in what CRT terms interest convergence. It facilitated the movement of aspirant workers from across the Empire to meet British labour shortages by creating a single category of citizenship 'of the United Kingdom and Colonies', thereby dissolving the formal citizenship boundary between those born in the UK and those born in Pakistan or Barbados. The 1948 Act was also passed shortly before the US clamped down on immigration from the Caribbean, which had the effect of reorientating Black Atlantic movement in that period.

However, as economic interests diverged, reversals in citizenship legislation began. The 1962 *Immigration Control Act*, passed by the Conservative government, and the 1968 *Commonwealth Immigration Act*, passed by Labour 6 years later, were both efforts to manage party political and popular anxieties over 'coloured' immigration. The 1962 and 1968 Acts (supplemented by further legislation during subsequent decades) did not only control numbers: they re-inscribed racialised boundaries around British identity and citizenship. These pieces of legislation set a marker for immigration policy that continues to the present: racialised and cyclical, revolving around interest convergence and divergence.

Powell's Britain: then and now

British debates around immigration continue to be embedded in discourses of numbers, cultural effects and postcolonial loss. To comprehend these discourses, it is necessary to reintroduce again the voice of Enoch Powell, Conservative Member of Parliament for Wolverhampton South West (1950–74) and later Ulster Unionist MP for South Down (1974–87). This is not to take the easy route of simply depicting Powell as a bogeyman but because Powell articulated an ensemble of arguments against Black and

Brown immigration and settlement that have remained lodged in British debates. This might, at first, seem a remarkable claim because Enoch Powell has, in one sense, become a byword for political notoriety, for unacceptable language and attitudes. On both Left and Right, Powell has been made a signifier of how far Britain has travelled in terms of its racial politics. It is true that his most lurid obsessions ('pickaninnies' harassing the elderly White widow who has excreta pushed through her letter box) would not normally find expression in mainstream public debate today. Even at the time, these were rejected by most of the political mainstream. After his 'rivers of blood' speech made in Birmingham in April 1968, Powell was sacked as Shadow Defence Secretary by Conservative Party Leader Edward Heath, though he continued to sit as an MP until 1987.

However, while British politicians tended to distance themselves publicly from Powell's rhetoric, his framing arguments have continued to inform the ground rules of immigration debates, as successive UK governments have cast around for ways to avoid being associated with high immigration. Powell's speeches on immigration were determinedly racist, in that they were concerned not with the mechanics of immigration policy in general but specifically with Caribbean and South Asian settlement. The Birmingham speech of 1968, for example, was concerned with 'Negro' and 'Sikh' communities establishing themselves in Britain. It was also designed as a critique of the Labour Government's then in process 1968 Race Relations Bill. Powell's concern was with Black and Brown *presence*. He presented a framework for constructing the material interests of Black and White working-class people as opposed to one another but his was also a framework that proposed a way of incorporating popular racism into mainstream political representation, by representing that racism as the authentic, collective and unchanging view of the White working class. The importance of Powell's schema is in its placing of Black and Brown communities outside the bounds of the authentic and legitimate working class, recasting them as a legitimate grievance available to 'authentic' Britons.

It is important to say that Enoch Powell did not singlehandedly develop what became known as Powellism (see Corthorn, 2019). The rearticulation of concerns about the numbers of Black and Brown people settling in Britain into a putative concern with the effects of that presence on working-class White communities was embedded in debates on race before Powell – including the period when Powell, as Minister of Health (1960–63), was amenable to recruiting nurses from the Commonwealth. Racist, anti-immigrant views certainly existed in Britain, and not only within working-class communities. Ministers in both Conservative and Labour governments had expressed unhappiness over 'coloured' migration and settlement well before Powell (Fryer, 1984; Olusoga, 2021). What Powell did was to give these complaints unashamed expression and narrative skill.

Their effects within Caribbean and South Asian communities, of course, were not rhetorical; they contributed to a climate of fear, violence and exclusion recounted by many of those who lived through the period (see Hirsch, S., 2019).

Strangers in their own country: legitimate grievances

What were the key elements of Powell's position on race – his contribution to Britain's racial grammar – and how did his arguments elide numbers and culture? First, in terms of numbers, Powell was adamant that by the late 1960s too many 'coloured' immigrants had settled in Britain, and that their numbers should be reduced (Corthorn, 2019). The argument that there are 'too many' has receded from polite political discourse, at least as a generality; it is still permissible to argue that there are 'too many' people of particular categories, such as refugees, asylum seekers or speakers of English as a second language. Second, Powell's apologists sometimes claim that since he avoided appeals to scientific racism, his concerns were not racist at all but were rooted but merely in concerns about lack of integration and other social effects. However, racism has never been purely about pseudo-scientific claims; it is also based on definitions of cultural alienness and/or cultural inferiority. It was here that Powell staked his claim for the elision between numbers, race and culture. What Britain should be concerned about, said Powell, were the numbers of settlers from the Indian sub-continent, the Caribbean and Africa whose cultures were inherently alien and could never be assimilated.

The concern with numbers thereby bleeds into culture, and into the narrative of imposition. According to Powell (although he offered minimal evidence), the numbers of Caribbean and South Asian people in Britain's (specifically England's) major towns imposed material losses upon the authentic White working class, in terms of jobs, healthcare and housing (Tomlinson, 2018). In addition, he argued that the imposition of 'alien' cultures and of legislation outlawing racial discrimination – that is, the imposition of both factual and state multiculturalism – had the effect of making authentic Britons strangers in their own country.

The converging narratives of imposition, competition and loss become the defining features of legitimate grievance. The search for legitimate grievance, in a sense, carries with it a public disavowal of racism, or at least an acknowledgment that overt racism cannot be made respectable. A premium is placed on establishing that whatever antipathy is felt towards Black and Brown communities, it is not racially motivated per se but is a reaction to change, difference and loss of status – anything but racism. In his role as the champion of the legitimately aggrieved, perhaps Powell – that most 'racial' of British politicians – was also a kind of prophet of facile postracialism.

Arguably, the most resilient aspect of Powell's framework is the link made between injury and 'imposition' within the discourse of legitimate grievance. As Jenny Bourne has written, Powell depicted Commonwealth immigration as 'a grand conspiracy (that) had taken place behind the backs and without the consent of the British people' (Bourne, 2008: 86). In the narrative that Powell came to embody, Whites were 'the real effective victims three times over – by being robbed physically, culturally and morally' (Bourne, 2008: 85). Here were the beginnings of the narrative of the White 'left behind' that has become dominant in 21st-century Britain. The White working class is portrayed as a static, homogeneous part of Britain's social fabric, whose unbroken culture was without fissures or disruption until the arrival of Black and Brown faces. Indeed, the conflation of race and immigration remains even more powerful in Britain than in the US. In the US the populist Right can use the language of concern about immigration to account for *some* of its racial anxieties, but in Britain, a melancholic discourse of indigeneity can be applied to make racism seem to be entirely about legitimate concerns over the numbers and cultures of immigrants.

What often goes unremarked in accounts of Powell's career was that his narrative was not a straightforward *appeal to* the White working class, based on a paternalistic respect for working-class views. With literary flair, Powell was also in the business of confecting convincing *stories about* the White working class for his own class fraction, to whom he gave adequate space to ventriloquise as champions of ordinary White Britons. Born solidly middle-class, Powell was a scholar at Cambridge and at the School of Oriental and African Studies, University of London. He was a Professor of Greek and a brigadier in the British army. Powell did not pretend to be working class and there was no need or desire for that pretence. As a Conservative MP, Powell was not interested in Leftist class politics but in racebound, cross-class definitions of British and/or English identity.

Neo-Powellism's triadic populism later found some expression in the 'legitimate grievances' of the Brexit campaign against membership of the European Union (see Chapter 5). The Brexit campaign invoked Powellite political obsessions: sovereignty and immigration. Neither could the arguments over the EU that came to consume Britain from the mid-2010s be entirely separated from the old concerns over non-EU (Black and Brown) immigration. For as Sally Tomlinson states: 'By 2016, settled citizens from former colonies and their descendants, especially if "non-white", economic migrants from the EU, legal migrants from outside the EU, illegal migrants, refugees and asylum seekers were all lumped together as targets for anti-immigrant rhetoric and activities' (Tomlinson, 2018: 5).

Tomlinson (2018, 2019) emphasises the continual recycling of Powellite themes in British politics and policy. They have been repurposed not only in relation to borders and entry, but to anxieties over settled communities of colour. In debates over culture, faith, integration and protest there is continued drawing of internal borders between those deemed authentically British and those whose Britishness is provisional.

Post-industrial race relations

In terms of precarious belonging, Enoch Powell was not the only class problem facing Windrush-era communities by the end of the 1960s. In speeches such as the Birmingham one, Powell had put Black children to rhetorical use (his 'wide-grinning pickaninnies'), the implication being that it was the descendants of first-generation immigrants that Britain should fear most: those who could not in any easy sense be 'sent back'. However, by the time of Powell's 1968 Birmingham speech the children of Commonwealth migrants, who had been born and/or schooled in Britain, were directly confronting the question of how they were to fit into Britain's working class (see Warmington, 2014).

In 1977 sociologist Paul Willis published his classic study *Learning to Labour*. Willis's book was a high point of mid-70s Marxist educational theory. Subtitled 'How Working Class Kids Get Working Jobs', the book theorised the cultural processes through which schooling reproduces a consenting working-class labour force. It did so through a critical ethnography of a group of White working-class lads in England's industrial West Midlands, not far from Powell's parliamentary constituency. Their subculture – masculine, rebellious and disdainful of what they saw as irrelevant academic education – equipped them for their futures on the shop floor. If Willis had written *Learning to Labour* in the 1950s, the book might not have looked much different but it could not have been written 20 years later, still less today. The capitalist structures that Willis depicted turned his working-class lads out into what seemed fairly secure employment, of a kind that today cannot be promised even to middle-class graduates, let alone their working-class contemporaries.

I have written previously about the resurgence during the 2010s of neo-Marxist structural analyses of schooling and employment in education research (Warmington, 2015a). Academics such as David J. Blacker, Pauline Lipman and John Marsh have focused on schooling as a system constituted by the specific social universe of capital: a social universe whose substance is not intellectual endeavour, self-realisation or social mobility but *value*. They acknowledge the lessons of cultural theory, feminism and critical race studies, but are unafraid to suggest that correspondence, determinism and pessimism may again need to enter our theoretical worldviews. Theirs is a *dystopian* social theory, conveying a sense that the 21st century will not right itself: that the socio-economic turmoil that we have lived through since the 2008 financial crash is not a blip but a symptom of what Blacker (2013) calls terminal capitalism.

Blacker's most dystopian claims concern terminal capitalism's tendency towards *eliminationism*. He argues that for reasons involving both technology and the drive for profit, the formal economies of the future will simply require fewer active participants: far less labour and far less education and training for a place in the labour process. In short, the growing global underclass will in the not too distant future be eliminated from the decaying neoliberal equation of education, training and work (Blacker, 2013). In this, Blacker's analysis has something in common with Achille Mbembe's (2019) *Necropolitics*, and with Feagin's (2020) theory of societal waste. The idea of learning to labour – and labouring for financial security, social status and modest social mobility – will be merely a fossil of bygone social democracy, amidst a future of disinvestment and hollowed out communities.

The theoretical implication of a terminal capitalism that produces an expanding underclass, rather than a disciplined labour force, is that classical Marxist theories of social reproduction need to be rethought. The new social theorists of education and employment also point to the ways in which the pathologisation of welfare recipients, single parent families and liberal permissiveness has served ideologically in the domination and regulation of those who may have been insufficiently disciplined through the routines of school and work. Importantly, all these sociologists offer some recognition of the ways in which people of colour, along with people with disabilities, have been advance parties in the march to social disposability (redressing the relative neglect of race by earlier theorists of education, such as Willis).

Second generation problems

These dystopian analyses of the disposability of working-class communities of colour are important because in Britain, as far back as the 1970s, Black communities were among the first to experience post-industrialism (even before the dismembering of the mining communities in the 1980s). Within a few years of the publication of Willis's *Learning to Labour*, many young Britons were to encounter the misery of not being exploited. By the late 1970s the full impacts of the 1973–4 oil crises had begun to bite. Then came the Thatcher government's early experiments in neoliberal economics. By spring of 1984 unemployment stood at almost 12 per cent (over 3 million people of working age) with youth unemployment considerably higher.

But, in fact, even as Willis was researching *Learning to Labour*, fractions of Britain's young Black working class were already being labelled surplus to capitalism's requirements. First among these were the underemployed children of post-Second World War Caribbean immigrants in the inner cities (Dhondy et al, 1985). By the mid- to late 1970s, young African-Caribbeans had become the most visible fraction of Britain's minority ethnic population, in terms both of sociological analysis and policy deliberation. In 1976 and

1977 the daily street conflict between police and young Blacks exploded at the Notting Hill Carnival. In early 1981, large scale uprisings in Brixton, South London were followed by disturbances in Liverpool, Birmingham and other major cities. There were similar conflicts in summer 1985.

During the 1970s, increasing numbers of Black school leavers found themselves entering a shrinking youth labour market. In 1979, the total unemployment rate rose by 2.5 per cent but among those of Pakistani heritage it rose by 10.1 per cent and among African-Caribbeans it rose by 13.5 per cent (Runnymede Trust, 1980). Over the following year, unemployment rose nationally by around 66 per cent but increased by 82 per cent among Black and Brown workers (Runnymede Trust, 1980). When Brixton erupted in 1981, unemployment among Black males aged 16–19 stood at an estimated 55 per cent (Scarman, 1981). For many young Black people, their place within the working class in 'multicultural' Britain was precarious in the extreme. It is worth remembering, as noted in Chapter 1 of this book, that at the end of 2020, in the economic downturn caused by the COVID-19 pandemic, 41.6 per cent of Black people aged 16–24 were unemployed, compared to 12.4 per cent of their White peers (ONS, 2020). In 2020 there was no *Scarman Report* to detail the effects of this level of unemployment.

At state level in the 1970s and 1980s there was some recognition that the Commonwealth immigration of the preceding decades had produced a new social fraction, who were barely being inserted into British capitalism. In fact, before the 1960s were out, the House of Commons Select Committee on Race Relations and Immigration (SCRRI) had reported on barriers Black school leavers faced in entering the labour market (in its 1969 green paper, *The Problem of Coloured School-Leavers*). For policy makers and communities alike, issues of race, education and employment were increasingly conflated with broader questions about the socialisation of 'Black youth' within British society. Questions around teachers' expectations, school disciplinary processes, a monocultural curriculum and underemployment informed documents such as SCRRI's *Report on The West Indian Community* (1977) and the Department for Education and Science's Green Paper, *Education in Schools* (1977) (see Warmington, 2014).

The emergence of second generation Black and Brown Britons also intensified the tendency in political and social policy discourse to reach for cultural deficit explanations of racial inequalities in Britain. There was a sense in which those who arrived from the Commonwealth between the 1940s and the early 1970s were defined principally by their 'alien' character. Regardless of whether they came from Jamaica, Uganda or Pakistan, they were most often grouped together as 'coloured immigrants', as a singular problem for British society. As another CCCS alumnus Errol Lawrence (1982) noted, after the confrontations between African-Caribbean youth and police in 1976 and 1981 racist discourses increasingly emphasised 'the sense that different communities pose different problems for the state and for "British society"' (Lawrence, 1982: 97). The denial of structural and institutional racism encouraged 'cultural' and 'ethnic' explanations of conflict and inequality. Policing, schooling and unemployment were held to be less important than African-Caribbean family and community structures, and a supposed lack of a clearly rooted identity among the second generation, who were, it was said, neither migrants nor fully British.

In the case of African-Caribbean communities a sometime claim was that the conflicts they experienced in British society were due to the fact that as Anglophone Christians who had lived under British rule for more than three centuries, they believed they were more British than they, in fact, were – hence their supposed sense of culture shock (Lawrence, 1982). This was colourblind logic *avant la lettre*, in its scratching around for 'anything but racism' to account for racial inequalities. Yet it exemplified the political need to place Black and Brown communities outside of the working class of which they were objectively part. The fact that in 1976 and 1981 'Asian' communities (at this point there was rarely nuanced differentiation between communities originating from the Indian subcontinent) had not been involved in similar unrest was attributed to the strong role of patriarchy and faith in those communities. Of course, by the early 2000s, after disturbances in Bradford, Oldham and Burnley, it was precisely such social features that led to 'Muslim' communities being accused of unwillingness to integrate, of living parallel lives. Now they were often compared unfavourably to the more 'integrated' Caribbean communities. The discursive location of Black and Brown communities as 'outside' class identity would be renewed at the start of the 2000s, a period by which Britain's 'working class' category had been dramatically reconfigured, not least in the increasingly overt claim that the authentic working class was, by definition, White.

From whence they came

As a coda, in the 21st century, British society had one remaining trick to play on the generation of Caribbeans that, in the 1960s, 1970s and 1980s, it had kept at arm's length from authentic working-class identity. Now middle aged, the victims were people who as young children had accompanied their parents to Britain from the Caribbean, and who as young adults had often experienced poor schooling, underemployment and police harassment but who had nevertheless raised families and contributed to life in Britain. They learned that the cyclical nature of Britain's immigration policy and debates makes it unwise to regard 1948, 1962 or 1968 as antique history.

In 2012, the same year in which Britain celebrated its diversity at the opening ceremony of the London Olympics, the UK government ushered in its 'hostile environment' policy on immigration: a gaggle of procedures aimed at identifying and removing migrants adjudged to have no right to remain (Goodfellow, 2019). Among the targets of the hostile environment policy (it was later used euphemised as the 'compliant environment' policy) were those who became, through no fault of their own, entangled in what became known as the Windrush scandal. They had in the main arrived in Britain between 1948 and 1971 as minors and therefore lacked the documentation that the UK government now demanded as proof of right to remain. As a result, hundreds were denied access to healthcare, housing, work and benefits; a substantial number were either deported or threatened with deportation (Gentleman, 2020).

The 2020 report by the Equalities and Human Rights Commission (EHRC) into the hostile environment policy summarised the Windrush scandal:

> In 2018, it came to public attention that hundreds of people, mostly of Black Caribbean heritage, had found it increasingly difficult to live, work and access services in the UK, often with life-changing consequences. People who had lived and raised families in Britain for most or all of their lives lost their homes and jobs, were refused vital healthcare, and were even removed or deported to places with which they did not have meaningful ties. Many were led to question their British identity as a result. (EHRC, 2020: 3)

The EHRC's report concluded that the hostile environment had 'accelerated the impact of decades of complex policy and practice based on *a history of white and black immigrants being treated differently*' (EHRC, 2020: 3, emphasis added). Compensation figures remain low, with only around 400 out of 2,000 applications resulting in payments. Dozens are known to have died before investigation into the scandal was completed, some dying in effective exile, having been refused the right to return to their homes in Britain (Gentleman, 2023).

Britain's record on immigration policy has rested on a bed of triadic populism but there are instances of what CRT calls interest convergence too. The UK government's acknowledgment of the Windrush scandal came about when campaigning journalists who had the ear of mainstream news media began to recount the story of the Windrush victims. When this one very specific strand of the hostile environment policy was cast by the press as a scandal, continuing to ignore the Windrush cases began for the state to carry a greater cost than backtracking. Interest convergence produced the Windrush investigation, report and compensation. The government's sudden rush of sympathy also offered contradiction closure. The Windrush case comprised a very clear cut and limited case, impacting upon a very specific fraction of Black Britons and it had been 'resolved' eventually by government intervention.

However, even after the Windrush scandal the UK's 'compliant environment' immigration policy continued. Mistreated migrants who fell outside of the circle drawn around the Windrush case disappeared into the depths of media indifference. Interest convergence and contradiction closure were accompanied by weakly worded and poorly enforced policy measures. At the beginning of 2023 the Conservative government moved to abandon several of the commitments it had made in response to the *EHRC Report*, including the appointment of a migrants' commissioner and extension of the powers of the independent Chief Inspector of Borders and Immigration. Anthony Williams, one of those affected by the Windrush scandal, reflected: 'They're just stringing us along until people lose interest, and we die out' (Gentleman, 2023).

The Windrush scandal and the hostile environment policy of which it was a part are salutary reminders that Britain's immigration policies still target particular fractions of its 'non-White' population for removal. Such policies are, as the *EHRC Report* (2020) concluded, embedded in a decades long history of racialised policies around immigration, citizenship, belonging and authenticity.

Inside/outside

The identity-based definition of social class positions the 'White working class' as Britain's authentic working class. This has a number of critically important stabilising effects. First, because it is a racial category rather than a class one, it offers identification across class fractions. In contemporary political discourse the 'White working class' category might include, for instance, a young renter on a zero hours contract but also a retired home owner in a 'red wall' seat. Second, it is a racial category that both constitutes and is constituted by triadic populism. The White working class has become the emblem of a postimperial Britain in which change has been too rapid, heritage and history are under attack, and White Britons have lost out culturally and economically in the multicultural realignment. Non-membership does not merely connote an asymmetrical relationship between groups: the 'White' working class and the 'Black' or 'Brown' working class; it constitutes a qualitative distinction between the authentic White working class and something other, something outside and potentially undeserving. Reflecting on his mixed heritage background, British historian David Olusoga has said of the current racial grammar: 'The term "working class", which my grandparents would have regarded as a simple descriptor of them and their community, in an age before mass migration, has become, with the addition of "white", a loaded political label, often used interchangeably with a new term, "the left behind"' (Olusoga, 2019).

In Britain, discussion of 'left behind' White communities became prominent in media and policy in the early 2000s. In the US the term had first been popularised in Christian evangelical circles via a series of dystopian cult novels about those who would be left behind when the Rapture occurred, left to face social chaos and environmental catastrophe (Frykholm, 2004); thus the phrase carried significant recognition value as it filtered into US political discourse. In Britain its connotations were less apocalyptic but still suggested a profound sense of abandonment and powerlessness, focusing on the social exclusion experienced by communities hollowed out by post-industrialism and left out of the embourgeoisement promised by post-1979 Conservative and New Labour governments. A number of discursive markers defined membership of the 'left behind' in racialised terms. These included educational underachievement among poor White students; a focus on communities in towns and small cities, as opposed to the big urban centres; antipathy to perceived metropolitan elitism; the notion that multiculturalism had privileged 'non-Whites' over Whites while, at the same time, leaving second and third generation communities of colour insufficiently integrated and still alien, hence the parallel lives supposedly led by different ethnic communities. The 'left behind' discourse was both a recognition of real social exclusion and a narrative about where White working-class anger should be directed.

Parallel lives

In summer 2001 there were disturbances involving Pakistani and Bangladeshi youth in the northern English towns of Bradford, Oldham and Burnley. While these were often headlined as 'race riots', the more thoughtful commentators identified a complex mix of factors, including inter-community tensions, the growth of far-right activity in some towns and the underlying poverty and deprivation of towns in which the old textile industries had long decayed. At state level the government cleaved to the long-established race relations framework in which different minority ethnic communities were perceived to embody different problems for the state and for wider British society. The 'cultural' problems in post-industrial Lancashire were not the problems identified, for example, among Brixton's African-Caribbean communities by Lord Scarman 20 years previously. So how were these community tensions understood?

Prominent policy and media themes included supposed self-segregation in poor Pakistani and Bangladeshi neighbourhoods and the influence of conservative forms of Islam in those communities (Kundnani, 2015). The implication was that British South Asians in Bradford, Oldham, and Burnley had actively placed themselves outside of normal community relations (including the recognised bonds of class). In previous decades the diverse ethnic makeup and class location of Pakistani and Bangladeshi communities was conflated into the category of 'Asians', now even that broad category was redrawn so that they were predominantly understood as 'Muslim' communities, obscuring ethnicity and class.

In advance of the December 2001 publication of the *Cantle Report* into the northern riots, the recently appointed Home Secretary David Blunkett offered a comment on lessons to be learned in an interview with the *Independent on Sunday*: 'We have norms of acceptability and those who come into our home – for that is what it is – should accept those norms just as we would have to do if we went elsewhere' (Blunkett, quoted in Grice, 2001).

It was a remarkable statement to make about long settled communities in which the majority of young people were British born. For journalist Gary Younge, Blunkett's comments and indeed much of the surrounding debate marked a retreat from the level of analysis of race in Britain that had been encouraged by the 1999 *Macpherson Report* into the murder of Stephen Lawrence, 'regressing towards the pitiful level it was before Stephen's birth in the 1970s' (Younge, 2002). Noting the return to ideas about communities of colour as an alien presence imposed upon British society, and also Blunkett's appeal to tropes of 'political correctness' and 'White middle-class guilt', Younge commented that:

> Blunkett appears to have misunderstood or just plain missed the debates on race, nationality and ethnicity that have been taking place for the past 20 years. ... Second and third generations who have been trying to turn Britain from a house into a home are once again being shown the visitors' entrance. (Younge, 2002: 13)

The *Cantle Report* (2001) itself, while containing more nuance than sometimes suggested, foregrounded the idea that White and South Asian communities in the northern towns 'operate on the basis of a series of parallel lives. These lives often do not seem to touch at any point, let alone overlap and promote any meaningful interchanges' (Cantle, 2001: 7).

While the *Cantle Report* acknowledged the deprivation that had afflicted poor communities in the northern towns over generations, the terms 'class' and 'working class' were almost absent from the report and at times Cantle's report seemed to regress to a 1960s concept of race relations, in which there was an emphasis on educating away prejudice and estrangement between distinct communities:

> We believe that there is an urgent need to promote community cohesion, based upon a greater knowledge of, contact between, and respect for, the various cultures that now make Great Britain such a rich and diverse nation. ... It is also essential to establish a greater

sense of citizenship, based on (a few) common principles which are shared and observed by all sections of the community. This concept of citizenship would also place a higher value on cultural differences. (Cantle, 2001: 10)

The theme of community cohesion might not have been unreasonable in itself but was allied to ideas about citizenship and British values that would dominate, or perhaps obscure, policy debates on race in Britain during the latter part of the New Labour administration (1997–2010) and the Conservative–Liberal Democrat coalition that succeeded it from 2010–15. Cantle may have written of the need for 'common principles' of citizenship but in the context of the time, and alongside the widely reported comments of Home Secretary Blunkett, it was difficult to escape the conclusion that the lack of commonly understood principles of British citizenship was not symmetrical, and that the problem lay particularly with those who had 'come into our home'. In large part, British social policy and its parallel political discourses were turning away from *Macpherson* and issues of institutional racism towards the older race relations framework in which materially opposed communities competed with each other for social resources.

Left out and left behind

The Cantle Report (2001) did not simply reflect communities living parallel lives; it also constructed a certain parallelism, in its references to 'left out' White communities. This was a valid area of concern but it was also an integral part of the race relations thesis, in which understandings of race and class were abstracted from structures of power and rearticulated in terms of identity. Culture and identity are, to paraphrase Stuart Hall, the modes in which class is lived but to understand class *only* as a form of cultural identity is inadequate. Nevertheless, by the 2010s the term 'left behind' had become voguish in both Britain and the US. The political appeal of the term was readily apparent. It was a passive descriptor wherein commentators could acknowledge societal waste, without being precise about the neoliberal structures that had seen the poor and marginalised become 'left behind'.

Moreover, in a gradual regression, the term 'left behind' became explicitly racialised. Rhetorically speaking, the true 'left behind' were White communities, particularly in former industrial towns in the north and midlands; the category did not usually extend to, for instance, those working on low, paid temporary contracts in the service industries of London. In part, this designation was an example of the kind of murky talking points through which race, class and capitalism were discussed in Britain. If different communities posed different problems for the state, then Pakistani or Bangladeshi communities could be depicted in terms of Islamic conservatism and self-segregation; Black Caribbeans and Africans in major cities could be referenced through policing, gangs and knife crime; White Britons in the towns and villages were the 'left behind'. In a sense, race was now offered to White people, while colourblindness was offered to Black and Brown people.

The White working class

The language of class analysis was eroded during the Thatcherite 1980s and 1990s and was not restored during the New Labour period (Jones, 2020). In that period, class identity had been stripped away from Black and White folk alike and what was left was 'cultural diversity'. Thus when in the early 2000s class made its partial reappearance in public debate, it returned as a form of cultural identity attached to White communities. It was a restricted reclaiming of the language of class, since in conservative discourses poor White families and communities had long been subjected to class-blind cultural deficit analysis (their failures were, we were told, the result not of social class reproduction, but of lack of aspiration and discipline). In short, the White working class was no longer, to use Marxist terms, a class for itself but another cultural identity, alongside other cultural groups defined in media and policy.

In a Runnymede Trust Report, Kjartan Páll Sveinsson (2009) noted the widespread criticism from Conservative politicians and the centre-right press levelled at Harriet Harman, then Labour Minister for Equalities, when she included discussion of *structural* inequalities in her speech to the Trades Union Congress (TUC) conference in September 2008. Harman's message was derided because it conflicted ideologically with the tactical reclaiming of social class, wherein, wrote Sveinsson:

> the issue of class is not a problem of structure, but a problem of culture. There is no working class anymore, only an underclass. Unless, of course, we are talking about multiculturalism, in which case the working class resurfaces from the depths of British history. In other words, it is permissible to use class as a stick to beat multiculturalism with, but not as a demand for increased equality for all. (Sveinsson, 2009: 4)

Sveinsson (2009) was pointing to the sense in which the reclaiming of social class abstracted class identity from class struggle and attributed social dislocation to Black and Brown immigration and settlement. Cultural critic Lynsey Hanley says of the same discursive reduction: 'Here, the "white working class" becomes "the left behind": those perceived to be uniformly bewildered by change, whose sense of loss began in the era of mass immigration and not hundreds of years before, in the time of land enclosures, rapid industrialisation and continual migration and violence' (Hanley, 2017: 8).

The caricature of the 'left behind' White working class has been predicated on a selective recall of British class history and upon Powellite zero-sum thinking. Policy attention to racism is viewed as always potentially conspiratorial; perceived gains for Black and Brown communities are losses for the White working class. In this depiction the White working class is authentic but the discourse also relies on a particular definition of what it is to be authentically White working class (see, for instance, Goodhart, 2013, 2017; Goodwin, 2023). The preferred features are homogeneity; social conservatism; suspicion of cultural diversity; living outside the major multicultural cities; Englishness (where the Welsh, Scots and Northern Irish White working class sit is never quite configured); and, quite probably, opposition to Britain's membership of the EU. The 'left behind' discourse professes fascination with White working-class people but is also limited and incurious, relying on a narrow set of tropes often used to ventriloquise right-wing concerns that are as much a part of elite thinking as they are a mark of Britain's working class.

Us and them

By the mid-2000s the depictions to which Sveinsson (2009) and later Hanley (2017) referred had become ubiquitous. In 2004 writer and TV producer Michael Collins's book *The Likes of Us: A Biography of the Working Class* (Collins, 2004b) was widely covered in Britain's media. For Collins, the White working class was a particular cultural identity, its features largely extrapolated from his own South London background. In the book's narrative the pivotal post-war social shift in Britain was South Asian, African and Caribbean immigration and no section of British society had been as affected as much as the White working class. Their loss of status was, argued Collins, largely due to the replacement of the old class settlement with a new liberal, multicultural consensus. The White working class was now Britain's 'forgotten tribe' (Collins, 2004a).

Collins's book was developed into an episode in a multipart Channel 4 TV documentary on class identity in Britain in 2005. Its depiction of Britain's class matrix was purposefully monoethnic, reinforcing the view that Black and Brown communities somehow existed outside class. The influence of the 'left behind' thesis was felt also in BBC TV's documentary series *The White Season* (2008). The trailer was provocative and drew considerable criticism, comprising as it did a single shot of a White man's face being graffitied by pens held in Black and Brown hands until it became invisible against a Black background. In the *Daily Mail*, one of Britain's highest selling newspapers, BBC series producer Richard Klein explained the rationale behind the series:

> Over the past two decades, Britain has been through a revolution. The extent of the change, in both scale and speed, has probably been unique in the peacetime history of our country. Globalisation, mass immigration and economic upheaval have helped to transform the fabric of our nation. ... Today, we are one of the most culturally and racially diverse places in Europe.
>
> These changes have been the subject of noisy debate within the media, politics and academia, yet it is a curious irony that, in all the heated discussion about the consequences of this revolution, one voice has been largely absent: that of the white working class. ... Politicians pontificate and academics argue, yet the voices of the British working-class public have been all but ignored: that of the white working class. (Klein, 2008)

Klein's tropes were embedded in the familiar discourse of legitimate grievance. Globalism and immigration had brought unprecedented change to a previously static society. The White working class bore the brunt of this change and were uniquely ill-equipped for it. Moreover, this fraction of society apparently shared a homogeneous 'White working-class opinion', one that was marginalised in the liberal media. Klein (2008) added that 'In metropolitan circles, where sneering at any minority ethnic group would be regarded as an outrage, this White working-class opinion is all too often treated with suspicion or contempt'. It was a remark that passed over the growing acceptability of Islamophobia in middle-class circles, described by Kundnani (2015). In actuality, it was questionable whether all of the films in the season fit Klein's description. In some episodes voice overs appeared grafted on rather artificially as a reminder of the themes promoted in the BBC's press releases. This raised questions as to whether the *White Season* was planned as a thematically coherent series or whether it was collated and ventriloquised *post hoc* to meet the mood of the period (Warmington and Grosvenor, 2011).

A decade and more later, this restricted definition of Britain's working class (one very particular mode of the culturalisation of labour) has become a robust presence in elite journalistic and academic circles. Among the better reviewed takes are David Goodhart's arguments about the impact of immigration and cultural diversity on Britain's social contract (Goodhart, 2013, 2017); Matthew Goodwin's writing on political tensions between British liberal elites and the White working class (Goodwin, 2023); and numerous 'Blue Labour' claims that politicians on the Left have pivoted too far to the concerns of multicultural urban constituencies, abandoning their 'traditional' support base (Embery, 2020).

A persistent theme in the discourse of the 'left behind' has been that socially conservative views (that are, by definition, held to be the authentic views of the White working class) have been marginalised by liberal media. This claim overlooks the still substantial influence of the UK's print media. Of the UK's 22 national daily and Sunday papers, 14 are firmly placed in the centre-right of the politics, including those with the very highest circulation, such as *The Daily Mail*, *The Sun* and *The Sunday Times*. These outlets are not known for liberal coverage of, for example, immigration, asylum seekers or Muslim communities. Such views have been displayed over years in front page headlines, such as 'Migrants Grab 12,000 Jobs a Month' (*Express*, 17 November 2011 [Little, 2011]), '4,000 foreign criminals including murderers and rapists we can't throw out … and, yes, you can blame human rights again' (*Daily Mail*, 2 January 2013 [Shipman and Doyle, 2013]), 'Ending channel migrant crisis can win election' (*Express*, 6 March 2023 [Brown, 2023]) and, in a notorious and later retracted headline, '1 in 5 Brit Muslims' sympathy for jihadis' (*The Sun*, 23 November 2015 [BBC News, 2016]).

In addition, the language of senior politicians is often less than temperate. In August 2015 journalist David Shariamadari noted comments by then Prime Minister David Cameron and his Chancellor Philip Hammond:

> David Cameron recently spoke of a 'swarm of people coming across the Mediterranean'. His foreign secretary, Philip Hammond, labelled migrants 'marauding' and one recent headline in the *Daily Mail* fretted that 'this tidal wave of migrants could be the biggest threat to Europe since the war'. The *Daily Express* frequently talks of the migrant 'flood' – even the BBC used 'flood' and 'stream' as verbs to describe the movement of people north out of Italy. (Shariamadari, 2015)

Nor is it the case, as sometimes claimed, that Powell's interventions in the 1960s somehow placed issues of immigration out of bounds politically. Since 1968, UK governments have passed some 15 major pieces of immigration legislation, supplemented by a vast number of supplementary rules and amendments (Girvan, 2018; National Archives, 2023).

Underachievement and betrayal

One of the discursive spaces that Britain's print media has opened up is the persistent suggestion that White working-class children are the lowest achievers in Britain's education system. The claim has its origins in the early 2000s, when it fitted with emerging policy on social exclusion. Media coverage of White working-class underachievement has provided a putative evidence base for those who have argued that policy focus on multiculturalism and other areas of equality and diversity has left behind White working-class communities (Williams, 2022). The performance of working-class children within the education system is a profoundly important issue. However, the claim that White working-class children fare worst in British schools has been based upon a misreading of data. Many of the data on 'class' gaps in educational performance actually refer to measures of *poverty* rather than to social class per se. In particular, the Department for Education and related social policy units frequently use *eligibility for free school meals* (FSM) as a somewhat crude proxy measure of poverty. However, the FSM measure is not a proxy for *social class*, since in most social surveys around 60 per cent of British adults consider themselves working class but only around 10 per cent of White British school students are eligible for FSM. The majority of White working class pupils are non-FSM. In addition, White pupils are one of the groups less likely to be on FSM (CRRE, 2020). Britain's news media has tended to misreport statistics relating to specific FSM measures of poverty as if they apply to White working-class children in general.

In every ethnic group, FSM students achieve lower average test results than their non-FSM peers. However, the majority of pupils – and the majority of *working-class* pupils – are non-FSM. Among non-FSM pupils, the lowest attaining ethnic groups are consistently Gypsy, Roma and Traveller; Black Caribbean; White/Black Caribbean dual heritage; and Pakistani students (Gillborn et al, 2016; CRRE, 2020). The continual focus on very small differences within the minority of pupils who are FSM obscures the far larger disparity between non-FSM pupils and those on FSM. However, focusing on the FSM/non-FSM gap would open up a quite different race/class analysis than the one preferred in conservative news media, apparent in headlines such as 'Betrayal of White Pupils' (*Daily Mail*, 4 April 2016 [Harris, 2016]) or 'White working-class children are UK's most deprived pupils' (*Daily Mail*, 19 September 2020 [Henry, 2020]). It is also worth noting that despite the claim that policy makers have overlooked the needs of White working-class pupils, since 2010 the only two House of Commons Education Committee inquiries to have focused on a single ethnic group have both concerned White pupils (CRRE, 2020). The issue of educational achievement among disadvantaged children has rightly been a focus of education policy in successive governments but there is little doubt that it has also been repurposed, to use Sveinsson's words, 'as a stick to beat multiculturalism with, but not as a demand for increased equality for all' (Sveinsson, 2009: 4).

Classlessness and social death

Since the early 2000s the discursive elimination of communities of colour from the social class matrix has become fixed in Britain's racial politics (Chen, 2013; Hanley, 2017). The phenomenological disappearance of Black and Brown working-class people has reinforced their 'in' but not 'of' positioning. In Britain being placed discursively 'outside' of class identity confers precarious status: the danger of being constructed as an interloping presence, as a unique social burden and even as part of a conspiracy wrought against the authentic working class.

There is a sense in which Black classlessness is, in Britain, a kind of *social death*. Those who have not come across this term before may initially find it perturbing but it is, in fact, one that has considerable history in social theory. The concept of social death, as distinct from physical death, has been widely used in studies of social being and social membership (Patterson, 1982/2018; Bauman, 1992; Cacho, 2012; Králová, 2015). Indeed, it might be argued that the idea of social death is necessary to any theorisation of social existence, insofar as it denotes the negation of social existence, the absence of social being.

As a concept, social death denotes a profound loss of social connectedness and identity, one that results in abject non-personhood and the loss of social birth rights. Králová (2015) explains that since the concept of social death entered the lexicon of the social sciences in the 1960s, it has been applied in myriad instances: to the terminally ill, to those with dementia, to refugees, to communities that are targets of genocide and to the enslaved. For Králová (2015), its diverse usages have meant that its conceptual clarity has sometimes been blurred (for instance, around whether social death refers to self-perception or how one is perceived by others). Králová's review of the literature provides both a valuable genealogy of the concept and an attempt to clarify the conceptual framework, defining it as 'the antithesis of well-being' (Králová, 2015: 246). However, rather than reiterating general arguments, what I wish to do here is to consider the strand of the theorisation of social death that has had particular influence in Black Atlantic thought. This strand, which begins conceptually by aligning social death to conditions of slavery and colonialism, derives from the writing of Jamaican sociologist and novelist, Orlando Patterson.

I first encountered Orlando Patterson's work through his literary fiction. Patterson's 1965 novel *The Children of Sisyphus* is an iconic post-independence Jamaican novel, depicting the lives of the most marginalised communities of 1950s Kingston (Patterson, 1965/1986). These included the urban poor displaced by slum clearance and those living at the edges even of those communities: the orphaned and abandoned, sex workers and the then ostracised Rastafari. These destitute characters exist in the slipstream of colonialism and slavery. Almost two decades later, Patterson published *Slavery and Social Death*, a comparative historical study of the status of slaves in diverse slaveholding societies (Patterson, 1982, republished in 2018). The book theorised social being and non-being by equating slavery with social death. Patterson's central premise was that in slaveholding societies slaves became 'nonpeople' because the slave 'had no socially recognized existence outside of his master, he *[sic]* became a social nonperson' (Patterson, 1982/2018: 5). Patterson explained slavery not primarily as a legal category but as a social relationship of domination. In the slaveholding societies that he examined, slavery often emerged as a conditional commutation or suspension of a death sentence (for example, captives in war might be enslaved, rather than slaughtered on the battlefield). Death was commuted as long as the slave was surrendered into a state of powerlessness; the conditional nature of the commutation was reinforced by subjection both to physical and symbolic violence. As a non-being, it is impossible to comprehend the slave outside of the master–slave relationship (Hall, 2017).

Integral to the status of nonperson was what Patterson termed 'natal alienation' (Patterson, 1982/2018: 7). Stuart Hall, who regarded Patterson's concept of social death as a significant contribution to postcolonial understandings of Atlantic slavery, empire and identity, regarded natal alienation as signifying 'a situation in which the elemental ties of birth were severed, and the enslaved were forcibly separated from the dynamics of those human qualities which, otherwise, we imagine to be bestowed on us when we are born' (Hall, 2017: 71). In short, natal alienation signified a separation from human rights and identity. Hall also pointed to enslavement as an ontological transformation, homing in on Patterson's understanding of slavery as a very particular form of violence, of violation. While force is a factor in all societies, in slave societies, such as the plantations that were the foundation of Hall and Patterson's shared Jamaican history:

> non-slaves had to be transformed into the social being of the slave, signalling the *work* – the pre-conditional absolute, the historical mission – of the planter class. It proved necessary continually to repeat the founding act of violence, ensuring that the transformation of the freed person into the slave became a daily task. *All of which was conducted under the banner of race*. ... The primary purpose of the violence inflicted was to impress upon the slave the knowledge that they had being only as that: as slaves with no existence conceivable except as an appendage to the master. (Hall, 2017: 70, emphasis added)

The influence of Patterson's reading of social death stretches beyond the study of plantation slavery into other contexts in which power is 'structured under the banner of race' (Hall, 2017: 70). Patterson's own writing examines what he terms the *afterlife* of slavery in colonial and postcolonial contexts, and has influenced current scholarship in areas such as racial capitalism and Afropessimism (see Chapter 2 of this book). Patterson has argued that sociologists working on present problems have paid minimal attention to slavery as a basis for understanding contemporary structures of power, being and identity (Patterson, 2019). This, Patterson has suggested, applies even to many sociologists who are concerned with contemporary problems of race and racism.

There is insufficient space in this book to embark on extensive theorisation of classlessness (*under the banner of race*) as a form of social death, but the concept is potentially useful in understanding contemporary problems of race and racism, particularly the precarity of identity among Black and Brown Britons. In contemporary Britain the political fascination with the 'White working class' has been bound up with a discursive stripping away of class identity from people of colour. In depictions of White working-class communities, race and class have become virtually indivisible in discursive terms, while in portrayals of communities of colour, race and class have become distanced from each other. *Natal alienation* here is twofold. In policy and media discourses Black and Brown working-class people are identified in ways that sever them from their actual place in the labour process. In turn, that alienation places a question mark over their authenticity, rendering their Britishness provisional. Perhaps above all, it is the category of *legitimate grievance* that carries the marker of social death. The role of the legitimate grievance affords no agency; it is to be perceived and defined directly as a negation, as the source of loss among the authentic, among the living. The legitimate grievance is wholly an object, not a subject and cannot be comprehended outside the majority–minority/authentic–alien relationship.

As Younge (2002) wrote in response to Home Secretary Blunkett's revival of the metaphor of 'our home', the conditional Britishness of communities of colour has meant that Black and Brown people can again and again be shown the visitors' entrance (literally so, in a case such as the Windrush scandal). It is an act of natal alienation; the founding act of being declared alien and other is repeated. In relation to the disqualification of people of colour from working-class identity, Black and Brown working-class people have ceased, in policy terms and in the wider culture, to exist as a category. They are located only as the negation of all that is contained in authentic White British working-class identity.

Conclusion

The danger for people of colour of the class-as-cultural-identity discourse, populated by categories such as the 'left behind' and the 'red wall', is that Blackness becomes coterminous with classlessness. We thus reach a stage whereby Black and Brown working-class identities cannot be narrativised, a state of affairs in which those Black and Brown identities become conceptually incoherent, unintelligible. The quote from historian David Olusoga (2019) early in this chapter speaks precisely to that negation. In CRT terms the disqualification of Black and Brown class identities has become a critically important stabilising factor, a condition of the social class matrix in Britain. It is a non-being that preserves a racialised conservative order, wherein Black and Brown communities hold a precarious and conditional relationship to the 'national interest' and to British identity. Under postracialism's race/class matrix there is a symbiosis between 'I don't see race', 'I don't see racism' and 'I don't see you'.

7
Conclusion: Black futures

CRT does not lend itself to neat conclusions or to neat concluding chapters. Derrick Bell saw the political tradition in which he worked as 'a story less of success than of survival through unremitting struggle that leaves no room for giving up' (Bell, 1992: 200). Moreover, it was, he said, a story that was still unfolding. This may not please every academic or activist and it will not please all those working adjacent to policy makers. However, as Sriprakash et al (2022) have cautioned, there is good reason to resist the pressure to write and research in ways that aim to produce policy fixes. In fields such as education, social policy and indeed the wider public sector, managerialist ideologies of 'what works' and 'effectiveness' have long been dominant and have impinged on even the most 'critical' scholarship.

In addition, because matters of race and racism are sources of discomfort, provoking in some that mythic desire for contradiction closure, there is a particular racialised dimension to the call for such fixes. Wilderson et al (2016) remark that 'Black speech is always coerced speech, speech under house arrest. And the jailers insist that you don't bring them any bad news unless it has a solution embedded in it' (Wilderson et al, 2016: 8).

Those critics of CRT who have taken the trouble to read at least some of the literature (and there really are not very many who fall into that category) have argued variously that CRT over relies on the category of race or that it homogenises White interests or that it is overly cynical about reform. But one of the main reasons that CRT remains unendorsed is simply that it refuses to play the role of butler to managers, policy makers and mainstream academics. CRT sometimes brings bad news and, following Derrick Bell's approach, it shies away from confecting social blueprints. This final chapter avoids a conclusive end, as it were, but it reflects on some of the ideas and issues that have recurred in the text, relating them to Britain's current political and policy directions, and it returns to the question of what we should make of Bell's insistence on the permanence of racism.

The Conversation

I was asked recently whether it was useful to tell young Black and Brown people that racism is permanent. First off, it seemed odd to me to suggest that 'young Black and Brown people' would not already be familiar with the impacts of racism by the time they came to a book such as this. Racism's mutability, the double-dealing of postraciality and the too-familiar patterns of progress and reversal – none of these were invented by Derrick Bell or by CRT.

Critical race theorists are often accused of claiming that 'everything' is about race and racism. That criticism is unsurprising. In a world in which the social relationship of race is normalised and in which racism tends to be acknowledged only when it shows itself in shocking and extreme incidents, the pervasive forms of racism – structural and institutional – mostly go unremarked. Race is, as Mills (2022) argued, the unseen backdrop against which other phenomena, those that count as politically important, are understood. Consequently, critical race analyses that focus on the sheer ordinariness of racism must indeed make it seem as if race is 'suddenly' everywhere. What was considered noise, if heard at all, is repositioned as signal.

Perhaps the best way to think of this book is as another iteration of The Conversation. What is The Conversation? It is that moment in the lives of Black and Brown parents, that unavoidable moment, when we explain to our children that they will, in all probability, have to work twice as hard for half the reward, when we must explain why figures of authority may not always treat them with the respect that should be their due – and why despite all of this, they should remain proud, self-caring and undefeated. It is the conversation my father had with me. Then I thought he was unduly pessimistic; now, I know that he was merely realistic. Truth is, I hope, useful to all, as is the message to speak freely, not to be, in Wilderson's words, coerced.

In short, The Conversation warns its listeners what they will be up against. This book endeavours to warn those committed to racial justice, particularly in the British context, what they are likely to be up against in the near future. First, there will be many thin symbols of postracialism to navigate and we shall all need to refuse their seduction, remembering, as Lewis Gordon reminds us that 'so-called "postracialism", a buzzword into the second decade of the twenty-first century, is little more than a way of referring to continued racism that is simply now ashamed of itself' (Gordon, 2015: 18).

Second, we shall come toe-to-toe with postracialism's pit bull: the 'contras', with their mix of derision and state sanctions. While we are told repeatedly that 'political correctness' and 'woke' ideology have captured our institutions and silenced debate; in fact, antiracism is increasingly being positioned outside the bounds of legitimate political speech. The space for critical thought on race and racism is vanishingly small, and the postracial project is directing us to a small corner in which there is little that can be said about racism except that it is deplorable and that, thank heavens, we are largely protected from it by British exceptionalism.

This far and no further

The novelty of 'the culture wars' is often exaggerated, while their political seriousness is underestimated. Those who lived in Britain in the 1980s, for instance, will remember the tactics of the Right in those times: a combination of derision ('the loony Left', the claim that the Greater London Council had banned the nursery rhyme, 'Ba Ba Black Sheep') and state intervention (Section 28, introduced by the Thatcher government to prohibit schools from promoting 'the acceptability of homosexuality as a pretended family relationship'). The culture war strategy is not particularly new. It is also easy to find much that is ridiculous in some of its manufactured controversies. However, as this book has argued, in regard to the politics of race and racism, culture as a 'contra-' space is a very real phenomenon.

Since 2020 the 'contra-' project has focused on BLM, CRT and so forth as 'woke' signifiers but it is also a renewed effort to break the tradition of Black Atlantic politics that informed the likes of New Beacon, the Institute of Race Relations and Southall Black Sisters, and that was also a significant presence in the anti-apartheid movement, in trade unions, and in struggles over education, policing and immigration. The influence of that Black Atlantic political tradition is, to the dismay of some, still present in BLM, CRT and the Colston protests. What is at issue is not, as some have claimed, changing demographics within communities of colour but a battle over Black politics.

Postracialism, with its reliance on rhetoric that depicts Britain as a model for other White-majority nations and reassures us that racism has no place in our society, is also a project to divorce models of social change from the actions of social movements. Addressing racism, we are told, does not require actions by antiracist campaigns or programmatic leadership by governments (for these might favour the interloper over the authentic Briton). Apparently, racism will wither from natural wastage and any unfortunate gaps or behaviours that remain are either not racism at all or must simply be accepted because Britain has gone as far as it can in meeting demands for racial justice. Our 'this far and no further' discourse is both self-congratulatory (it holds that multiculturalism has been adequately achieved) and deterministic (racism has receded but we have now met our non-racist limits). Here we return to Gillborn's CRT analysis of educational and social policy as too often maintaining racial inequality but at manageable levels (Gillborn, 2008). The insistence that race equality policy goes this far and no further offers a stabilising effect, speaking both to triadic populism and to the mythic conclusive end. It also speaks to the limits of the liberal imagination; it is one thing to identify briefly with, say, Black History Month but when profound questions are asked about current social arrangements, then antiracism has indeed 'gone too far'.

Conclusion

While CRT, BLM and so forth are often used as empty signifiers, fuzzily connoting race talk as something that 'ordinary' Britons should disdain, there are also more solid electoral calculations in play. In Britain, as in many comparable nations, the old centre-right has shown signs in the past decade of being eclipsed by a harder right-wing, not least in Britain's Conservative Party, wherein 'one nation Conservatism' has waned and 'National Conservativism' is emergent. There is now an argument for using a term such as 'conservative race politics' in the British context to denote something closer to the 'hard' sense in which it is understood in the US, not least because Britain's culture warriors have taken much from the US playbook (see Gillborn et al, 2022).

It should be borne in mind also that conservative views on race do not always map on neatly to traditional Left/Right divides, although the Right has, of course, had a more programmatic commitment to 'contra-' antiracism. In the UK, the Conservative Party has, at time of writing, been in power for 13 years. It is not the only source of conservatism and 'contra-' positions in British society but it has been a principal force in constructing a centre-right social order (one that has historically maintained space for traditional conservatism, its sometime bedfellow neoliberalism and the emergent hard Right). In first-past-the-post electoral politics the stability of that conservative coalition is dependent on securing an electoral alliance that will hit the 40 per cent support mark generally required to achieve a term in government.

Political commentator Paul Mason has argued that, to this end, recent Conservative governments have aimed to construct a 'mass reactionary movement', among whose targets are 'migrants, Black Lives Matter protesters ... and that perennial racist euphemism "communities with large households"' (Mason, 2020). This reactionary movement has rested in part upon hard Right conservatives depicting themselves as tribunes of the White working class (defined 'culturally', not of course in Marxist terms) and, more recently, on mobilising 'anti-woke' sentiments. CRT is sometimes accused of homogenising White communities' interests but what CRT, in fact, offers is an *analysis* of the ways in which White interests are homogenised in the cause of stabilising conservative political power. Racialised alliances do not require the buy-in of White people en masse; they merely require enough buy-in to maintain stability.

However, as previously noted, socially conservative views on race equality do not map on neatly to traditional Left/Right divides. In seeking to appeal to the 'red wall' voters lost to the Conservatives in the 2019 election, Britain's Labour Party has not entirely shied away from racially restricted definitions of the working class and Labour's 'traditional' support base. The political usefulness of warring over British culture may prove to be durable because in Britain (and particularly in England) melancholic appeals to British exceptionalism and spotless readings of history endure. While numerous arguments have been made for 'progressive patriotism', writers such as David Wearing maintain that too much has been said and done to make such a position easily achievable:

> In practice, these myths of national or civilisational greatness have been indivisible from racism and xenophobia. 'Our' greatness has been defined – through the formative centuries of colonialism right up to the present day – by drawing contrasts with 'their' inferiority, be 'they' black people, south Asians, Arabs, Muslims, or whoever else needed to be denigrated in a specific historical moment or political-economic context. (Wearing, 2021)

Our contemporary culture wars, which rest in substantial part on antagonism to antiracist movements, are not merely a handy political or media hook; they have been about the search for a larger discursive space to develop restricted definitions of Britishness and belonging, but in ways that are politely distanced from the deplorability of the far-right. To return to the idea of a mass reactionary bloc, the possibility that sufficient opposition to its purported values might endanger the 40 per cent electoral baseline is a direct, material threat. As Wearing argues: 'If a genuine, substantive antiracist politics went truly mainstream and became the common sense of the age, conservatism as we know it would be rendered unviable' (Wearing, 2021).

What remains in question in CRT is whether substantive antiracist politics (something quite different from an easy postracial consensus) have the potential to become truly mainstream. As stated in Chapter 1 of this book, it is not that antiracist action is pointless but that positional victories do not imply that race as a line of social conflict ceases to exist.

Conclusion

In contemplating the permanence of racism, Derrick Bell maintained that the moral arc of the universe might or might not bend toward social justice. Either way, a promise is not a political programme, so bracket it for the moment. Bell seemed to be urging a different kind of struggle, one that required:

> a more realistic perspective from which to gauge the present and future worth of our race-related activities. Freed of the stifling rigidity of relying unthinkingly on the slogan 'we shall overcome,' we are impelled *both* to live each day more fully *and* to examine critically the actual effectiveness of traditional civil rights remedies. Indeed, the humility required by genuine service will not permit us to urge remedies that

we may think appropriate and the law may even require, but that the victims of discrimination have rejected. (Bell, 1992: 199)

Bell's realist position is, in a sense, a fork in the road. We might return to the well-worn idea derived by Mark Fisher from Fredric Jameson: that it is now easier to imagine the end of the world than it is to imagine the end of capitalism (Fisher, 2009). Bell's racial realism took a similar line, or at least posed a similar set of questions in relation to race and racism as modes of social organisation. How politically realistic was the 'long-held dream of attaining a society free of racism' (Bell, 1992: 199)? In immediate terms, were our energies better directed towards millenarian goals or, as in the case of Mrs MacDonald, the elderly African-American woman whom Bell met as a young civil rights activist, should our realistic goal be daily defiance, daily resistance, undertaken in the knowledge that the struggle against racism is a grinding one, subject to reversal and likely without conclusive end?

We might therefore ask the same type of questions of Bell as many have asked of Fisher's work. Did Fisher's vision of capitalist realism actually suggest that capitalism was now the only attainable mode of social organisation or did capitalist realism refer to the ideological limits that capitalism set on our thinking: a robustly policed boundary that anti-capitalists were dared to cross? In Bell's case, was racism with its interlocking structures and hierarchies simply permanent, case closed – or did racialised societies (their facile gestures towards postracialism notwithstanding) reproduce themselves, in part, by the strength of their ideological insistence on race as a permanent mode of social organisation? Remember that Bell said the 'permanence of racism' was a descriptive, not a prescriptive term. In other words, perhaps Bell was arguing that racism is durable but not eternal. If so, then it is possible, just possible, that Bell's 'permanence' was a veil that could be torn. Perhaps we might say that Bell's CRT project was to harass the 'really existing' world of race equality claims. By encouraging us to see where legislation and policy provided symbolic rather than actual achievements, he sought to hasten the crisis of symbolic efficiency. As Bell wrote:

> It is not a matter of choosing between the pragmatic recognition that racism is permanent no matter what we do, or an idealism based on the long-held dream of attaining a society free of racism. Rather it is a question of *both, and*. *Both* the recognition of the futility of action – where action is more civil rights strategies destined to fail – *and* the unalterable conviction that something must be done, that action must be taken. (Bell, 1992: 199)

Bell's thought was pessimistic and non-utopian, insofar as deferred utopianism too often became another kind of contradiction closure, a slight consolation for the failures of present politics. However, Bell's writing might also suggest that pessimism about current social arrangements was the precondition for new imaginaries. In Bell's work these new possibilities are understated. There are, however, contemporary writers – a diverse spread variously characterised as Afro-optimists and Afrofuturists – who have been much more explicit about the possibilities, indeed the necessity, of radical disordering of society as the way to a meaningful postracialism. Alex Zamalin argues that, as yet, these ways forward are speculative, comprising 'fantastical meditation on untapped possibilities already embedded within society – unconditional freedom, equality, interracial intimacy, solidarity, and social democracy' (Zamalin, 2019: 10).

In the present day, we are still regrettably closer to Bell's realism than to these fantastic vistas. However, Bell's dialectic between pessimism and possibility does not bind us into political paralysis; it may, in fact, instead serve as the imperative for focused antiracist thought and action. Racial realism – the rejection of facile postracialism and contradiction closure – would, Bell believed, free us to redefine antiracist struggle in terms that were meaningful to people who experienced the impacts of racism. In short, we should cease wasting time and energy on the wrong game and put new ways of struggle into play. For, as Bell's contemporary Audre Lorde cautioned, '*the master's tools will never dismantle the master's house.* They may allow us to temporarily beat him at his own game, but they will never enable us to bring about genuine change' (Lorde, 2017: 19). This perpetual motion, struggle with no room for giving up, might lead us to fugitive spaces that Bell and his peers did not yet imagine. In the current moment, the postracial is premature and so, as the old fighters used to say, *a luta continua*.

References

Abraham, E. (2022) 'Rishi Sunak's plans to refer people who "vilify" Britain to Prevent are being mocked', *indy100*, [online] 3 August, Available from: https://www.indy100.com/politics/rishi-sunak-vilify-britain-prevent [Accessed 10 December 2022].

Afzal, N. (2022) *Independent Culture Review of London Fire Brigade*, London: Independent Culture.

Aitken, A. and Butcher, B. (2020) 'Black Lives Matter: have racial inequality reviews led to action?', BBC News, [online] 25 June, Available from: https://www.bbc.co.uk/news/53053661 [Accessed 1 March 2021].

Allen Jnr., E. (1997) 'On the reading of riddles', in L.R. Gordon (ed) *Existence in Black: An Anthology of Black Existential Philosophy*, London: Routledge, pp 49–68.

Alves, J.A. (2014) 'Neither humans nor rights: some notes on the double negation of black life in Brazil', *Journal of Black Studies*, 45(2): 143–62.

Anderson, B. (1983) *Imagined Communities: Reflections on the Origin and Spread of Nationalism*, London: Verso.

Angiolini, Dame E. (2017) *Report of the Independent Review of Deaths and Serious Incidents in Police Custody*, London: HMSO.

Annamma, S.A., Connor, D. and Ferri, B. (2013) 'Dis/ability critical race studies (DisCrit): theorizing at the intersections of race and dis/ability', *Race Ethnicity & Education*, 16(1): 1–31.

Apple, M.W. (2001) *Educating the 'Right' Way: Markets, Standards, God and Inequality*, New York: Routledge Falmer.

Apple, M.W. (2018) *Ideology and Curriculum* (4th edn), London: Routledge.

Badenoch, K. (2020) 'Contribution to debate on Black History Month', *Hansard (2020) [HC]* vol. 682, column 1011–12 [online], Available from: https://hansard.parliament.uk/Commons/2020-10-20/debates/5B0E393E-8778-4973-B318-C17797DFBB22/BlackHistoryMonth [Accessed 11 January 2021].

Ball, S.J. (2017) *The Education Debate: Policy and Politics in the Twenty-First Century* (3rd edn), Bristol: Policy Press.

Barrett, D. and Ellicott, C. (2022) '"Statue protesters can't change our history": Boris Johnson insists people toppling effigies should not be allowed to alter nation's heritage following outcry over Colston trial verdict', *Mail Online*, [online] 6 January, Available from: https://www.dailymail.co.uk/news/article-10376711/Boris-Johnson-insists-people-toppling-effigies-not-allowed-alter-nations-heritage.html [Accessed 10 December 2022].

Batty, D. and Parveen, N. (2021) 'UK schools record more than 60,000 racist incidents in five years', *The Guardian*, [online] 28 March, Available from: https://www.theguardian.com/education/2021/mar/28/uk-schools-record-more-than-60000-racist-incidents-five-years [Accessed 29 March 2021].

Bauman, Z. (1992) *Mortality, Immortality and Other Life Strategies*, Cambridge: Polity.

BBC (2011) 'Analysis: A New Black Politics', transcript of broadcast, *BBC Radio 4*, 31 October, London: BBC.

BBC News (2005) 'UK economy ends 2004 with a spurt', *BBC News*, [online] 26 January, Available from: http://news.bbc.co.uk/1/hi/business/4208499.stm [Accessed 9 March 2023].

BBC News (2010) 'BNP vote increases, but fails to win seat', *BBC News*, [online] 7 May, Available from: http://news.bbc.co.uk/1/hi/uk_politics/election_2010/8667231.stm [Accessed 26 January 2023].

BBC News (2016) 'The Sun's UK Muslim "jihadi sympathy" article "misleading", Ipso rules', *BBC News*, [online] 26 March, Available from: https://www.bbc.co.uk/news/uk-35903066 [Accessed 31 July 2023].

BBC News (2021) 'Race report: "UK not deliberately rigged against ethnic minorities"', *BBC News*, [online] 31 March, Available from: https://www.bbc.co.uk/news/uk-56585538 [Accessed 5 February 2022].

Begum, H. (2021) 'Opinion: Here's everything Britain's report on racism got wrong', *Thompson Reuters Foundation News*, [online] 1 April, Available from: https://news.trust.org/item/20210401161436-7nfxk [Accessed 20 February 2023].

Bell, D. (1973) *Race, Racism and American Law*, Boston: Little, Brown.

Bell, D. (1980) 'Brown v. Board of Education and the interest convergence dilemma', *Harvard Law Review*, 93: 518–33.

Bell, D. (1987) *And We Are Not Saved: The Elusive Quest For Racial Justice*, New York: Basic.

Bell, D. (1991) 'Racism is here to stay: now what', *Howard Law Journal*, 35(1): 79–94.

Bell, D. (1992) *Faces at the Bottom of The Well: The Permanence of Racism*, New York: Basic.

Bell, D. (1993) 'The racism is permanent thesis: courageous revelation or unconscious denial of racial genocide', *Capital University Law Review*, 22(3): 571–88.

Bell, D. (1995a) 'Brown v. Board of Education and the interest convergence dilemma', *Harvard Law Review*, 93: 518–33. Reprinted in K. Crenshaw, N. Gotanda, G. Peller and K. Thomas (eds) *Critical Race Theory: The Key Writings that Formed the Movement*, New York: New Press, pp 20–29.

Bell, D. (1995b) 'Racial realism', in K. Crenshaw, N. Gotanda, G. Peller and K. Thomas (eds) *Critical Race Theory: The Key Writings that Formed the Movement*, New York: New Press, pp 302–12.

Bell, D. (1995c) 'Who's afraid of Critical Race Theory', *University of Illinois Law Review*, 1995(4): 893–910.

Bell, D. (2004) *Silent Covenants: Brown v. Board of Education and the Unfulfilled Hopes for Racial Reform*, New York: Oxford University Press.

Bell, T. (2021) 'On pay and wealth, damaging race inequalities prevail', *The Guardian*, [online] 11 April, Available from: https://www.theguardian.com/commentisfree/2021/apr/11/on-pay-and-wealth-damaging-race-inequalities-prevail [Accessed 10 January 2023].

Bernstein, F.A. (2011) 'Derrick Bell, law professor and rights advocate, dies at 80', *New York Times*, [online] 6 October, Available from: https://www.nytimes.com/2011/10/06/us/derrick-bell-pioneering-harvard-law-professor-dies-at-80.html [Accessed 18 March 2021].

Bhattacharyya, G. (2018) *Rethinking Racial Capitalism: Questions of Reproduction and Survival*, London: Rowman and Littlefield.

Bhopal, K. (2018) *White Privilege: The Myth of a Post-Racial Society*, Bristol: Policy Press.

Bhopal, K. (2021) 'The Sewell report displays a basic misunderstanding of how racism works', *The Guardian*, [online] 31 March, Available from: https://www.theguardian.com/commentisfree/2021/mar/31/sewell-report-racism-government-racial-disparity-uk [Accessed 10 November 2021].

Blacker, D.J. (2013) *The Falling Rate of Learning and the Neoliberal Endgame*, Alresford: Zero.

Bonilla-Silva, E. (2010) *Racism Without Racists: Color-Blind Racism and the Persistence of Racial Inequality in the United States* (3rd edn), Plymouth: Rowman and Littlefield.

Bonilla-Silva, E. (2012) 'The invisible weight of whiteness: the racial grammar of everyday life in contemporary America', *Ethnic and Racial Studies*, 35(2): 173–94.

Bonilla-Silva, E. (2015) 'More than prejudice: restatement, reflections, and new directions in Critical Race Theory', *Sociology of Race and Ethnicity*, 1(1): 75–89.

Bonilla-Silva, E. and Dietrich, D. (2011) 'The sweet enchantment of color-blind racism in Obamerica', *The ANNALS of the American Academy of Political and Social Science*, 634(1): 190–206.

Booth, R. (2020) 'Black Lives Matter has increased racial tension, 55% say in UK poll', *The Guardian*, [online] 27 November, Available from: https://www.theguardian.com/world/2020/nov/27/black-lives-matter-has-increased-racial-tension-55-say-in-uk-poll [Accessed 30 December 2022].

Bourne, J. (2007) *In Defence of Multiculturalism*. IRR Briefing Paper No.2, London: Institute of Race Relations.

Bourne, J. (2008) 'The beatification of Enoch Powell', *Race and Class*, 49(4): 82–7.

Boyd, J. (2020) 'UK minister: teaching White privilege and Critical Race Theory in schools is illegal', *The Federalist*, [online] 21 October, Available from: https://thefederalist.com/2020/10/21/uk-minister-teaching-white-privilege-and-critical-race-theory-in-schools-is-illegal/ [Accessed 1 August, 2023].

Brayboy, B.M.J. (2005) 'Toward a Tribal Critical Race Theory in education', *Urban Review*, 37: 425–46.

Bristow, A. (2021) *Meeting the Housing Needs of BAME Households in England: The Role of the Planning System – Executive Summary*, Edinburgh: Heriot Watt/ I-Sphere.

Brown, M. (2022) 'Rishi Sunak: "I won't let Left bulldoze our history"', *Express*, [online] 30 July, Available from: https://www.express.co.uk/news/politics/1648204/rishi-sunak-britain-tory-leadership-Boris-Johnson [Accessed 5 November 2022].

Brown, M. (2023) 'Ending channel migrant crisis can win election', *Express*, [online via Magzter.com] 6 March, Available from: https://www.magzter.com/stories%252Fnewspaper%252FDaily-Express%252FENDING-CHANNEL%25C2%25A0MIGRANT%25C2%25A0CRISIS%25C2%25A0CAN-WIN%25C2%25A0ELECTION%2F/ [Accessed 31 July 2023].

Bryan, B., Dadzie, S. and Scafe, S. (1985) *The Heart of the Race: Black Women's Lives in Britain*, London: Virago.

Buenavista, T. (2016) 'Model (undocumented) minorities and "illegal" immigrants: centering Asian-Americans and US carcerality in undocumented student discourse', *Race, Ethnicity and Education*, 21(1): 78–91.

Bunting, M. (2011) 'Cameron is wrong. Multicapitalism is to blame, and not multiculturalism', *The Guardian*, 7 February, p 25.

Burn-Murdoch, J. (2022) 'Britain and the US are poor societies with some very rich people', *Financial Times* [online], Available from: https://www.ft.com/content/ef265420-45e8-497b-b308-c951baa68945 [Accessed 8 February 2023].

Cacho, L.M. (2012) *Social Death: Racialized Rightlessness and the Criminalization of the Unprotected*, London: New York University Press.

Cantle, T. (2001) *Community Cohesion: A Report of the Independent Review Team*, London: Home Office.

Carby, H. (1982) 'Schooling in Babylon', in Centre for Contemporary Cultural Studies (eds) *The Empire Strikes Back: Race and Racism in 70s Britain*, London: Hutchinson, pp 183–211.

Carby, H. (1999) *Cultures in Babylon: Black Britain and African America*, London: Verso.

Carmichael, S. and Hamilton, C. (1967) *Black Power: The Politics of Liberation in America*, New York: Vintage.

Casey, L. (Baroness Casey of Blackstock) (2023) *An Independent Review into the Standards of Behaviour and Internal Culture of the Metropolitan Police Service: Final Report*, London: Metropolitan Police.

Centre for Contemporary Cultural Studies Education Group (CCCS) (1981) *Unpopular Education: Schooling and Social Democracy in England Since 1944*, Birmingham: University of Birmingham.

Centre for Research in Race and Education (CRRE) (2013) *Inquiry into Underachievement in Education by White Working Class Children: Written Evidence Submitted by the Centre for Research in Race and Education (CRRE) at the University Of Birmingham*, Birmingham: University of Birmingham.

CRRE (2020) *Evidence for the Commission on Race and Ethnic Disparities*, Birmingham: University of Birmingham.

Charters, C. (2022) 'Almost half of young people in Britain are too frightened to dispute the idea of white privilege and some even feared being EXPELLED from school', *Mail Online*, [online] 20 November, Available from: https://www.dailymail.co.uk/news/article-11448541/Almost-half-young-people-Britain-frightened-dispute-idea-white-privilege.html [Accessed 1 August, 2023].

Chen, A. (2013) 'Working class history's been ethnically cleansed', *The Guardian*, 17 July, p 28.

Church, J. (2022) 'The fatalistic cynicism of Derrick Bell's interest convergence thesis', *Counterweight*, [online] 10 January, Available from: https://counterweightsupport.com/2022/01/10/the-fatalistic-cynicism-of-derrick-bells-interest-convergence-thesis/ [Accessed 26 February 2023].

Clegg, D. (2019) 'Boris Johnson "uses racist language to gain far-right support" claims Anas Anwar', *Daily Record*, [online] 9 July, Available from: https://www.dailyrecord.co.uk/news/politics/boris-johnson-uses-racist-language-17609201 [Accessed 2 March 2023].

Coates, T.N. (2015) *Between the World and Me*, Melbourne: Text Publishing.

Collins, M. (2004a) 'Forgotten tribe', *The Guardian*, [online] 3 July, Available from: https://www.theguardian.com/world/2004/jul/03/race.britishidentity [Accessed 7 March 2023].

Collins, M. (2004b) *The Likes Of Us: A Biography of the White Working Class*, London: Granta.

Collins, P.H. and Solomos, J. (2010) 'Introduction: situating race and ethnic studies', in P.H. Collins and J. Solomos (eds) *The SAGE Handbook of Race and Ethnic Studies*, London: Sage, pp 1–16.

Commission on Race and Ethnic Disparities (CRED) (2021) *The Report*, London: CRED.

Cook T., Kursumovic E. and Lennane S. (2020) 'Deaths of NHS staff from Covid-19 analysed', *Health Service Journal*, [online] 22 April, Available from: https://www.hsj.co.uk/exclusive-deaths-of-nhs-staff-from-covid-19-analysed/7027471.article [Accessed 28 February 2022].

Corthorn, P. (2019) *Enoch Powell: Politics and Ideas in Modern Britain*, Oxford: Oxford University Press.

Crabtree, E. (2022) '"Detached from reality": Javid shuts down "simply wrong" Sunak narrative by US TV host', *Express*, [online] 27 October, Available from: https://www.express.co.uk/news/us/1688808/sajid-javid-rishi-sunak-narrative-the-daily-show-trevor-noah-united-states-dxus [Accessed 1 November 2022].

Crenshaw, K.W. (2019) 'How colorblindness flourished in the age of Obama', in K.W. Crenshaw, L.C. Harris, D.M. HoSang and G. Lipsitz (eds) *Seeing Race Again: Countering Colorblindness across the Disciplines*, Oakland: University of California Press, pp 128–51.

Crenshaw, K.W. (2023) 'Mapping the margins: intersectionality, identity politics, and violence against women of color', in E. Taylor, D. Gillborn and G. Ladson-Billings (eds) *Foundations of Critical Race Theory in Education* (3rd edn), London: Routledge, pp 273–307.

Crenshaw, K., Gotanda, N., Peller, G. and Thomas, K. (eds) (1995) *Critical Race Theory: The Key Writings that Formed the Movement*, New York: New Press.

Crenshaw, K.W., Harris, L.C., HoSang, D.M. and Lipsitz, G. (eds) (2019) *Seeing Race Again: Countering Colorblindness across the Disciplines*, Oakland: University of California Press.

Da Costa, A.E. (2016) 'Confounding anti-racism: mixture, racial democracy, and post-racial politics in Brazil', *Critical Sociology*, 42(4–5) 495–513.

Davies, H.C. and MacRae, S.E. (2023) 'An anatomy of the British war on woke', *Race and Class* [online], Available from: https://journals.sagepub.com/doi/full/10.1177/03063968231164905 [Accessed 30 June 2023].

Dearden, L. (2022) 'Suella Braverman says it is her "dream" and "obsession" to see a flight take asylum seekers to Rwanda', *Independent*, [online] 5 October, Available from: https://www.independent.co.uk/news/uk/politics/suella-braverman-rwanda-dream-obsession-b2195296.html [Accessed 30 December 2022].

Delgado, R. (1996) *The Rodrigo Chronicles: Conversations about America and Race*, New York: New York University Press.

Delgado, R. and Stefancic, J. (2001) *Critical Race Theory: An Introduction*, London: New York University Press.

Department for Business and Trade (2017) *Race in the Workplace: The McGregor-Smith Review*, London: HMSO.

Department for Education [DfE] (2019) *Timpson Review of School Exclusion*, CP92. DfE-00090-2019, London: DfE.

Department for Education and Science (1977) *Education in Schools: A Consultative Document*, London: HMSO.

Dhondy, F., Beese, B. and Hassan, L. (1985) *The Black Explosion in British Schools*, London: Race Today.

Dixson, A.D. and Rousseau Anderson, C. (2018) 'Where are we? Critical Race Theory in education 20 years later', *Peabody Journal of Education*, 93(1): 121–31.

Dixson, A.D., Gillborn, D., Ladson-Billings, G., Parker, L., Rollock, N. and Warmington, P. (2018) *Critical Race Theory in Education: Major Themes in Education*, Vol 1–4, London: Routledge.

Dolan, A. (2016) 'Warning on "UK Muslim ghettoes": nation within a nation developing says former equalities watchdog', *Mail Online*, [online] 10 April, Available from: https://www.dailymail.co.uk/news/article-3533041/Warning-UK-Muslim-ghettoes-Nation-nation-developing-says-former-equalities-watchdog.html [Accessed 30 July 2023].

Dubois, W.E.B. (1903) *The Souls of Black Folk*, Chicago: A.C. McClurg [page numbers from 1995 Signet Classic 100th Anniversary edition].

Dumas, M.J. and ross, k. (2016) '"Be real black for me": imagining blackcrit in Education', *Urban Education*, 51(4): 415–42.

Eddo-Lodge, R. (2017) *Why I'm No Longer Talking to White People About Race*, London: Bloomsbury.

Ehrman, B.D. (1999) *Jesus: Apocalyptic Prophet of the New Millennium*, New York: Oxford University Press.

El-Enany, N. (2021) *Bordering Britain: Law, Race and Empire*, Manchester: Manchester University Press.

Embery, P. (2020) *Despised: Why the Modern Left Loathes the Working Class*, Cambridge: Polity.

Equality and Human Rights Commission (EHRC) (2020) *Public Sector Equality Duty Assessment of Hostile Environment Policies*, London: EHRC.

Essed, P. and Goldberg, D.T. (eds) (2002) *Race Critical Theories: Text and Context*, Oxford: Blackwell.

Fanon, F. (1963) *The Wretched of the Earth*, Harmondsworth: Penguin.

Fanon, F. (1967) *Black Skin, White Masks*, London: Pluto.

Feagin, J.R. (2020) *The White Racial Frame: Centuries of Racial Framing and Counter-Framing* (3rd edn), Abingdon: Routledge.

Ferreira da Silva, D. (2015) 'Before Man: Sylvia Wynter's rewriting of the modern episteme', in K. McKittrick (ed) *Sylvia Wynter: On Being Human as Praxis*, London: Duke University Press, pp 90–105.

Finney, N., Nazroo, J., Bécares, L., Kapadia, D. and Shlomo, N. (2023) *Racism and Ethnic Inequality in a Time of Crisis: Findings from the Evidence for Equality National Survey*, Bristol: Policy Press.

Fisher, M. (2009) *Capitalist Realism. Is There No Alternative?*, Winchester: Zero.

Fisher, M. (2014) *Ghosts of My Life: Writings on Depression, Hauntology and Lost Futures*, Winchester: Zero.

Fredricksen, P. (2018) *When Christians Were Jews: The First Generation*, London: Yale University Press.

Fryer, P. (1984) *Staying Power: The History of Black People in Britain*, London: Pluto.

Frykholm, A.J. (2004) *Rapture Culture: Left Behind in Evangelical America*, New York: Oxford University Press.

Gay, R. (2014) *Bad Feminist*, London: Corsair.

Gentleman, A. (2020) *The Windrush Betrayal: Exposing the Hostile Environment*, London: Guardian Faber.

Gentleman, A. (2023) 'Stringing us along: Windrush u-turns let down those whose lives were ruined', *The Guardian*, [online] 26 January, Available from: https://www.theguardian.com/uk-news/2023/jan/26/stringing-us-along-windrush-u-turns-disappoint-those-whose-lives-were-ruined [Accessed 26 January 2023].

Gibson, N.C. (2019) 'Toward a radical humanities for a radical humanity (for Lewis R. Gordon)', in D. Davis (ed) *Black Existentialism: Essays on the Transformative Thought of Lewis R. Gordon*, London: Rowman and Littlefield, pp 7–24.

Gillborn, D. (2005) 'Education policy as an act of white supremacy: whiteness, critical race theory and education reform', *Journal of Education Policy*, 20(4): 485–505.

Gillborn, D. (2008) *Racism and Education: Coincidence or Conspiracy?*, Abingdon: Routledge.

Gillborn, D. (2010) 'The White working class, racism and respectability: victims, degenerates and interest-convergence', *British Journal of Educational Studies*, 58(1): 2–25.

Gillborn, D. (2024) *White Lies: Racism, Education and Critical Race Theory*, London: Routledge.

Gillborn, D., Warmington, P. and Demack, S. (2018) 'QuantCrit: education, policy, "big data" and principles for a critical race theory of statistics', *Race Ethnicity and Education*, 21(2): 158–79.

Gillborn, D., McGimpsey, I. and Warmington, P. (2022) 'The fringe is the centre: racism, pseudoscience and authoritarianism in the dominant English education policy network', *International Journal of Educational Research*, 115: 1–16.

Gillborn, D., Rollock, N., Warmington, P. and Demack, S. (2016) *Race, Racism and Education: Inequality, Resilience and Reform in Policy and Practice*. Report to Society for Educational Studies, Birmingham: University of Birmingham.

Gillborn, D., Demack, S., Rollock, N. and Warmington, P. (2017) 'Moving the goalposts: education policy and twenty-five years of the black/white achievement gap', *British Educational Research Journal*, 43(5): 848–74.

Gilroy, P. (1993) *The Black Atlantic: Modernity and Double Consciousness*, London: Verso.

Gilroy, P. (2000) *Against Race: Imagining Political Culture Beyond the Color Line*, Cambridge, MA: Harvard University Press.

Gilroy, P. (2004) *After Empire: Melancholia or Convivial Culture?*, Abingdon: Routledge.

Girvan, A. (2018) 'The history of British immigration policy (1905–2016) Timeline Resource, June 2018', *Refugee History* [online], Available from: https://docslib.org/doc/10765729/the-history-of-british-immigration-policy-1905-2016-timeline-resource-june-2018 [Accessed 10 January 2023].

Giusti, S. (2022) *The Fall and Rise of National Interest: A Contemporary Approach*, London: Palgrave Macmillan.

Goldberg, D.T. (2015) *Are We All Postracial Yet?*, Cambridge: Polity.

Goldberg, D.T. (2021) 'The war on Critical Race Theory', *Boston Review*, [online] 7 May, Available from: https://www.bostonreview.net/articles/the-war-on-critical-race-theory/ [Accessed 13 December 2022].

Goodfellow, M. (2019) *Hostile Environment: How Immigrants Became Scapegoats*, London: Verso.

Goodfellow, M. (2022) 'Labour have always been just as bad as Tories', *Novara Media*, [online] 13 November, Available from: https://novaramedia.com/2022/11/13/immigration-labour-have-always-been-just-as-bad-as-tories-ash-meets-maya-goodfellow/ [Accessed 8 March 2023].

Goodhart, D. (2013) *The British Dream: Successes and Failures of Post-War Immigration*, London: Atlantic.

Goodhart, D. (2017) *The Road to Somewhere: The New Tribes Shaping British Politics*, London: Hurst and Co.

Goodhart, D. (2021) 'The Sewell commission is a game-changer for how Britain talks about race', *Policy Exchange*, [online] 30 March, Available from: https://policyexchange.org.uk/blogs/the-sewell-commission-is-a-game-changer-for-how-britain-talks-about-race/ [Accessed 28 February 2022].

Goodwin, M. (2023) *Values, Voice and Virtue: The New British Politics*, London: Penguin.

Gordon, L.R. (1995) *Fanon and the Crisis of European Man: An Essay on Philosophy and the Human Sciences*, London: Routledge.

Gordon, L.R. (2011) 'A short history of the "Critical" in Critical Race Theory', *American Philosophy Association Newsletter, Habermas.org* [online], Available from: http://dearhabermas.org/critraceth01bk.htm [Accessed 21 February 2023].

Gordon, L.R. (2015) *What Fanon Said: A Philosophical Introduction to his Life and Thought*, New York: Fordham University Press.

Gordon, L.R. (2022) *Fear of Black Consciousness*, London: Allen Lane.

Graham, D.A. (2012) 'Breitbart.com's massive Barack Obama-Derrick Bell video fail', *The Atlantic*, [online] 8 March, Available from: https://www.theatlantic.com/politics/archive/2012/03/breitbartcoms-massive-barack-obama-derrick-bell-video-fail/254213/ [Accessed 24 February 2023].

Grant, C.A., Woodson, A.N. and Dumas, M.J. (eds) (2021) *The Future is Black: Afropessimism, Fugitivity, and Radical Hope in Education*, London: Routledge.

Grice, A. (2001) 'Blunkett under fire for backing "British norms"', *The Independent*, [online] 10 December, Available from: https://www.independent.co.uk/news/uk/politics/blunkett-under-fire-for-backing-british-norms-9256806.html [Accessed 15 December 2022].

Gunaratnam, Y. (2003) *Researching 'Race' and Ethnicity: Methods, Knowledge and Power*, London: Sage.

Hall, M. (2009) 'Muslim schools ban our culture', *Express*, [online] 20 February, Available from: https://www.express.co.uk/news/uk/85553/Muslim-schools-ban-our-culture [Accessed 30 July 2023].

Hall, S. (1996) 'Cultural studies and its theoretical legacies', in D. Morley and K-H. Chen (eds) *Stuart Hall: Critical Dialogues*, Abingdon: Routledge, pp 261–74.

Hall, S. and Jhally, S. (1997) *Race, The Floating Signifier: Transcript*, Northampton: Media Education Foundation.

Hall, S. (with Schwarz, B.) (2017) *Familiar Stranger: A Life Between Two Islands*, London: Allen Lane.

Hall, S., Critcher, C., Jefferson, T., Clarke, J. and Roberts, B. (1978) *Policing the Crisis: Mugging, the State, and Law and Order*, Basingstoke: Macmillan.

Han, C. (2008) 'No fats, femmes, or Asians: the utility of critical race theory in examining the role of gay stock stories in the marginalization of gay Asian men', *Contemporary Justice Review*, 11(1): 11–22.

Hanley, L. (2017) 'Class is not a black and white issue', *The Guardian*, 23 March, pp 6–9.

Harney, S. and Moten, F. (2013) *The Undercommons: Fugitive Planning and Black Study*, Brooklyn: Minor Compositions.

Harris, A. (2021) 'The GOP's "Critical Race Theory" obsession', *The Atlantic*, [online] 7 May, Available from: https://www.theatlantic.com/politics/archive/2021/05/gops-critical-race-theory-fixation-explained/618828/ [Accessed 8 March 2023].

Harris, S. (2016) 'Betrayal of white pupils', *Daily Mail*, and 'Pupils let down by their parents', *Mail Online*, [online] 4 April, Available from: https://www.dailymail.co.uk/news/article-3521989/Betrayal-white-pupils-16-white-British-children-lag-12-ethnic-groups-alarming-report-says-let-schools-parents.html [Accessed 31 July 2023].

Hartman, S. (2021) *Lose Your Mother: A Journey Along the Atlantic Slave Route*, London: Serpent's Tail.

References

Harvard Law School News (2011) 'Derrick Bell (1930–2011): an iconoclast and a community builder', *Harvard Law Bulletin*, [online] Winter 2012, Available from: https://hls.harvard.edu/today/derrick-bell-1930-2011/ [Accessed 18 March 2021].

Heath, A.F. and Di Stasio, V. (2019) 'Racial discrimination in Britain, 1969–2017: a meta-analysis of field experiments on racial discrimination in the British labour market', *British Journal of Sociology*, 70(5): 1774–98.

Henehan, K. and Rose, H. (2018) *Opportunities Knocked? Exploring Pay Penalties among the UK's Ethnic Minorities*, London: Resolution Foundation.

Henry, J. (2020) 'White working-class children are UK's most deprived pupils – and they'll be hardest hit by Covid fallout too, researchers warn MPs', *Mail Online*, [online] 19 September, Available from: https://www.dailymail.co.uk/news/article-8751131/White-working-class-children-UKs-deprived-pupils-MPs-warned.html [Accessed 31 July 2023].

Henry, K.L. and Powell, S.N. (2021) 'Kissing cousins: Critical Race Theory's racial realism and Afropessimism's social death', in C.A. Grant, A.N. Woodson and M.J. Dumas (eds) *The Future is Black: Afropessimism, Fugitivity, and Radical Hope in Education*, London: Routledge, pp 79–86.

Hensher, P. (2017) 'How the straight majority still silences gay people', *The Guardian*, 22 July, p 33.

Higgins, T.E. (1992) 'Derrick Bell's radical realism', *Fordham Law Review*, 61(3): 683–92.

Hirsch, A. (2018) *Brit(ish): On Race, Identity and Belonging*, London: Jonathan Cape.

Hirsch, S. (2019) *In the Shadow of Enoch Powell: Race, Locality and Resistance*, Manchester: Manchester University Press.

Hogan, B. (2018) 'Derrick Bell's dilemma', *Berkeley Journal of African-American Law and Policy*, 20(1): 1–26.

Holland, D., Lachicotte, W., Skinner, D. and Cain, C. (1998) *Identity and Agency in Cultural Worlds*, Cambridge, MA: Harvard University Press.

Home Office (2022) *Policy paper – Protest Powers: Police, Crime, Sentencing and Courts Act 2022 Factsheet*, [online], Available from: https://www.gov.uk/government/publications/police-crime-sentencing-and-courts-bill-2021-factsheets/police-crime-sentencing-and-courts-bill-2021-protest-powers-factsheet [Accessed 12 January 2023].

House of Commons Education Committee (2021) *The Forgotten: How White Working-Class Pupils Have Been Let Down, and How to Change It. First Report of Session 2021–22*. HC85, London: House of Commons.

Hughey, M.H. (2014) 'White backlash in the "post-racial" United States', *Ethnic and Racial Studies*, 37(5): 721–30.

Hylton, K., Pilkington, A., Warmington, P. and Housee, S. (eds) (2011) *Atlantic Crossings: International Dialogues on Critical Race Theory*, Birmingham: CSAP/Higher Education Academy.

Ignatiev, N. (2008) *How the Irish Became White*, London: Routledge.

INQUEST (2023) *I Can't Breathe: Race, Death and British Policing*, London: INQUEST.

Institute of Economic Affairs (IEA) (2020) 'Amy Gallagher sues woke NHS Tavistock Clinic – Parallax Views', *IEA* [online], Available from: https://iea.org.uk/films/amy-gallagher-sues-woke-nhs-tavistock-clinic-parallax-views/ [Accessed 1 August, 2023].

John, T. (2021) 'Campaigners slam UK government report into racial disparities as a "whitewash"', *CNN*, [online] 31 March, Available from: https://edition.cnn.com/2021/03/31/uk/uk-racial-disparity-report-intl-gbr/index.html [Accessed 20 November 2022].

Joint Parliamentary Committee on Human Rights (2020) *Black People, Racism and Human Rights: Eleventh Report of Session 2019–21*, HC 559/ HL Paper 165, London: House of Commons and the House of Lords.

Jones, O. (2020) *Chavs: The Demonization of the Working Class*, London: Verso.

Joseph-Salisbury, R., Connelly, L. and Wangari-Jones, P. (2021) '"The UK is not innocent": Black Lives Matter, policing and abolition in the UK', *Equality, Diversity and Inclusion*, 40(1): 21–8.

Judis, J. (2016) *The Populist Explosion: How the Great Recession Transformed American and European Politics*, New York: Columbia Global Reports.

Kelley, R.D.G. (1996) *Race Rebels: Culture, Politics, and the Black Working Class*, New York: Free Press.

Kelley, R.D.G. (2022) 'There are no utopias', *Throughline*, [online] 24 February, Available from: https://www.npr.org/2022/02/20/1082030426/there-are-no-utopias [Accessed 1 December 2022].

Kirp, D. (1979) *Doing Good by Doing Little: Race and Schooling in Britain*, Berkeley: University of California Press.

Klein, R. (2008) 'White and working class ... the one ethnic group the BBC has ignored', *Mail Online*, [online] 29 February, Available from: https://www.dailymail.co.uk/news/article-523351/White-working-class---ethnic-group-BBC-ignored.html [Accessed 8 March 2023].

Králová, J. (2015) 'What is social death?', *Contemporary Social Science*, 10(3): 235–48.

Kundnani, A. (2007) *The End of Tolerance: Racism in 21st Century Britain*, London: Pluto.

Kundnani, A. (2015) *The Muslims are Coming! Islamophobia, Extremism, and the Domestic War on Terror*, London: Verso.

Kundnani, A. (2020) '"What is racial capitalism?" Arun Kundnani on race, culture, and empire', *Kundnani.org*, [online] 23 October, Available from: https://www.kundnani.org/what-is-racial-capitalism/ [Accessed 26 April 2021].

Ladson-Billings, G. (1998) 'Just what is critical race theory and what's it doing in a nice field like education?', *International Journal of Qualitative Studies in Education*, 11(1): 7–24.

Ladson-Billings, G. (2013) 'Critical Race Theory – what it is not!', in M. Lynn and A.D. Dixson (eds) *Handbook of Critical Race Theory in Education*, New York: Routledge, pp 34–47.

Ladson-Billings, G. and Tate, W. (1995) 'Towards a Critical Race Theory of education', *Teachers College Record*, 97(1): 47–68.

Laing, O. (2020) *Funny Weather: Art in an Emergency*, London: Picador.

Lammy, D. (2017) *The Lammy Review: An Independent Review into the Treatment of, and Outcomes for, Black, Asian and Minority Ethnic Individuals in the Criminal Justice System*, London: Lammy Review.

Lander, V. (2016) 'Introduction to fundamental British values', *Journal of Education for Teaching*, 42(3): 274–9.

Lawrence, E. (1982) 'In the abundance of water the fool is thirsty: sociology and the black "pathology"', in Centre for Contemporary Cultural Studies (CCCS) (eds) *The Empire Strikes Back: Race and Racism in 70s Britain*, London: Hutchinson, pp 95–142.

Lentin, A. (2004) *Racism and Anti-Racism in Europe*, London: Pluto.

Lentin, A. (2020) *Why Race Still Matters*, Cambridge: Polity.

Lentin, A. (2021) 'The egregious Sewell report only bolsters those who want to discredit antiracism', *The Guardian*, [online] 6 April, Available from: https://www.theguardian.com/commentisfree/2021/apr/06/sewell-report-discredit-antiracism-racism [Accessed 20 December 2022].

Leonardo, Z. (2009) *Race, Whiteness and Education*, Abingdon: Routledge.

Leonardo, Z. (2011) 'After the Glow: race ambivalence and other educational prognoses', *Educational Philosophy and Theory*, 43(6): 675–98.

Leonardo, Z. (2012) 'The race for class: reflections on a Critical Raceclass Theory of education', *Educational Studies*, 48(5): 427–49.

Leonardo, Z. and Manning, L. (2017) 'White historical activity theory: toward a critical understanding of white zones of proximal development', *Race Ethnicity and Education*, 200(1): 15–29.

Lipman, P. (2011) *The New Political Economy of Urban Education: Neoliberalism, Race, and the Right to the City*, New York: Routledge.

Lipsiszt, G. (2019) 'The sounds of silence: how race neutrality preserves white supremacy', in K.W. Crenshaw, L.C. Harris, D.M. HoSang and G. Lipsitz (eds) *Seeing Race Again: Countering Colorblindness across the Disciplines*, Oakland: University of California Press, pp 128–51.

Little, A. (2011) 'Migrants grab 12,000 jobs a month', *Express*, [online] 17 November, Available from: https://www.express.co.uk/news/uk/284200/Migrants-grab-12-000-jobs-a-month [Accessed 30 July 2023].

Lorde, A. (2017) *The Master's Tools Will Never Dismantle the Master's House*, London: Penguin Modern.

Lothian-McLean, M. (2020) 'Fury as Afua Hirsch calls out Britain's racism and Nick Ferrari asks: "Why do you stay in this country?"' *indy100*, [online] 10 June, Available from: https://www.indy100.com/news/afua-hirsch-nick-ferrari-sky-news-statues-racism-black-lives-matter-9558071 [Accessed 20 April 2022].

Macpherson, W. (1999) *The Stephen Lawrence Inquiry: Report of an Inquiry by Sir William Macpherson of Cluny*, Cmd 4262, London: Home Office.

Malcolmson, S. (2000) *One Drop of Blood: The American Misadventure of Race*, New York: Farrar, Straus, Giroux.

Malik, K. (2009) *From Fatwa to Jihad: The Rushdie Affair and its Legacy*, London: Atlantic.

Malik, N. (2021) 'The right is winning the culture war because its opponents don't know the rules', *The Guardian*, [online] 19 July, Available from: https://www.theguardian.com/commentisfree/2021/jul/19/right-winning-culture-war [Accessed 10 December 2022].

Malik, N. (2022a) 'For Labour and the Conservatives, racism is really all about reputation management', *The Guardian*, [online] 2 January, Available from: https://www.theguardian.com/commentisfree/2022/jan/02/labour-conservatives-racism-stephen-lawrence-inquiry-rightwing-press [Accessed 10 December 2022].

Malik, N. (2022b) 'The Colston Four's critics are deluded to think Britain owes no apology for its past', *The Guardian*, [online] 10 January, Available from: https://www.theguardian.com/commentisfree/2022/jan/10/colston-four-britain-apology-for-past [Accessed 27 December 2022].

Malik, N. (2023) 'Is a British pub racist for displaying golliwogs? Think how that question makes people of colour like me feel', *The Guardian*, [online] 17 April, Available from: https://www.theguardian.com/commentisfree/2023/apr/17/british-pub-right-golliwogs-rightwing-politicians-press-racism-people-colour [Accessed 16 June 2023].

Manning, A. and Rose, R. (2021) 'Ethnic minorities and the UK labour market: are things getting better?', *Economics Observatory* [online], Available from: https://www.economicsobservatory.com/ethnic-minorities-and-the-uk-labour-market-are-things-getting-better [Accessed 9 March 2023].

Mansell, W. (2021) 'Government's race report failed to include findings saying pupils experience discrimination, in education research it commissioned', *Education Uncovered*, [online] 21 July, Available from: https://www.educationuncovered.co.uk/news/151671/governments-race-report-failed-to-include-findings-saying-pupils-experience-discrimination-in-education-research-it-commissioned.thtml [Accessed 5 February 2022].

Marsh, J. (2011) *Class Dismissed: Why We Cannot Teach our Way out of Inequality*, New York: Monthly Review Press.

Marx, K. (1883/1976) *Capital: A Critique of Political Economy, Volume 1*, London: Penguin.

Mason, P. (2020) 'The Tories aim to get through the pandemic by blaming the public', *New Statesman*, [online] 23 December, Available from: https://www.newstatesman.com/politics/2020/12/the-tories-aim-to-get-through-the-pandemic-by-blaming-the-public [Accessed 8 March 2023].

Mbembe, A. (2019) *Necropolitics*, Durham, NC: Duke University Press.

McWhorter, J. (2021) 'Race in America: John McWhorter on how Critical Race Theory poorly serves its intended beneficiaries', *The Economist*, [online] 24 May, Available from: https://www.economist.com/by-invitation/2021/05/24/john-mcwhorter-on-how-critical-race-theory-poorly-serves-its-intended-beneficiaries [Accessed 3 March 2023].

Meer, N., Akhtar, S. and Davidson, N. (eds) (2020) *Taking Stock: Race Equality in Scotland*, London: Runnymede.

Mills, C.W. (2022) *The Racial Contract*, London: Cornell University Press.

Ministry of Justice (2007) *The Governance of Britain*. CM7170, presented to Parliament by the Secretary of State for Justice and Lord Chancellor July 2007, Norwich: HMSO.

Modood, T. (2005) 'A defence of multiculturalism', *Soundings*, 29 [online], Available from: https://journals.lwbooks.co.uk/soundings/vol-2005-issue-29/ [Accessed 9 March 2023].

Mohdin, A. and Walker, P. (2021) 'Bodies credited in UK race review distance themselves from findings', *The Guardian*, [online] 12 April, Available from: https://www.theguardian.com/world/2021/apr/12/bodies-credited-in-uk-race-review-distance-themselves-from-findings [Accessed 20 December 2022].

Morrison, T. (2019) *Mouth Full of Blood: Essays, Speeches and Meditations*, London: Chatto and Windus.

Mosley, H. (1978) 'The new Communist opposition: Rudolf Bahro's critique of the "Really Existing Socialism"', *New German Critique*, 15(Autumn): 25–36.

Moten, F. (2008) 'The case of blackness', *Criticism*, 50(2): 177–218.

NatCon UK (2023) 'National Conservatism: A Conference in London, UK, May 15–17 2023 – About NatCon UK', *National Conservatism* [online], Available from: https://nationalconservatism.org/natcon-uk-2023/about/ [Accessed 17 May 2023].

National Archives (2023) *Immigration: Primary and Secondary Legislation*, *legislation.gov.uk* [online], Available from: https://www.legislation.gov.uk/primary+secondary?title=immigration [Accessed 1 February 2023].

Nelson, F. (2020) 'Kemi Badenoch: the problem with critical race theory', *The Spectator*, [online] 24 October, Available from: https://www.spectator.co.uk/article/kemi-badenoch-the-problem-with-critical-race-theory/ [Accessed 5 January 2023].

Nicholson, K. (2022) 'Rishi Sunak's latest plan to punish those who "vilify" UK is being completely torn apart', *Huffpost*, [online] 3 August, Available from: https://www.huffingtonpost.co.uk/entry/rishi-sunak-tory-leadership-policy-torn-apart_uk_62ea4a54e4b00f4cf235e32e [Accessed 5 March 2023].

Office for National Statistics [ONS] (2020) 'Why have black and South Asian people been hit hardest by COVID-19?', *Office for National Statistics* [online], Available from: https://www.ons.gov.uk/peoplepopulationandcommunity/healthandsocialcare/conditionsanddiseases/articles/whyhaveblackandsouthasianpeoplebeenhithardestbycovid19/2020-12-14 [Accessed 28 February 2023].

ONS (2023) 'Cost of living latest insights', *Office for National Statistics* [online], Available from: https://www.ons.gov.uk/economy/inflationandpriceindices/articles/costofliving/latestinsights [Accessed 9 March 2023].

Olaloku-Teriba, A. (2018) 'Afro-Pessimism and the (un)logic of anti-blackness', *Historical Materialism*, 26(2): 96–122.

Olusoga, D. (2017) 'Bristol's Colston Hall is an affront to a multicultural city. Let's rename it now', *The Observer*, 26 February, p 33.

Olusoga, D. (2019) 'I was born black and working class. The identities need not be in opposition' *The Observer*, [online] 13 April, Available from: https://www.theguardian.com/commentisfree/2019/apr/13/i-was-born-black-and-working-class-the-identities-need-not-be-in-opposition [Accessed 2 January 2023].

Olusoga, D. (2021) *Black and British: A Forgotten History*, London: Picador.

Oluwole, F. (2020) 'Boris Johnson wants to "change the narrative" on racism, but he isn't prepared to change the reality', *iNews*, [online] 30 July, Available from: https://inews.co.uk/opinion/boris-johnson-wants-to-change-the-narrative-on-racism-but-he-isnt-prepared-to-change-the-reality-564058 [Accessed 18 February 2023].

Omi, M. and Winant, H. (1986) *Racial Formation in the United States: From the 1960s to the 1980s*, New York: Routledge.

O'Toole, F. (2019) *Heroic Failure: Brexit and the Politics of Pain*, London: Head of Zeus.

Outlaw, L. (1996) *On Race and Philosophy*, London: Routledge.

Parekh, B. (2000) *The Future of Multi-Ethnic Britain: Report of the Commission on the Future of Multi-Ethnic Britain*, London: Profile.

Parekh, B. (2006) *Rethinking Multiculturalism: Cultural Diversity and Political Theory* (2nd edn), Basingstoke: Palgrave Macmillan.

Parker, L. and Gillborn, D. (eds) (2020) *Critical Race Theory in Education*, London: Routledge.

Patterson, O. (1965/1986) *The Children of Sisyphus*, Harlow: Longman.

Patterson, O. (1982/2018) *Slavery and Social Death: A Comparative Study*, Cambridge, MA: Harvard University Press.

Patterson, O. (2019) 'The denial of slavery in contemporary American sociology', *Theory and Society*, 48: 903–14.

Phillips, M. (2020) '"Taking a knee" to the destroyers of worlds', *Melaniephillips.com*, [online] 10 June, Available from: https://www.melaniephillips.com/taking-knee-destroyers-worlds/ [Accessed 28 December 2022].

Poku, V. (2022) *Black Student Teachers' Experiences of Racism in the White School: Strategies of Resilience and Survival*, Cham: Palgrave Macmillan.

Police, Crime, Sentencing and Courts Act (2022) [online], Available from: https://www.legislation.gov.uk/ukpga/2022/32/contents [Accessed 27 July 2023].

Pollock, M. (2004) *Colormute: Race Talk Dilemmas in an American School*, Princeton: Princeton University Press.

Postone, M. (1996) *Time, Labor and Social Domination: A Reinterpretation of Marx's Critical Theory*, New York: Cambridge University Press.

Powell, E. (1968) 'Rivers of Blood', speech to Conservative Party Association, Birmingham, 20 April, reprinted in *The Telegraph*, [online] 6 November 2007, Available from: http://www.telegraph.co.uk/comment/3643823/Enoch-Powells-Rivers-of-Blood-speech.html [Accessed 21 February 2023].

Preston, J. (2008) *Whiteness and Class in Education*, Dordrecht: Springer.

Public Health England (2020) *Beyond the Data: Understanding the Impact of COVID-19 on BAME Groups*, London: Public Health England.

Race Disparity Audit (2018) *Summary Findings from the Ethnicity Facts and Figures Website*, London: Cabinet Office.

Race Relations (Amendment) Act (2000) [online], Available from: https://www.legislation.gov.uk/ukpga/2000/34/contents [Accessed 26 July 2023].

R.L. (2013) 'Wanderings of the slave: black life and social death', *Mute*, [online] 13 June, Available from: https://www.metamute.org/editorial/articles/wanderings-slave-black-life-and-social-death [Accessed 9 March 2023].

Ramdin, R. (1987) *The Making of the Black Working Class in Britain*, Aldershot: Wildwood House.

Rattansi, A. (2011) *Multiculturalism: A Very Short Introduction*, Oxford: Oxford University Press.

Rawlinson, K. and Davies, C. (2021) 'Downing Street initially opposed Stephen Lawrence inquiry', *The Guardian*, [online] 30 December, Available from: https://www.theguardian.com/uk-news/2021/dec/30/downing-street-initially-opposed-stephen-lawrence-inquiry [Accessed 30 December 2021].

Robinson, C. (1983) *Black Marxism: The Making of the Black Radical Tradition*, London: Zed.

Robinson, C. (2019) *On Racial Capitalism, Black Internationalism and Cultures of Resistance* (edited by H.L.T. Quan), London: Pluto.

Robinson, C. (2020a) 'Beware Critical Race Theory – the divisive ideology infiltrating school history lessons', *The Telegraph*, [online] 1 October, Available from: https://www.telegraph.co.uk/news/2020/10/01/beware-critical-race-theory-divisive-ideology-infiltrating/ [Accessed 1 August 2023].

Robinson, C. (2020b) 'Time to end the teaching of divisive critical race theory in British schools', *The Telegraph*, [online] 21 October, Available from: https://www.telegraph.co.uk/news/2020/10/21/time-end-teaching-divisive-critical-race-theory-british-schools/ [Accessed 1 August, 2023].

Rubin, D.I. (2020) 'Hebcrit: a new dimension of critical race theory', *Social Identities*, 26(4): 499–514.

Rufo, C.F. (2021) 'What critical race theory is really about', *New York Post*, [online] 6 May, Available from: https://nypost.com/2021/05/06/what-critical-race-theory-is-really-about/ [Accessed 3 March 2023].

Runnymede Trust (1980) *Britain's Black Population*, London: Heinemann.

Rutherford, A. (2020) *How to Argue with a Racist: History, Science, Race and Reality*, London: Weidenfield and Nicolson.

Saed (2016) 'The enduring relevance of state-socialism', *Capitalism Nature Socialism*, 27(4): 1–15.

Saini, A. (2019) *Superior: The Return of Race Science*, London: 4th Estate.

Scarman, Lord L.G. (1981) *The Scarman Report: The Brixton Disorders 10–12 April 1981*, Harmondsworth: Pelican.

Schuessler, J. (2021) 'Bans on critical race theory threaten free speech, advocacy group says', *New York Times*, [online] 9 November, Available from: https://www.nytimes.com/2021/11/08/arts/critical-race-theory-bans.html [Accessed 8 March 2023].

Select Committee on Race Relations and Immigration (SCRRI) (1977) *Report on the West Indian Community*, London: HMSO.

Sexton, J. (2016) 'Afro-pessimism: the unclear word', *Rhizomes: Cultural Studies in Emerging Knowledge*, 29 [online], Available from: http://www.rhizomes.net/issue29/sexton.html [Accessed 23 February 2023].

Shariamadari, D. (2015) 'Swarms, floods and marauders: the toxic metaphors of the migration debate', *The Guardian*, [online] 10 August, Available from: https://www.theguardian.com/commentisfree/2015/aug/10/migration-debate-metaphors-swarms-floods-marauders-migrants [Accessed 7 January 2023].

Shelby, T. (2022) Foreword to Mills, C.W. *The Racial Contract*, 25th anniversary edition with new material, London: Cornell University Press.

Shipman, T. and Doyle, J. (2013) '4,000 foreign criminals including murderers and rapists we can't throw out … and, yes, you can blame human rights again', *Mail Online*, [online] 2 January, Available from: https://www.dailymail.co.uk/news/article-2256285/4-000-foreign-criminals-including-murderers-rapists-throw--yes-blame-human-rights-again.html [Accessed 30 July 2023].

Singh, N.P. (2015) 'A note on race and the left', *Social Text*, [online] 31 July, Available from: https://socialtextjournal.org/a-note-on-race-and-the-left/ [Accessed 23 February 2023].

Sivanandan, A. (1982) *A Different Hunger: Writings on Black Resistance*, London: Pluto.

Social Metrics Commission (SMC) (2020) *Measuring Poverty 2020: A Report of the Social Metrics Commission*, London: SMC.

Solórzano, D.G. and Bernal, D.D. (2001) 'Examining transformational resistance through a Critical Race and Latcrit Theory framework: Chicana and Chicano students in an urban context', *Urban Education*, 36(3): 308–42.

Sriprakash, A., Rudolph, S. and Gerrard, J. (2022) *Learning Whiteness: Education and the Settler Colonial State*, London: Pluto.

St. Louis, B. (2007) *Rethinking Race, Politics, and Poetics: C.L.R. James' Critique of Modernity*, London: Routledge.

Starmer, K. (2022) Contribution to Prime Minister's Engagements, debated 26 October, *Hansard* Vol. 721 [online], Available from: https://hansard.parliament.uk/Commons/2022-10-26/debates [Accessed 18 February 2023].

Stout, C. and Wilburn, T. (2022) 'CRT map: efforts to restrict teaching racism and bias have multiplied across the US', *Chalkbeat*, [online] 2 February, Available from: https://www.chalkbeat.org/22525983/map-critical-race-theory-legislation-teaching-racism [Accessed 3 March 2023].

Sturge, G. (2022) *UK Prison Population Statistics: Research Briefing, 25 October*, London: House of Commons Library.

Swann, M. (1985) *The Swann Report. Education for All: Report of the Committee of Enquiry into the Education of Children from Ethnic Minority Groups*, London: HMSO.

Sveinsson, K.P. (2009) 'Introduction: The white working class and multiculturalism. Is there space for a progressive agenda?' in K.P. Sveinsson (ed) *Who Cares about the White Working Class?*, London: Runnymede Trust, pp 3–6.

Taylor, B. (2020) *Real Life*, London: Daunt.

Taylor, E., Gillborn, D. and Ladson-Billings, G. (eds) (2023) *Foundations of Critical Race Theory in Education* (3rd edn), Abingdon: Routledge, pp 1–16.

Thomas, T. (2021) 'Black youth unemployment rate of 40% similar to time of Brixton riots, data shows', *The Guardian*, [online] 11 April, Available from: https://www.theguardian.com/society/2021/apr/11/black-youth-unemployment-rate-brixton-riots-covid [Accessed 12 April 2023].

Timms, S. and Caddick, D. (2022) 'Losing the inflation race: poorly targeted policy is failing to prevent an income crisis', *New Economics Foundation*, [online] 5 May, Available from: https://neweconomics.org/2022/05/losing-the-inflation-race [Accessed 9 March 2023].

Tomlinson, S. (2018) 'Enoch Powell, empires, immigrants and education', *Race Ethnicity and Education*, 21(1): 1–14.

Tomlinson, S. (2019) *Education and Race: From Empire to Brexit*, Bristol: Policy Press.

Toscano, A. (2023) 'Gramsci in Florida: how the US right stole the ideas of the Italian Marxist in its war on the woke', *New Statesman*, [online] 4 March, Available from: https://www.newstatesman.com/the-weekend-essay/2023/03/gramsci-florida-republican-party [Accessed 7 March 2023].

Unger, R.M. (2015) *The Critical Legal Studies Movement: Another Time, A Greater Task*, London: Verso.

Vann, K. (2006) 'Learning into labor', *Psychologie and Gesellschaftskritik*, 30(1): 73–110.

Vieler-Porter, C.G. (2022) *The Under-Representation of Black and Minority Ethnic Educators in Education: Chance, Coincidence or Design?*, London: Routledge.

Virdee, S. and McGeever, B. (2018) 'Racism, crisis, Brexit', *Ethnic and Racial Studies*, 41(10): 1802–19.

Vought, R. (2020) *Training in the Federal Government: Memorandum for The Heads Of Executive Departments and Agencies, 4 September*, Washington DC: Office of the President.

Walker, B. (2023) 'Rishi Sunak at day 100: the least popular prime minister in recent history', *New Statesman*, [online] 2 February, Available from: https://sotn.newstatesman.com/2023/02/rishi-sunak-day-100-least-popular-prime-minister [Accessed 18 February 2023].

Wallace-Wells, B. (2021) 'How a conservative activist invented the conflict over critical race theory', *New Yorker*, [online] 18 June, Available from: https://www.newyorker.com/news/annals-of-inquiry/how-a-conservative-activist-invented-the-conflict-over-critical-race-theory [Accessed 20 December 2022].

Warmington, P. (2009) 'Taking race out of scare quotes: race conscious social analysis in an ostensibly post-racial world', *Race Ethnicity and Education*, 12(3): 281–96.

Warmington, P. (2011) '"Some of my best friends are Marxists": CRT, sociocultural theory and the "figured worlds" of race', in K. Hylton, A. Pilkington, P. Warmington and S. Housee (eds) *Atlantic Crossings: International Dialogues on Critical Race Theory*, Birmingham, CSAP/Higher Education Academy, pp 262–83.

Warmington, P. (2012) '"A tradition in ceaseless motion": Critical Race Theory and black British intellectual spaces', *Race, Ethnicity & Education*, 15(11): 5–21.

Warmington, P. (2014) *Black British Intellectuals and Education: Multiculturalism's Hidden History*, London: Routledge.

Warmington, P. (2015a) 'Dystopian social theory and education', *Educational Theory*, 65(3): 265–81.

Warmington, P. (2015b) 'The emergence of black British social conservatism', *Ethnic and Racial Studies*, 38(7): 1152–68.

Warmington, P. (2020) 'Critical Race Theory in England: impact and opposition', *Identities: Global Studies in Culture and Power*, 27(1): 20–37.

Warmington, P. and Grosvenor, I. (2011) '"A very historical mode of understanding": examining editorial and ethnographic relations in The Primary (2008)', *Paedagogica Historica*, 47(4): 543–58.

Warmington, P., Gillborn, D., Rollock, N. and Demack, S. (2018) '"They can't handle the race agenda": stakeholders' reflections on race and education policy, 1993–2013', *Educational Review*, 70(4): 409–26.

Watts, K. (2022) 'Colston 4 judgment: "The government is tearing up our protest rights"', *Bristol Cable*, [online] 28 September, Available from: https://thebristolcable.org/2022/09/colston-4-judgement-the-government-is-tearing-up-our-protest-rights/ [Accessed 28 December 2022].

Wearing, D. (2021) 'The right are panicking about anti-racism – as well they should be', *Novara Media*, [online] 24 July, Available from: https://novaramedia.com/2021/07/24/the-right-are-panicking-about-anti-racism-as-well-they-should-be/ [Accessed 15 August 2021].

Weigel, M. (2016) 'Political correctness: how the right invented a phantom enemy', *The Guardian*, 30 November, pp 31–3.

Welsh Government/Llywodraeth Cymru (2022) *Anti-racist Wales Action Plan*, Cardiff: Gov.Wales.

West, C. (1992) 'Nihilism in Black America', in M. Wallace and G. Dent (eds) *Black Popular Culture*, Seattle: Bay Press, pp 37–47.

Wiedorn, M. (2018) *Think Like an Archipelago: Paradox in the Work of Édouard Glissant*, Albany: SUNY.

Wilderson, F.B. (2015) 'Afropessimism and the end of redemption', *Humanities Futures* [online], Available from: https://humanitiesfutures.org/papers/afro-pessimism-end-redemption/ [Accessed 23 February 2023].

Wilderson, F.B. (2020) *Afropessimism*, New York: Liveright.

Wilderson, F.B., Spatzek, S. and von Gleich, P. (2016) '"The inside-outside of civil society": an interview with Frank B. Wilderson III', *Black Studies Papers* 2(1): 4–22.

Williams, Z. (2022) 'The phrase "white working class" is a fiction – so why are the Tories obsessed with it?', *The Guardian*, [online] 4 August, Available from: https://www.theguardian.com/commentisfree/2022/aug/04/white-working-class-fiction-tories-obsessed [Accessed 5 August 2022].

Willis, P. (1977) *Learning to Labour: How Working Class Kids Get Working Class Jobs*, Aldershot: Gower.

Winder, R. (2013) *Bloody Foreigners: The Story of Immigration to Britain*, London: Abacus.

Wynter, S. (2003) 'Unsettling the coloniality of being/power/truth/freedom: towards the human, after man, its overrepresentation – an argument', *New Centennial Review*, 3(3): 257–337.

Wynter, S. and McKittrick, K. (2015) 'Unparalleled catastrophe for our species? Or, to give humanness a different future: conversations', in K. McKittrick (ed) *Sylvia Wynter: On Being Human as Praxis*, London: Duke University Press, pp 9–89.

Younge, G. (2002) 'Britain is again white', *The Guardian*, 18 February, p 13.

Zamalin, A. (2019) *Black Utopia: The History of an Idea from Black Nationalism to Afrofuturism*, New York: Columbia University Press.

Index

A

Afrofuturism 62, 72, 73, 150
Afropessimism xvi, 16, 32, 42–4, 63, 72, 141–42
Afropessimism and the End of Redemption (Frank B. Wilderson) 42–3
After Empire (Paul Gilroy) 14–15
AIDS 96
Allen, Ernest 72
And We Are Not Saved: The Elusive Quest for Racial Justice (Derrick Bell) 46
Angiolini Review 82
antiracism
  antifascism and 14
  Bell and 50, 51, 52, 62, 67, 150
  Britain 42, 65, 87, 89, 92, 95–6, 98–100, 103, 109, 110–13, 117, 146, 148
  colourblindness and 49
  contra-antiracism and xvi–xvii, 9, 95, 96, 145
  CRED Report (2021) and 82
  criticism of xiv, xvii, 49, 63, 95, 101, 105, 107, 108, 109
  CRT 65, 70, 97, 103, 148
  decolonisation and xiv
  delegitimization of 81, 82–3, 95, 96
  'gone-too-far' xiii, xvii, 58, 95, 97, 113, 146
  institutional racism and 71
  multiculturalism and 89, 98, 109
  non-racism and 71, 116
  postracialism and 6, 9, 14, 58, 69, 72, 75, 94–6, 116, 117, 145, 146
Apple, Michael 28–9, 31
Asians
  BAME xv
  CRT and 3, 18, 34, 63
  first Asian PM in Britain 11, 114
  immigration xv, 120, 123, 128, 136
  meaning 24
  race and 28

B

Badenoch, Kemi 101, 102
BAME *see* Black, Asian and minority ethnic
Black, Asian and minority ethnic (BAME) xv, 79
Begum, Halima 81
Bell, Derrick
  antiracism and 50, 51, 52, 62, 67, 150
  civil rights movement and 51, 52, 55, 56, 144, 149
  colourblindness and 50, 91
  contradiction closure 5, 45, 47, 51, 67, 89, 149–50
  criticism of 62–3
  CRT and xii–xiii, xvi, 2–4, 16, 45, 53, 62
  cyclical progress and regression xiii, xiv, 51, 92
  early life 46
  economic theme 51, 54
  influence of Frantz Fanon 67
  interest convergence 45, 50, 55–7, 58, 89
  non-utopianism 52, 62, 73, 107, 149
  permanence of racism xiii, xvi, xvii, 2, 3–4, 32, 44, 45, 51, 52–3, 64–5, 144, 148–9
  pessimism 67, 149–50
  postracialism and xiii, xvi
  racial realism xvi, 3–4, 7, 16, 33, 44–5, 47, 50–2, 56, 62–3, 87, 149–50
Berkeley, Rob 93
Bhattacharyya, Gargi 38
Bhopal, Kalwant 74, 81
Black Atlantic thought
  Black disposability 61
  Britain and 17, 19–20, 66
  CRT and 16, 17, 22, 27, 65, 146
  influence of 17, 18, 19–20
  Marxism and 37, 39
  slavery and 23, 26
  social death and 43, 59, 140
Black Atlantic, The: Modernity and Double Consciousness (Paul Gilroy) 18
Black History Month 20, 59, 101, 102, 146
Black Marxism (Cedric Robinson) 26, 37–8
Black People, Racism and Human Rights (JCHR) 76
Black Skin, White Masks (Frantz Fanon) 52
Blacker, David J. 126–7
Black Lives Matter (BLM)
  2020 protests xii, xiii, xvii, 5, 7, 82, 101, 104, 110
  Britain and xiii–xiv, xvi, 49, 74, 75, 82, 95–6, 101, 103–4, 109, 110–13, 146–7
  Contra-antiracism and 95, 97, 99, 146
  contradiction closure and 112
  CRED Report (2021) and 75, 82
  'imported' from USA 20
  liberalism and 110–11, 112
  movement becoming prominent 13, 19, 98
  organisational sympathy with 85
  taking the knee 89, 101, 104, 110, 111

Black people
  accused of lack of aspiration 7, 103–4
  Britain
    Africans xv, 12, 18–20, 23, 26, 118, 120, 124, 135–6
    Caribbeans xv, 12–13, 18–20, 42, 78, 88, 118, 120, 122–4, 127–30, 132, 135–6, 139
  education and 13, 65, 82, 91–3, 129
  identity 36–7, 63–4, 72, 119, 129, 130, 140, 142
  immigration and xv, 10, 14, 20, 43, 65, 100, 118, 120, 122–3, 124–5, 126–8, 130–1, 135, 136
  multiculturalism and 9, 10, 128
  as racial category 23–8, 39–44
  police force and xiv, 13, 19, 76, 82, 90, 93, 128, 129
  poverty xvi, 9, 12–13
  slavery and 26
  social class matrix and xvii, 9, 117–8, 139
  terminology xv
  unemployment xiv, 9, 12, 85, 118, 128
  US (African-Americans) 19, 23, 25–6, 33, 40, 46, 52, 54–7, 61–3, 65, 119
  Working-class 129, 139–40
Blair, Tony 90
BLM *see* Black Lives Matter
Blunkett, David 133, 134, 142
Bonilla-Silva, Eduardo 7, 17, 85, 86, 91
Bourne, Jenny 69, 99, 125
Braverman, Suella 110
Brexit xvi, 15, 100, 125
Bristol bus boycott 88, 120
Britain
  antiracism 42, 65, 87, 89, 92, 95–6, 98–100, 103, 109, 110–13, 117, 146, 148
  Black Atlantic thought and 17, 19–20, 66
  Black people
    Africans xv, 12, 18, 19, 20, 23, 26, 118, 120, 124, 135, 136
    Caribbeans xv, 12–13, 18–20, 42, 78, 88, 118, 120, 122–4, 127–30, 132, 135–6, 139
  BLM and xiii–xiv, xvi, 49, 74, 75, 82, 95–6, 101, 103–4, 109, 110–13, 146–7
  capitalism 118, 126, 128, 134
  class matrix xii, xvii, 1, 9, 16, 29, 116, 117–19, 136, 139, 143
  'colour bar' 48
  colourblindness 49, 69, 70, 92, 129, 135
  contra-antiracism 83, 95, 96–7, 105, 109, 110, 116, 146, 148
  CRT and xvi, 16–20, 36, 45, 65–6, 95–8, 101–3, 109, 146, 147
  culture wars 9, 11, 83, 89, 97, 104–5, 111, 113, 146–8

  education 4, 65, 66, 82, 102, 126, 132, 138–9
  Empire xvi, 14–15
  exceptionalism 4, 18, 45, 145
  identity xii, 1, 10, 40, 100, 118–19, 121–2, 143
  inequalities 7, 12, 55, 79, 81–2, 86–7, 92–3, 101, 103, 128–9, 135
  interest convergence 87, 90–2, 95, 112, 122, 130–1
  Irish and 25
  multiculturalism 4–5, 9–10, 14, 76, 87–9, 92–3, 98–100, 109, 128, 131, 135–9, 146
  national interest 10, 121, 143
  postcolonial 14–15, 66
  postracialism xiv, 1–2, 5, 14, 16, 68, 69–87, 91, 94, 95–7, 116, 117, 143, 145, 146
  race relations legislation 87–8
  racism xiii, xiv, 1, 2, 9, 70, 77–85, 91, 93, 96, 115, 121, 123–4
  slavery 16, 19, 59, 89, 110, 114
  social class matrix xii, xvii, 1, 9
BritCrit 16, 18, 27, 66
British Nationality Act (UK 1948) 122
Brockway, Fenner 87
Brown, Gordon 88
Brown v. Board of Education 46, 49, 55–6, 57
Bryan, Beverley 117

C

Cameron, David 76, 138
Cantle Report 88, 92, 133–4
capitalism
  Britain 118, 126, 128, 134
  CLS and 47
  CRT and 38
  CTR and 35
  inequalities 36
  Marx and 8, 34, 35, 38
  racial xvi, 22, 26, 35, 37–9, 53, 60, 121, 141
  racism and 1, 35, 38, 39
  terminal 61, 126–7
  US 106
  violent 17
Carby, Hazel 4, 10, 37, 120–1
Carmichael, Stokely 84
Casey, Baroness Louise xiv, 79
CCCS *see* Centre for Contemporary Cultural Studies
Centre for Contemporary Cultural Studies (CCCS) 10, 37, 120, 128
Centre for Research on Race and Education (CRRE) 78, 91–3, 139
Césaire, Aimé 23, 44, 53
Chakrabarty, Namita 66
Christianity 59–60

Index

civil rights
  Bell and 51, 52, 55, 56, 144, 149
  contradiction closure and 51
  critique of 45, 47, 50, 51, 54, 64, 148–9
  legislation 14, 34, 39, 45–7, 49, 50, 51, 55, 56, 64
  movement xii, 41, 51, 53, 59–60, 108
  struggle 2, 3, 23, 34, 42, 51, 55, 64, 106
  USA xii, 14, 20, 23, 39, 41–2, 45–7, 49, 51
CLS *see* Critical Legal Studies
Coates, Ta–Nehisi 25–6
Collins, Michael 136
colonialism *see* imperialism
colourblindness
  antiracism and 49
  Britain 49, 69, 70, 92, 129, 135
  CRED Report (2021) and 7, 76, 79
  CRT and 3, 33, 47, 48–9, 108
  inequalities and 1, 5, 7
  law and 48–9, 50
  liberalism and 49, 71
  multiculturalism and 71
  non-racism and 71, 83
  postracialism and xii, 1, 5, 6–7, 70, 83, 115
  racism and 83, 85–7, 91, 115
  US 7, 49, 91
Colston, Edward xiv, 19, 82, 95, 97, 105, 109, 110, 113
Colston Four xvii, 109, 111, 112
Commission on Race and Ethnic Disparity xv, 75, 104
Commonwealth xv, 20, 87–8, 118, 120, 122–3, 125, 126, 128
Commonwealth Immigration Act (UK 1968) 122
conservativism 25, 34, 47, 49, 51, 54, 66, 76, 79–80, 89, 98, 105–6, 110, 147
contra-antiracism
  antiracism and xvi–xvii, 9, 95, 96, 145
  BLM and 95, 97, 99, 146
  Britain 83, 95, 96–7, 105, 109, 110, 116, 146, 148
  CRT and xvii, 95, 97, 109, 146
  culture wars and 9
  multiculturalism and xvii, 95
  postracialism and xii, xvii, 1, 70, 95, 96–7, 116, 145
  USA 102, 105, 109
contradiction closure
  abolition of slavery and 59
  Bell and 5, 45, 47, 51, 67, 89, 149–50
  BLM and 112
  civil rights and 51
  CRT and 3, 5, 10, 39, 45, 47, 58, 90
  Macpherson Report and 90–1
  postracialism and 5, 58, 91, 94
  symbolic achievements 5
  Windrush scandal and 130–1
COVID-19 xiv, 12, 15, 67, 81, 101, 112, 128

CRED *see* Commission on Race and Ethnic Disparity
CRED Report (2021)
  antiracism and 82
  Black unemployment and 12
  colourblindness and 7, 76, 79
  education and 75–6, 78, 81
  inequalities and 79, 81
  institutional racism and xv, 49, 70, 76–82
  Macpherson Report and 91
  postracialism and 9, 77
  response to BLM protests 75, 82
Crenshaw, Kimberlé 2, 3, 6, 7, 16, 27–8, 44, 45, 47, 48, 49, 84, 86, 87, 91, 108
CRRE *see* Centre for Research on Race and Education
Critical Race Theory (CRT)
  antiracism 65, 70, 97, 103, 148
  Bell and xii–xiii, xvi, 2–4, 16, 45, 53, 62
  Black Atlantic thought and 16, 17, 22, 27, 65, 146
  Britain and xvi, 16–20, 36, 45, 65–6, 95–8, 101–3, 109, 146, 147
  capitalism and 38
  CLS and 47, 48
  colourblindness and 3, 33, 47, 48–9, 108
  contra-antiracism and xvii, 95, 97, 109, 146
  contradiction closure 3, 5, 10, 39, 45, 47, 58, 90
  criticism of 51, 62–4, 98, 105–8, 109
  culture wars and 66, 67, 104
  education and 2–3, 16, 48, 58, 63, 65–6, 84, 101–2
  'imported' from US 101, 109
  institutional racism and 2, 4, 45, 54, 84–7
  interest convergence 3, 4, 10, 39, 45, 47, 58, 62, 122, 130
  liberalism and 102, 107, 108
  off-shoots 18, 34, 54, 63, 65
  origins 16, 17, 18, 39, 42, 45, 53
  permanence of racism 10, 33, 39, 45
  postracialism and 44, 98
  racial realism and 4, 14, 16, 33, 44, 50, 64
  racism and 33–4, 41, 84–5
  US xii, xvi, 2, 17, 18, 45, 65, 66, 98, 101, 105–8, 109
CRRE *see* Centre for Research on Race and Education
CRT *see* Critical Race Theory
Critical Theory of Race (CRT) 34–5, 36
CTR *see* Critical Theory of Race
culture wars 9, 11, 83, 89, 97, 104–5, 111, 113, 146–8

D

decolonisation xiv, 9, 98
Delgado, Richard 2, 24, 45, 49, 84
DiAngelo, Robin 103, 105, 107

DisCrit 18, 63
Dixson, Adrienne 65, 66
Douglass, Frederick 32
Dubois, W.E.B. 17, 18, 32, 33, 34, 41, 48, 108, 119
Duggan, Mark 93
Dumas, Michael 63

E

Eddo-Lodge, Reni 4, 85, 91, 103
education
  Asians and 81
  Black people and 13, 65, 82, 91–3, 129
  Britain 4, 65, 66, 82, 102, 126, 132, 138–9
  CRED Report (2021) 75–6, 78, 81
  CRT and 2–3, 16, 48, 58, 63, 65–6, 84, 101–2
  decolonisation and 9
  inequalities 6, 9, 29, 30, 48, 66, 81, 91–2, 93
  multiculturalism and 88
  postracialism and 6, 74
  racialisation and 30
  segregation and 46, 49, 55–6, 57
  White privilege and 112–13
  White working class and 112, 132, 138–9
EHRC *see* Equalities and Human Rights Commission
Emboaba Da Costa, Alexandre 73–4
Engels, Friedrich 8, 30, 34
Equalities and Human Rights Commission (EHRC) 130, 131
Equality Act (UK 2010) 88, 90
Essed, Philomena 36
Eurocentrism 27, 35, 37, 39
Everard, Sarah 79, 82

F

Faces at the Bottom of The Well: The Permanence of Racism (Derrick Bell) 45, 46, 51, 52–3, 54, 60, 65
Fanon, Frantz 2, 17, 18, 22, 26, 28, 33, 34, 37, 44, 46, 48, 52–4, 64, 67, 73, 108
Ferrari, Nick 114, 115
Ferreira da Silva, Denise 40–1
Fisher, Mark 8–9, 64, 65, 73, 149
Floyd, George 5, 13, 19, 20, 85, 101
Freeman, Alan 2, 45
Fryer, Peter 117

G

Garvey, Amy Ashwood 42
Garvey, Marcus 41, 42
Gay, Roxanne 104
Gibson, Nigel C. 41, 67
Gillborn, David 18, 24, 30, 51, 58, 65, 66, 78, 83, 90, 91, 105, 108, 146
Gilmore, Ruth Wilson 38, 72

Gilroy, Paul 14–15, 17, 18–19, 22, 26, 28, 37, 69, 72–3
Glissant, Édouard 23, 42
Goldberg, David Theo 5–6, 36, 70, 108
Goodfellow, Maya 120, 121, 122, 130
Goodhart, David 7, 80, 103, 137
Gordon, Lewis R. 17, 26, 32, 33, 36, 54, 75, 145
Gramsci, Antonio 17, 105
Grunwick strike 96, 120
Gunaratnam, Yasmin 71
Guru-Murthy, Krishnan 114
Gypsy, Roma and Traveller people 13, 139

H

Hall, Stuart 10, 25, 35, 37, 52, 59, 120, 134, 141
Hamilton, Charles 84
Hammond, Philip 138
Hanley, Lynsey 117, 135–6
Harman, Harriett 135
Harney, Stefano 72, 73
Harris, Adam 98
Harris, Cheryl 2, 45
Hartman, Saidiya 23, 34
Hayles, Maxie 94
Hazarika, Ayesha 114–15
Hensher, Philip 96
Hirsch, Afua 40, 114–15, 124
Housee, Shirin 66
Hylton, Kevin 66

I

Ignatiev, Noel 25
immigration
  Asians xv, 120, 123, 128, 136
  Black Atlantic thought and 17, 146
  Black people and xv, 10, 14, 20, 43, 65, 100, 118, 120, 122–3, 124–5, 126–8, 130–1, 135, 136
  Brexit and 100, 125
  Commonwealth xv, 20, 87, 88, 118, 120, 122–3, 125, 126, 128
  cultural diversity and 137
  media and 93, 96–7, 98–9, 138
  policies 4, 9, 11, 14, 15, 20, 87, 88, 89, 91, 121–3, 129–31
  racism and 1, 82, 123, 147
  White working class and 135–7
Immigration Control Act (UK 1962) 122
imperialism
  European 23, 39
  post- xvi, 10, 14–15, 16, 20, 66, 72, 119, 131
Independent Review into the Standards of Behaviour and Internal Culture of the Metropolitan Police Service (Baroness Louise Casey) 7, 79

Indians 29, 85, 124, 129
inequalities
  antiracism and 70–1, 89
  Britain 7, 12, 55, 79, 81–2, 86–7, 92–3, 101, 103, 128–9, 135
  capitalism and 36, 38, 126–7
  colourblindness and 1, 5, 7
  CRED Report (2021) and 79, 81
  CRT and 33, 44, 48–9, 58, 70–1, 146
  culture wars and 112
  education 6, 9, 29, 30, 48, 66, 81, 91–2, 93
  multiculturalism and 89
  police force and 7, 82
  postracialism and 6, 7, 34, 44, 70, 91, 95
  racial
    antiracism and 70
    behaviourism and 74, 79, 87, 103, 128
    Britain 7, 12, 51, 54–5, 69, 79, 81–2, 87, 92, 93, 101, 128–9
    CRT and 49, 51, 58, 146
    education and 30
    persistence of 2, 69, 75, 83
    social reproduction of 3
  racism and 6, 86, 129
injustices *see* inequalities
interest convergence
  Bell 45, 50, 55–7, 58, 89
  CRT 3, 4, 10, 39, 45, 47, 58, 62, 122, 130
  Macpherson Report and 90, 92
  US 55–8, 61, 89
  Whites and 50, 57, 58, 61
Irish 25, 26, 38, 136

J

James, C.L.R. 4, 23, 26, 39, 42, 53
JCHR (Joint Parliamentary Committee on Human Rights) 76
Jews
  CRT and 2–3
  racism against xiii, 26, 27, 38
John, Gus 92
Johnson, Boris 7, 11, 15, 75, 76, 79, 100, 104, 109, 110, 113
Judis, John B. 55

K

Kelley, Robin D.G. 38, 62, 121
Kendi, Ibram X. 105, 107
King, Martin Luther 71, 103, 107, 108
Kirp, David 72
Klein, Richard 137
Králová, Jana 140
Kundnani, Arun 4–5, 25, 38, 69, 98, 99, 137

L

Ladson-Billings, Gloria 16, 65, 66, 84
Laing, Olivia 96
Lammy Review 7, 82

Lawrence, Errol 37, 128–9
Lawrence, Stephen xii, 70, 80, 90, 91, 133
Learning to Labour (Paul Willis) 126, 127
legal realism 50
legitimate grievance xvii, 9, 14, 55, 118–19, 123, 124–5, 137, 142
Lentin, Alana 81–2, 109
Leonardo, Zeus 16, 32–3, 34–5, 36, 44, 62, 65, 66
Leont'ev, A.N. 30
LGBTQIA+ 88, 96
liberalism
  abstract 86
  BLM and 110–11, 112
  colourblindness and 49, 71
  CRT and 102, 107, 108
  diversity and 2
  equality and 2, 33, 45, 53
  human rights and 33, 39
  imperialism and 39
  media and 103, 137, 138
  multiculturalism and 89, 99, 136
  neo- 8, 60, 74, 102, 127, 134, 147
  postracialism and 96
  racism and 23, 45, 67
Lipman, Pauline 126
Lipsistz, George 48–9, 115
Lorde, Audre 21, 150
Luria, A.R. 30
Lynn, Marvin 66

M

Macpherson Report
  analysis of race 133
  contradiction closure and 90–1
  CRED Report (2021) and 79, 80, 91
  inequalities and 78
  institutional racism xii, xvi, 70, 77, 78, 80, 83, 90, 93, 134
  interest convergence and 90, 92
  multiculturalism and 15
  police force and xii, 70, 80, 90
  policy gains 68, 69
  pushback against 68, 69, 70, 73, 78, 93, 134
  Race Relations (Amendment) Act (UK 2000) and 88
Malcolm X 46
Malik, Nesrine xiii, 88, 90, 91, 104–5, 111–12, 115
Marsh, John 126
Marx, Karl 8, 17, 29, 30, 34, 35, 38, 39
Marxism
  Black Marxism 26, 37–9, 121
  Black Atlantic thought and 37, 39
  capitalism and 8, 34, 35, 38
  CRT and 106
  CTR and 35
  'cultural Marxism' xiii, 106, 111
  really existing socialism and 8

Mason, Paul 147
Matsuda, Mari 2, 45
May, Theresa 82
Mbembe, Achille 127
McWhorter, John 107
Mills, Charles W. 17, 18, 27, 39, 53
Modood, Tariq 71, 72
Moody, Harold 42
Morrison, Toni 24, 26, 34, 42
Moten, Fred 43, 44, 72, 73
multiculturalism
  antiracism and 89, 98, 109
  backlash against 73, 76, 92, 98, 99
  Britain 4–5, 9–10, 14, 76, 87–9, 92–3, 98–100, 109, 128, 131, 135–9, 146
  colourblindness and 71
  contra–antiracism and xvii, 95
  criticism of 7, 93, 95, 97, 99, 103, 109
  definitions of 88, 97, 122, 124
  diversity 71, 72, 88
  education and 88
  factual 88, 97, 122, 124
  inequalities and 89
  liberalism and 89, 99, 136
  state 5, 9, 15, 69–70, 87–9, 97, 98, 99, 100, 103, 124
  Whites and 9, 93, 100, 131–2, 136–7, 138
Muslims 25, 93, 97, 99–100, 129, 132–3, 137, 138

N

New Beacon 96, 146
New Cross Fire Campaign 96
Non-racism
  antiracism and 71, 116
  colourblindness and 71, 83
  postracialism and 75, 77
Northern Ireland xvi, 15

O

Olusoga, David 19, 87, 110, 117, 131, 142
Outlaw, Lucius 28

P

Parker, Laurence 65, 66
Patterson, Orlando 10, 42, 59, 63, 140–2
Phillips, Melanie 110–11
Poku, Veronica 66
Police, Crime, Sentencing and Courts Crime Act (UK 2022) 82, 110
police force
  Black people and xiv, 13, 19, 76, 82, 90, 93, 128, 129
  institutional racism xiv, 13, 69, 79, 90
  Macpherson report and xii, 70, 80, 90
  Metropolitan xii, xiv, 7, 79, 90, 110
  US 13, 19

political correctness 96, 99, 106–7, 109, 133, 145
Pollock, Mica 24, 36
populism 55, 93, 97, 100, 116, 119, 120, 125, 130, 131, 146
postcolonialism 4, 5, 14–15, 42, 67, 122, 141
postracialism
  antiracism and 6, 9, 14, 58, 69, 72, 75, 94–6, 116, 117, 145, 146
  colourblindness and xii, 1, 5, 6–7, 70, 83, 115
  contra-antiracism and xii, xvii, 1, 70, 95, 96–7, 116, 145
  contradiction closure and 5, 58, 91, 94
  CRED Report (2021) and 9, 77
  CRT and 44, 98
  facile xii, xvi, 1, 6, 7, 9, 13, 14, 69, 73–4, 94, 95
  ideology 1, 58, 59, 73–4, 87, 94, 97
  inequalities and 6, 7, 34, 44, 70, 91, 95
  multiculturalism and xii, 4–5, 14, 70, 73, 94, 97, 146
  non-racism and 75, 77
  racism and xv, xvi, 70, 83, 115, 116
  radical 70, 72–3
  really existing xvi, 7–11, 14, 65, 70, 74, 75, 77, 91, 94–6, 116, 118
  state xii, xiv, xv, xvi, 1, 6–7, 9, 68–70, 73–4, 83, 87, 91, 94, 95, 116, 117
Powell, Enoch 9, 20, 119, 122–6, 138

Q

QueerCrit 18, 28, 63

R

race
  identity and 27–8, 36, 37, 70, 71, 72, 76, 106, 119, 121, 122
  invention of 17, 25, 40
  relations 3, 5, 30, 38, 56, 75, 87–8, 90–1, 96, 99, 101, 118, 126–8, 132–4
  science 24, 27
  social construct 22, 24, 30, 32, 70
  social relationship 28–30
  sociocultural mediation 30–1
Race Critical Theory (RCT) 34–5, 36–7
Race Relations Act (UK 1965) 87–88, 120
Race Relations (Amendment) Act (UK 2000) 67, 83, 88, 90, 92, 93
Racial Contract, The (Charles W. Mills) 39
racial realism
  Afropessimism and 63
  Bell and xvi, 3–4, 7, 16, 33, 44–5, 47, 50–2, 56, 62–3, 87, 149–50
  CRT and 4, 14, 16, 33, 44, 50, 64
  postracialism and 3
  racism and 14

racism
  Britain xiii, xiv, 1, 2, 9, 70, 77–85, 91, 93, 96, 115, 121, 123–4
  capitalism and 1, 35, 37, 38, 39, 53, 121
  colour-coded xv, xvi, 1, 22, 23, 26, 41, 63, 84, 115
  colourblindness and 83, 83, 85–7, 91, 115
  CRT and 33–4, 41, 84–5
  cultural 63, 86
  Europe 41
  institutional
    Britain 70, 77–82, 83, 93, 111, 129
    CRED Report (2021) and xv, 49, 70, 76–82
    CRT and 2, 4
    denial of xiii, 5, 6
    effects of 7
    Macpherson Report and xii, xvi
    persistence of 45, 117
    police force and xiv, 13, 69, 79, 90
    understanding of 86–7
  permanence of xiii, xvi, xvii, 2, 3–4, 32, 39, 44, 45, 51, 52–3, 64–5, 87, 144, 148–9
  postracialism and xv, xvi, 70, 83, 115
  stabilising role of 41, 45, 54, 55, 58–60
  see also antiracism; contra–antiracism
Ramdin, Ron 117
RCT *see* Race Critical Theory
Roberts, Lorna 66
Robinson, Cedric 23, 26, 27, 35, 37–9, 42, 121
Roma xiii, 26, 38, 139
'romance of abolition' 59
ross, kihana 63
RRAA *see Race Relations (Amendment) Act* (UK 2000)
Rufo, Christopher F. 105–7
Rushdie, Salman 99

S
Satanic Verses, The (Salman Rushdie) 99
Scarman Report 88, 93, 128
Schulman, Sarah 96
Sewell, Tony 75, 104
Sexton, Jared 42, 43, 54
Shelby County v. Holder 51
Shriprakash, Arathi 66, 144
Silent Covenants: Brown v Board of Education and the Unfulfilled Hopes for Racial Reform (Derrick Bell) 46
Singh, Nikhil Pak 35–6
Sivanandan, Ambalavaner 117
slavery 23, 24, 25, 26
  abolition 59
  Atlantic 1, 23, 26, 37, 39, 42, 110

Black Atlantic thought and 23, 26
Britain 16, 19, 59, 89, 110, 114
racism and 23, 24, 27, 31
social death and 42–3, 140–1
USA 19, 20, 26–7, 74
Slavery and Social Death (Orlando Patterson) 140–1
Slavs 26, 38
social death 10, 42–3, 59, 63, 119, 140–2
Solórzano, Daniel 65
Southall Black Sisters 96, 146
'Space Traders, The' (Derrick Bell) 45, 54, 60–2, 63
Starmer, Keir 11
Stefancic, Jean 24, 84
Stout, Cathryn 108
Sunak, Rishi 11–12, 19, 113–14
Sveinsson, Kjartan Páll 135, 136
Swann Report 88, 93

T
Tate, William 16, 65
Taylor, Brendan 115–16
Taylor, Edward 65
Thompson, E.P. 117
Tomlinson, Sally 98, 125
Trump, Donald 106, 108
Truss, Liz 11, 15, 19, 114

U
US
  Afropessimism 16
  antiracism 105–6, 107–8, 109
  Black Americans (African-Americans) 19, 23, 25–6, 33, 40, 46, 52, 54–7, 61–3, 65, 119
  BLM 101
  civil rights movement xii, 14, 20, 23, 39, 41–2, 45–7, 49, 51
  CLS 39
  colourblindness 7, 49, 91
  contra-antiracism 102, 105, 109
  CRT xii, xvi, 2, 17, 18, 45, 65, 66, 98, 101, 105–8, 109
  interest convergence 55–8, 61, 89
  Irish 25
  legislation 45–7, 74
  police force 13, 19
  postracialism 7
  racism 33, 74, 84, 113
  segregation 48, 50, 55–6, 57
  slavery 19, 20, 26–7, 74
  symbolic achievements 64–5
  White working class 132

V
Vann, Katie 31
Vieler-Porter, Christopher 66

Voting Rights Act (USA 1965) 51
Vygotsky, Lev 30

W

Wallace-Wells, Benjamin 105, 106, 108
Watts, Katy 110
Wearing, David 148
Wechsler, Herbert 55–6
Weigel, Moira 106
West, Cornel 79
White people
  Britain xiv, 1, 4, 12–13, 88–9, 93, 100, 111–12, 116–20, 123–6, 129, 131–9, 142
  CRT and 3, 19, 34, 66, 85, 144, 147
  education and 13, 29, 93, 112, 132, 138–9
  inequalities and 12–13, 85, 128
  interest convergence and 50, 57, 58, 61
  majority societies 1, 4, 33, 34, 50, 76, 81, 146
  multiculturalism and 9, 93, 100, 131–2, 136–7, 138
  postracialism and 1, 2, 69
  racism and xiv, 3, 26, 27, 33, 55, 85, 86
  supremacy 1, 27, 33, 40, 48, 52, 63
  US 33, 50, 56–8, 61, 103, 121, 132
  working class
    Britain xvii, 9, 93, 100, 111–12, 116–20, 123–6, 129, 131–9, 142
    education and 93, 112, 132, 138–9
    England 112, 117, 124, 126, 136
    'left behind' 9, 93, 119, 125, 132, 134, 135, 136
    liberalism and 117, 134, 136, 137
    USA 53, 58, 132
Why I'm No Longer Talking to White People About Race (Reni Eddo-Lodge) 4, 91, 103
Wilderson, Frank B. 16, 42–3, 54, 144, 145
Williams, Anthony 131
Williams, Eric 39
Williams, Patricia 45
Willis, Paul 126, 127
Windrush Generation 21, 94, 118, 119, 122, 126
Windrush scandal xiv, 15, 130–1, 142
'woke' xiii, 1, 4, 9, 75, 89, 102, 105, 107, 111, 145, 146, 147
Woolley, Simon 81
Wynter, Sylvia 16, 17, 23, 39, 40, 41, 42

Y

Yosso, Tara 65
Younge, Gary 133, 142

Z

Zamalin, Alex 150

www.ingramcontent.com/pod-product-compliance
Lightning Source LLC
Chambersburg PA
CBHW071201070526
44584CB00019B/2875